POWER AND DEPENDENCE

Social Audit on the safety of medicines

By Charles Medawar

Edited by Elaine Rassaby
and Brian Guthrie

Published by Social Audit Ltd

HNJA

M

POWER AND DEPENDENCE
Social Audit on the safety of medicines

This book is not a guide to medical treatment; nor are we (authors or editors) qualified to give advice about the possible advantages or disadvantages of specific treatments for any individual. If this book prompts questions about any treatment you are receiving, please discuss them with your own doctor. Only he/she would be in a position to give you good advice, since the benefits and risks of different treatments depend so much on individual medical history, present circumstances and needs.

Printed by Bath Press

ACKNOWLEDGEMENTS

My grandfather was a doctor, and naturally I believe he was a very good one. I imagine him caring for his patients, giving much of himself, and I take for granted that they were the better for it. But I also know that, by today's standards, my grandfather would have been profoundly limited in what he could offer patients, because there were so few effective drugs. That also explains why my grandfather and I never met: he died of tuberculosis shortly before the discovery of streptomycin, in 1944. Better drugs have since been introduced, but this was the first effective treatment for TB.

My father brought medicine to life in a different way: he was one of the founders of immunology and a philosopher of science, and he explored and explained medicine in ways which excited him and delighted others. He was not a clinician, but he did spend a lot of time in hospital - as a patient, after a massive stroke. Against nearly all the odds, my father made a remarkable recovery and, in spite of several further crises, he lived and worked to the full for another 18 years. He had extraordinary dignity as a patient, above all because he was treated and cared for as the person he was. [1] But that was possible only because, time and again, my father's life was saved by dedicated treatment and excellent drugs.

In this book I have focused attention on aspects of medicine which fall far short of these ideals - of good drugs used with real understanding and great care. If this seems a contradiction, even ungrateful, perhaps it is because I have seen so much of medicine at its best and hope for progress too much.

My understanding of medicine comes mainly from my family background, from personal experience of treatments which have ranged from inferior to inspired, and from a professional background in consumer protection. I started work in this field with a series of very depressing enquiries into the promotion and use of drugs in the third world. From the mid 1980s, I began to look at UK drug policy and to investigate cases of alleged drug injury as well.

My work in this field has led me to believe, above all, that the essence of medicine can be comprehensible to any lay person - and that the more widely medicine is understood, the better it will become. The fact that medicine involves vast areas of uncertainty in my view argues for, not against, the involvement of consumers in the process of its administration.

I accept full responsibility for this book, though it is of course mainly a synthesis and interpretation of many other peoples' ideas. Some are credited by name in the text - but others are not, though their influence has been profound. This is the place to acknowledge and thank them for their help, and to underline that this book would never have been written without it.

The book was conceived not as an end in itself, but as fuel for a movement towards greater understanding of medicine, and for more effective public participation in the system of medicines' control. The whole project was generously funded by the Joseph Rowntree Charitable Trust. I am deeply grateful to the Trustees and to the Secretary, Steven Burkeman, for making the project possible, and for their moral support throughout. It should go without saying that this does not imply any endorsement by JRCT - but it is worth saying, if only to thank them for taking the risk.

Elaine Rassaby and Brian Guthrie patiently and skilfully edited every word of countless drafts; time and again they made sense of ill-formed and over-elaborated ideas, sometimes in the face of wild opposition from me. Their good judgement and good humour prevailed.

Many people painstakingly read and commented on drafts of this book; inevitably there were bits they liked and bits they didn't, and points of disagreement between them. But they helped enormously to decide what the book should and could not say. Special thanks to my wife, Caroline - and to Maurice Frankel, Dr Andrew Herxheimer, Mark Mildred, Dr Ian Munro, Andrew Phillips, Michael Pountney, Anthony Sampson, Oliver Thorold, Sir Roger Walters, and Christopher Zealley.

Trish Daniel helped a lot with the research, as did Anna Vogel and Corinne Rossbotham in getting it organised. I am very grateful to them, and to Dan Vogel for his help too.

Finally, I have in mind, but will not mention their names, a number of other people - in medicine, academic departments, the pharmaceutical industry, the consumer movement, the press and media and beyond - whose example and understandings I have also tried to reflect.

This book is dedicated to a better and wider understanding of medicine - but what it actually might achieve must be decided by you and other readers. The book is intended partly as a consultation and as an interactive study; as you will see, its main conclusion is left to you. I would greatly welcome a quick reaction (using the FREEPOST card provided) to the central ideas in this book - as well as critical comment and feedback on any aspect of the safety of medicine, including this particular interpretation of what it seems to mean.

Charles Medawar, London, September 1991

1 Medawar J, 1990

CONTENTS

FOREWORD

Social audit on the safety of medicines

"Drugs are remarkably safe. Few patients would refuse an elective surgical operation with a risk of less than 1:10,000. Yet for medicines much greater safety is demanded and achieved ... Drug regulatory authorities should be immune from political and public pressure and above all free from the pressures of action groups." [Asscher, 1986]

This is the view of the present Chairman of the Committee on Safety of Medicines, and it reflects opinions that are widely held by the providers of medicine - doctors, manufacturers and government. They maintain that prescription drugs are safe enough, and that their benefits far outweigh the risks. They believe that the public expects drugs to be safer than they ever can be, and complain that the press and media greatly exaggerate the dangers. [1] On this basis, the providers argue against public accountability, and the law supports them.

We disagree. We believe that the authorities take the benefits of drug treatment too much for granted, and that risks and levels of drug injury are much higher than they should be. Drug risks are in some ways exaggerated, and it is true that the public does not consistently err on the side of safety - as resistance to vaccination campaigns sometimes shows. But public concern about drug safety ultimately reflects lack of trust in the authorities, and is surely related to their unwillingness to explain and justify what they do.

No-one really knows how many people are injured by prescribed drugs, nor how much damage is done. This is partly because drug injury is still largely a hidden problem - hard to detect, grossly underreported, and frequently impossible to verify. The problem is further obscured by the intensity of focus on benefit rather than risk; by the extent of secrecy; by pursuit of vested interests; and by the tendency to create monopolies of understanding:

> "... the health education approach often remains pater-
> nalistic and commandment-like ... This attitude, where it
> exists, perpetuates the elitist position of health-care
> providers who make plans, define objectives, and devel-
> op messages that aim at persuading people, thus creating
> a certain distance between health professionals and 'the
> receivers' ..." [Therefore, most health education pro-
> grammes have been] "basically concerned with 'telling
> people' what is good for them ... The underlying concept
> in this approach was that only a few people knew certain
> facts and that the majority of the population knew little
> or held the wrong views." [WHO, 1983]

Lack of public awareness and involvement must partly explain
why there is no systematic, independent investigation of the underlying causes of drug injury - nor even a rough estimate of its cost to the
UK economy. In the US, in the mid-1980s, the direct cost of adverse
drug reactions was put at over $5 billion per year - a figure close to
half the amount spent annually on prescription drugs. [2] But in the UK
drug injury has traditionally been regarded as of marginal economic
or social significance in relation to the overwhelming benefits that
drugs are believed to bring.

The benefits of drug treatment can undoubtedly be great, but there
are still appreciable risks. For the average person, the chances of serious drug injury do seem low, though far higher than official estimates
suggest. We would compare the overall risk to the likelihood of serious injury on the roads. Road accidents in Britain cause around 5,000
fatalities and 60,000 serious injuries (requiring hospital in-patient
treatment) each year. [3] Depending on the source, drug injury occurs
with "appalling frequency" or "astonishing rarity", or something in
between. [4] Even using the most conservative estimates, the figures
never quite add up; at best they suggest a range. The rough estimates
(facing page) of the annual incidence of serious adverse drug reactions (ADRs) are based on different methods, but all are derived from
industry or government sources.

Society is only beginning to get to grips with drug injury. So far the
problem has been defined mainly in terms of redress for injured par-
ties - for example, with no-fault compensation schemes. This would
be an advance, because it would help some patients whose needs are

Basis of estimate	Serious ADRs per year	Fatalities per year
Number of reported cases assuming (optimistically) that 10% of all ADRs are recognised and reported[5]	47,000	2,500
Incidence of ADRs noted in a major general practice survey, extrapolated for all prescriptions in UK [6]	180,000	?
Number of hospitalisations believed to result wholly or largely from drugs[7]	240,000	?

now overlooked, but it would still fail to get at the underlying problem, and would leave other patients at risk. The proposed no-fault approach aims to ameliorate distress, deliberately avoiding questions of responsibility or blame. There would therefore be little emphasis on prevention, and drug safety would continue to be defined essentially as a private matter rather than a public problem.

Again, this approach is worth comparing with what happens on the roads. As road safety is defined as a public problem - and because everyone knows that accidents will happen - third-party insurance is compulsory, and victims of road accidents generally get compensation. In addition, accidents involving injury are usually investigated by the police and by insurance companies; while the causes, effects and implications of more serious incidents may be examined in open court.

There is also a government minister responsible for road safety, and policies and priorities tend to be planned - but not just because road accidents are plain to see. It is also because accidents are often avoidable; because of some commitment to reduce risks; also because the authorities have determined that basic preventive measures are economically worthwhile. Department of Transport investments in road safety are partly based on estimates of the financial cost to the community of injury on the roads - and are now based on a valuation of £500,000 for each death. [8]

The stock reason for isolating the public from decision-making about the control of drug safety is that ordinary people cannot appreciate what it is about, and have no need to. Official policy is exemplified by the concealment of figures which register the number of reports from doctors of suspected adverse drug reactions. The Committee on Safety of Medicines (CSM) restricts their circulation on the grounds that even MPs would tend to misinterpret them - as indeed they would if they imagined the national reporting system to be more than a crude tool either for spotting problems or assessing risk. This reporting system sometimes does produce useful and important early warnings - but overall it tends to give a highly distorted reflection of only a small fraction of significant adverse drug effects. [9]

The CSM's policy on non-disclosure of adverse drug reaction data, agreed at a meeting in June 1989, is itself an official secret. And this underlines that the main point of openness and accountablity is not to provide, say, journalists or MPs with this or that piece of information. It is to encourage better practice, by reminding decison-makers that their work may always be scrutinised, and must pass some test of public acceptance.

Failing this, it seems to us that there will always be an unacceptable risk of neglect and abuse of power. It is often difficult to see this from the perspective of the individual patient, because medicine has so much to give, and because it is largely expressed and felt in highly personal ways. Nevertheless, medicine operates increasingly as a system, and in many ways resembles other limbs of power. This system cannot just be trusted to control itself. Medicine needs people to check, test and stimulate its performance.

With this in mind, we have tried to measure "the safety of medicines" - mainly by looking at what safety has actually meant, over the years, in relation to one particular class of drugs. We decided to focus attention on drugs for anxiety and insomnia, mainly because we wanted to make this book accessible to consumers and professionals alike. Though most of the evidence in this book is "scientific" data, reviewed with a straight bat, there is also a good story to be told about these drugs - which are well known medicines and widely used. Tranquillisers and sleeping pills tend to be prescribed for social as well as strictly medical reasons, and account for around one in ten of all drugs prescribed on the NHS.

We believe that the public is capable of understanding well enough what standards of safety apply - and that the major obstacle to better understanding is lack of cooperation and obstruction by the providers themselves. The providers generally do not welcome scrutiny, and protect themselves from it by custom, practice and law. The government, manufacturers and doctors seem pretty unanimous in their view that they alone should define how safe medicines should be - and insist that the public has good reason to trust them.

How far can the providers be trusted to deliver safe medicine ? The answer depends partly on what you make of the story unravelled in this book. It is mainly about one particular aspect of safety - the tendency of these drugs to cause what the experts call dependence and the public calls addiction. Drug dependence of one kind or another is a risk with many medicines, also an aspect of safety which anyone can understand.

The evidence suggests that the providers of medicine keep making the same mistakes, mainly because they have been allowed to deny how badly things have gone wrong. Virtually every anti-anxiety drug and sleeping pill ever prescribed has proved to be a drug of dependence - yet each one has been prescribed, often for many years, as if this risk did not exist. This pattern of error has been established over the past 100 years or more, and continues to this day. [10]

We suggest that the providers have failed to come to terms with this reality essentially because they have distanced themselves from the receivers, "the people out there". The providers have made a secret of drug safety and methods of drug control to an extent which seems unrivalled in any other area of public life. The secrecy, for the most part, has nothing to do with protecting legitimate trade secrets or personal privacy - nor is it compatible with what science should be. It seems to have much more to do with protecting professional, commercial and political reputations; we link it with the pursuit of unfair advantage and unjustified power.

There is clearly scope for a systematic parliamentary scrutiny of drug safety standards; but we avoid making specific recommendations. This is not to say that solutions do not exist, but to emphasise that there can never be solutions until a problem is recognised and defined for what it is. The problem goes beyond questions of drug safety and unhealthy dependence on medicine. It seems to be to do with the failure to reconcile, within the system of medicine, some of the guiding principles of both democracy and science.

On the basis of the following case-history, and the concluding overview, we hope more will be understood about what can be trusted in pharmaceutical medicine, and what can not. We have no doubt that the providers can do much better, and will do if they explain themselves, and justify the use of their powers. Medicine needs people to ask, and to keep asking, whether the standards that apply are good enough for them. The safety of medicines can never be achieved without this, nor can risks be properly defined.

1 Inman, 1984, von Wartburg 1984, Scrip 1985, Burley, 1986; D'Arcy & Griffin, 1986
2 D'Arcy, 1986
3 Department of Transport, 1988, 1991
4 Dukes and Swartz, 1988
5 Rawlins, 1988
6 Lumley & Walker, 1986
7 Davies, 1981; Rawlins, 1981; D'Arcy 1986; Dukes & Swartz, 1988
8 Department of Transport, 1988
9 Rawlins, 1988
10 Olivieri et al, 1986

POWER AND DEPENDENCE

Chapter I

LINES OF DESCENT

"Science is useful, indispensable sometimes, but whenever it moves forward it does so by producing a surprise; you cannot specify the surprise you'd like. Technology should be watched closely, monitored, criticised, even voted in or out by the electorate, but science itself must be given its head if we want it to work." [Thomas, 1983]

One addiction after another

RO 5-0690 looks like something you dial - an old-style American telephone number perhaps. Actually, it was the code the manufacturers used to identify a new molecule they had made, hoping it might prove effective as a medicinal drug. Later, this drug was given a proper chemical name: chlor - di - aze - ep - ox - ide.

Chlordiazepoxide was first synthesised in 1955 and then nothing happened. The research chemist who made it did not think it would be effective as a drug, so the two small bottles of white powder lay around in his lab for two years. Eventually, just before throwing it out, he arranged for a basic evaluation of the new compound in animal tests. Two years later, chlordiazepoxide was on the market - and has been sold under the brand name Librium ever since.

Librium was the first of a large family of closely related compounds called benzodiazepines. Two years after Librium came Valium; then Serenid, Mogadon, Ativan, Dalmane and at least a dozen more. (See Table.) For the past 20 - 30 years, drugs like these have been the mainstay of medical treatment for anxiety and insomnia, and have found many other uses besides. Around one in four adults in Britain has been prescribed a benzodiazepine, and many people have taken them for years.

The benzodiazepines were the latest in a long line of drugs used as

Benzodiazepines 1960-1983

BRAND manufacturer	Generic name (and main indication)	Approx NHS prescription 1980-89 (millions)
LIBRIUM Roche Products (Switzerland)	chlordiazepoxide (anxiety)	14
VALIUM Roche	diazepam (anxiety)	60
MOGADON Roche	nitrazepam (insomnia)	64
SERENID-D Wyeth Laboratories (US)	oxazepam (anxiety)	7
NOBRIUM Roche	medazepam (anxiety)	1
ATIVAN Wyeth	lorazepam (anxiety	28
TRANXENE Boehringer-Ingelheim (Germany)	clorazepate (anxiety)	6
DALMANE Roche	flurazepam (insomnia)	11
EUHYPNOS & NORMISON Farmitalia Carlo Erba (Italy) & Wyeth	temazepam (insomnia)	50
HALCION Upjohn Ltd (US)	triazolam (insomnia)	15
ANXON Beecham Research Laboratories	ketazolam (anxiety)	1
FRISIUM Hoechst UK Ltd	clobazam (anxiety)	3
LORAMET & NOCTAMID Wyeth & Schering Pharmaceuticals (US)	lormetazepam (insomnia)	2
LEXOTAN Roche	bromazepam (anxiety)	less than 1
CENTRAX William R Warner (UK)	prazepam (anxiety)	less than 1
ROHYPNOL Roche	fluritrazepam (insomnia)	less than 1
DORMONOCT Roussel Laboratories (France)	loprazolam (insomnia)	1
XANAX Upjohn	alprazolam (anxiety)	1

tranquillisers and sleeping pills. Such drugs used to be known as "sedative-hypnotics" - and in some ways this is a more helpful description, because it acknowledges that their effects very much depend on the size of the dose given. At relatively low dosages, these drugs reduce levels of anxiety and arousal; but if the dosage is increased, they promote sleep. At even higher dosages, sedative-hypnotics induce unconsciousness: this makes some of them useful as anaesthetics, but tends to make them dangerous in overdose as well.

If these drugs are used at the right dose, and for only a few days at a time, they are usually efficacious and often effective - ie they usually do exert a sedative or hypnotic effect and patients often benefit. But if sedative-hypnotics are used continuously for more than a week or so, their effects begin to wear off. From then on, there is the risk that drug dependence will develop, and that some users will find it increasingly hard to stop taking them.

The original sedative-hypnotic drugs were alcohol and opium; until the middle of the 19th century, there was nothing else. Today, derivatives of opium still play an important part in medicine, as strong pain killers; until the 1980s, alcohol was widely prescribed in tonic medicines as well. Both drugs are now recognised to be addictive - though, in its day, opium was in fact often used as a treatment for alcoholism. It didn't work, and because of the profound chemical differences between alcohol and opium, it meant that two different addictions could develop, instead of just the one.

Ever since those days - and right through to the age of the benzodiazepines - history has been repeating itself in a rather sinister way. A pattern has emerged in which one drug after another, used to treat addiction, proved in time to be a drug of addiction itself. Thus, from around the 1850s, doctors began to use morphine to treat addiction to both alcohol and opium. Morphine was not thought to be addicting, and doctors used it enthusiastically for many years.

When "morphinomania" was later revealed to be a problem, doctors tried a variety of other drugs - and the standard treatment for morphine addiction around the 1880s was a new drug from the Americas, called cocaine. In its day, cocaine was also said to be beneficial and safe - notably by Sigmund Freud. But it didn't work either and, because of the chemical differences between cocaine and the opiates, there was again the risk of producing two addictions instead of one.

When cocaine was found to be addictive, it was superseded by a new opiate called diamorphine. This drug, which was said to be espe-cially safe for infants, was known by its brand name, Heroin. By the turn of the 20th century, many doctors were using it to treat all the addictions gone before.

Eventually, the routine use of these major drugs of addiction was curbed, and that left the field open first for chloral hydrate, and then for the class of drugs known as the bromides. In their day, both chloral and the bromides were widely believed to be effective and safe, and they were copiously prescribed. But by the 1930s, doctors had begun to recognise their limitations - so they turned to a new class of drugs, the barbiturates, instead.

The barbiturates, in turn, were extensively prescribed in Britain, again in the belief that they were effective and non-addicting. Though they are now generally discredited as sedative-hypnotics, the barbitu-rates and many similar drugs were used well into the 1970s. It was then the turn of the benzodiazepines. Following their introduction into medicine in the 1960s and 1970s, the benzodiazepines were pro-moted as safe and non-addicting alternatives to the barbiturates, and to the many other sedative-hypnotics drugs used at that time.

Until the 1980s, the risk of becoming addicted to a benzodiazepine was officially considered remote. By then, these drugs had been wide-ly used for 20 years and the authorities had decided that addiction was theoretically possible but in practice would not happen. Follow-ing what it called a thorough review, the government's main watch-dog estimated in 1980 that the risks were so low that the average doc-tor might expect to see only one case of benzodiazepine addiction in a 40-year lifetime of general practice. [1] The manufacturers objected even to this rather uncritical assessment: they acknowledged that there were very occasional problems with patients who were "dependence-prone", but said that their products were otherwise remarkably safe - and most doctors went on prescribing them as if they were.

All that is now changing. By the end of the 1980s, the best estimates suggested that perhaps half a million people in Britain were more or less addicted to benzodiazepines. [2] The drugs most implicated were lorazepam (Ativan) and diazepam (Valium); however, the benzodi-azepines are very closely related and can all cause what is now for-mally described as "dependence".

In the early 1990s, the benzodiazepines are still by far the most widely prescribed sedative-hypnotics, though they are becoming less used as concern about dependence grows. Increasingly, the benzodi-azepines are being replaced by new kinds of anti-anxiety drugs and sleeping pills. Two of the main alternatives are mentioned later in this book: the manufacturers have claimed that they present little if any risk of dependence. Time will tell.

The relevance of yesterday

The history of medicine is rarely taught in medical schools. The real reason may be that "so much of it is an embarrassment", [3] but the con-ventional wisdom is that medicine has advanced so far since the early days that there would be little point in looking back. The force of this argument can be seen by comparing what medicine can achieve now with the standards of practice our grandparents might have known.

> "Somewhere between 1910 and 1912 in this country ... a random patient, with a random disease, consulting a doctor chosen at random had for the first time in history a better than 50-50 chance of profiting from the encounter." [Henderson, 1935]

On the other hand, if medicine continues to progress at such a rate, present-day practice itself will soon seem an embarrassment. When our grandchildren reach our age, they will probably feel much as we do when we contemplate the kinds of treatment our grandparents endured. Yet our grandparents would have seen little reason to com-plain, because everything would have seemed to them so much better than it had been in the past. The prevailing view in medicine is always that great strides have been made, and that patients have never had it so good. Had they consulted the *Encyclopedia Britannica*, this is what our grandparents would have read, for example, about the treatment of insanity.

> "The modern hospital for the insane does credit to latter-day civilisation. Physical restraint is no longer practised. The day of chains - even of wristlets, covered cribs and straight-jackets - is past. Neat dormitories, cosy single rooms, and sitting- and dining-rooms please the eye. In place of bare walls and floors and curtainless windows, are pictures, plants, rugs, birds, curtains, and in many asylums even the barred windows have been abolished." [Peterson, 1910]

The history of medicine reveals again and again the bias that exists towards proving the triumph of benefit over risk - and at times this has involved extraordinary denial of unpalatable truths. The case-history of sedative-hypnotic drugs also illustrates one of the most important reasons why failures in medicine have happened. The most serious problems have generally arisen not because doctors didn't know enough - but because so many behaved as if they did.

New and sometimes remarkable technologies have been introduced into pharmaceutical medicine over the years, and some treatments have been transformed as a result. And yet there are clear limits to what science and technology can achieve. In the end, it is the values of medicine which really matter - another reason why the past is so relevant to today. The relevance of the past is underlined by the fact that Hippocrates is still revered at least notionally as the father of medicine and the author of its constitution - even though he practised and preached over 2,000 years ago. Values define goals, and good technologies help to realise them.

Hippocrates advanced many ideas relevant to medicine today. One was his understanding that the human body is very adaptable and resilient, and that it contains great resources of healing power. Accordingly, Hippocrates advised that doctors intervene as little as possible and, above all, do no harm. Countless problems would have been avoided if doctors had heeded this, yet over-prescribing is still commonplace. And some doctors seem to take pride in intervening whenever they can.

> "Try listening to some dopey witterer and send him off with a catechism of advice but no prescription in his hand ... In 30 years of general practice I have only on three occasions managed to see patients out of my surgery without a scrip - the talisman, the reason for the visit and the evidence of the recognition of the seriousness of the complaint." [Swan, 1985]

Hippocrates favoured openness and the demystification of medicine. He specifically suggested that - with due regard to the patient's state of body and mind - doctors should explain to patients the treatments they gave. Hippocrates emphasised that any doctor who was unable to communicate with his patients, even the least-educated, had failed in the healing art.

> "Whoever treats of this art should treat of things which are familiar to the common people. For of nothing else

> will such a one have to inquire or treat, but of the dis-
> eases under which the common people have laboured,
> which diseases and the causes of their origin and depar-
> ture, illiterate persons cannot easily find out for them-
> selves, but still it is easy for them to understand these
> things when discovered and expounded by others. For it
> is nothing more than that everyone is put in mind of
> what has occurred to himself. But whoever does not
> reach the capacity of the illiterate vulgar and fails to
> make them listen to him, misses his mark." [4]

The underlying humanity of Hippocratic medicine, and its relevance now, is indicated by an aside in the old *Encyclopedia Britannica*.
It suggested that the great advances claimed for psychiatry in the
early 20th century had in fact been realised many centuries before,
when: "a Greek physician protested against mechanical restraint in
the care of the insane, and advocated kindly treatment, the use of
music and some sorts of manual labour". [5] Older technologies may
have been rudimentary - but the treatments were almost certainly
more effective than some used even today. [6] This is because they
reflected care and good intent, and values which patients shared.

Medicine began to lose sight of such ideals just a few centuries after
the death of Hippocrates, as tidal waves of religion brought new and
backward-looking ideas. The leaders of the new orders appropriated
and systematically perverted medicine, creating vast amounts of ill-
health as they did so. Underlying their beliefs was the idea that the
human body was the property of a divine being, and that it should
therefore be left to his more important representatives on earth to
decide how to treat it.

To protect and augment their power, these mal-practitioners developed to extremes the practice of blaming patients. Mental illness was
interpreted as possession by the devil and treatment was severe and
cruel as a result. Routine torture and explicit punishment have now
stopped, though the tendency to hold patients responsible for treatment failures still seems quite strong. Certainly many doctors still
believe that the patients who get hooked on prescribed drugs are
mainly the "dependence prone".

At the time our story starts, around 200 years ago, medicine was
still sick - the outcome of centuries of repression of scientific enquiry
and profound confusion between illness and sin. Only towards the

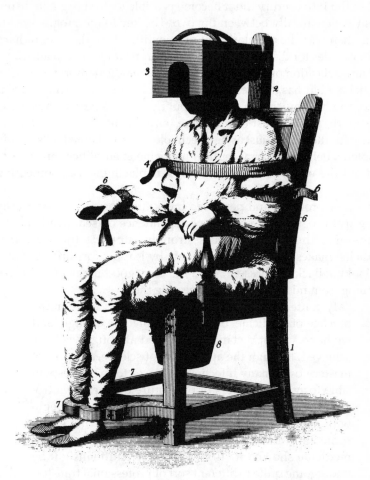

The first tranqillizer - "the most complete restraint of a patient's every movement ever devised" - was the invention of the father of American psychiatry, Benjamin Rush, in 1811. It comprised a chair (1) stapled to the floor, behind which was an adjustable board (2) to which was fixed a wooden frame (3) stuffed with linen to prevent movement of the head. Strong leather bands over the chest and belly (4, 5) secured the patient to the chair. Other bands (6) confined the arms and hands, and a wooden projection at the base of the chair (7) prevented movement of the feet. Under the chair was a stool pan, half filled with water (8), which could be emptied and replaced "without removing, or disturbing the patient".

end of the 19th century did it become possible to even begin to distinguish systematically between the two. The key to the progress made since then was the development of scientific method - a set of hard and fast rules for distinguishing between appearance and reality.

The application of scientific method led to radical improvements in medicine - but has also tended to obscure how much further there is to go, and how much remains to be put right. At its best, medicine can be superb, yet the best of medicine tends still to be be used as an excuse for the worst - just as new technologies are claimed to leave old problems behind. Pharmaceutical medicine exemplifies this urge to blot out the worst of the past, always displacing it with something new.

Yet new products and perceived breakthroughs do not necessarily bring real progress. The history of dependence on sedative-hypnotic drugs over the past 200 years strongly supports the view that medicine makes real progress not only by leaping forward - but also by looking back. At present, as in the past, good medicine involves learning from mistakes and not repeating them.

> "My contention is that we do have some science in the practice of medicine, but not anything like enough, and we have a great distance to go. And although we have achieved, through the application of science, a degree of mastery over many infectious diseases formerly responsible for great numbers of premature deaths, the introduction of science into medicine did not really begin with management of infection. Long before that event, some time in the middle of the nineteenth century, medicine showed its first signs of scientific insight by undergoing quite a different sort of professional transformation. It stopped doing some things." [Thomas, 1986]

The power of suggestion

At least until the turn of the 20th century, any benefit patients felt from medical treatment would have been mainly due to the placebo effect. In essence, the placebo effect is a response elicited through suggestion, reinforced in turn by early conditioning. Beyond that, little is known about how or why, only that placebo effects can be pervasive, subtle and very strong. If a doctor reflects confidence that some treatment will work, the results may be very impressive indeed.

"I was once told by a distinguished old professor of medicine ... that it was his practice to paint gentian violet (a brilliant dye) over a wart and then assure the patient firmly that it would be gone in a week, and he never saw it fail. There have been several meticulous studies by good clinical investigators, with proper controls. In one of these, fourteen patients with seemingly intractable generalised warts on both sides of the body were hypnotised, and the suggestion was made that all the warts on one side of the body would begin to go away. Within several weeks, the results were indisputably positive; in nine patients, all or nearly all of the warts on the suggested side had vanished, while the control side had just as many as ever." [Thomas, 1979]

The word placebo is Latin for "I will please". The classic placebo is a dummy drug, an inert substance used in a clinical trial as a yardstick by which to measure the effects of an active drug. Countless trials have demonstrated beyond question the healing power of placebo pills: they have often proved quite as effective as pharmacologically active treatments in numerous organic diseases, as well as in relief of severe pain and mental illness of many kinds. And many trials have failed to demonstrate any significant difference in the long-term effectiveness of sedative-hypnotic drugs compared with placebo. [7]

The placebo effect gave medicine some standing, not only because of its effect on patients, but also because it pleased doctors and empowered them. Because they did not understand human nature, many doctors assumed that they and their treatments were responsible for the successes they seemed to achieve. In practice, if a treatment seemed to work well, it was usually because the patient recovered in spite of it.

"A Dr. Raymond at the Salpetriere (a mental asylum) in Paris found 70 per cent of patients suffering from a variety of diseases ... were treated successfully by suspending them by their feet, causing the blood to flow into their heads. A collaborator of Bernheim at Nancy reversed the procedure and suspended the patient's head upwards and obtained a similar per cent success in a variety of organic and nervous diseases." [Volgyesi, 1954]

One cannot be precise, but perhaps a third of all drugs are now prescribed mainly for their placebo effect, and sedative-hypnotic drugs much more than most. The standard explanation for this has been "patient demand", but the manufacturers' promotion to doctors has also played an important part. When promoting a drug, manufacturers seek to elicit a placebo response from the doctor, by reassuring, providing and pleasing in many ways. Drug advertisements reveal something of the forces in play, and a fine example is the centrefold advertisement that appeared in the British Medical Journal [1969]. Twice lifesize and in colour, it showed just the tips of the doctor's fingers on the patient's pulse; and only the size of the fingers and the shape of the fingernails reveal that the doctor is a man, the patient a woman. The caption suggested that the doctor could do no wrong: "WHATEVER THE DIAGNOSIS ... LIBRIUM".

Do they go on working ?

The placebo effect is central to any discussion of dependence on sedative-hypnotic drugs - because a key question in this story is whether these drugs actually maintain their original therapeutic effect if used for more than a few days. Until recently, this was taken for granted, but doubts have grown as the nature of drug dependence and the significance of the placebo effect have become better understood. Even after 30 years' extensive use, the long-term effectiveness of benzodiazepines has not been proved, and doubts are growing rather than going away. There is increasing evidence that benzodiazepines and similar drugs appear to go on working only because dependence has developed, or because of the placebo effect, or both.

There is no doubt that benzodiazepines work when used for short periods, but most of their initial effects begin to wear off after only a few days' use - and dependence is undoubtedly the only effect which wears on. The orthodox view is that, although the body has a diminished response to some drug effects, other effects persist. It is still generally believed that tranquillisers go on tranquillising, even if some of their other effects, such as drowsiness or muscle relaxation, soon disappear. On this basis, many patients have been prescribed benzodiazepines for years.

The evidence that the placebo effect and drug dependence have been misinterpreted as signs that these drugs go on working is not conclusive, but it looks quite strong. The gist of it can be fairly simply illustrated, by imagining what might happen if a large group of more and less anxious people took normal doses of a benzodiazepine for about a year - at the end of which the drug was withdrawn. What would happen?

Enough is now known to be able to make several reliable predictions about the outcome. One is that the individual patient's response would be greatly affected by how the drug was stopped. The negative response to withdrawal would certainly be more marked if the drug was stopped abruptly, rather than slowly tapered off. It would also be stronger if the patient anticipated deprivation or if the drug was withheld in a seemingly callous way. The placebo (or nocebo) response can work both ways: good or bad feelings can be generated, depending on the stimulus applied.

However, if the active drug was surreptitiously withdrawn, and replaced by an identical-looking placebo, patients would react in one of three ways. Most would probably not be conscious of the difference. Others would experience increased levels of anxiety, insomnia and marked discomfort. And a small minority would suffer from extreme anxiety, plus a range of more severe and distinctive symptoms, such as tremors and vomiting and possibly seizures or psychotic episodes. In each case, though, the patients' response is open to entirely different interpretations - the difference between them depending as much as anything on the interest of the interpreter in a pleasing outcome.

For example, there would be two quite different ways of interpreting what happened to the majority of patients, those who did not react to withdrawal. The conventional clinical interpretation would be that the drug had done its job and that the patient had got better because of it. But the less comfortable (and less obvious) explanation would be that patients who never noticed the difference had thereby proved that the benzodiazepine was no more effective than placebo for them. If withdrawal of the active drug made no difference, there would be no reason to think that it had gone on exerting any real effect - even if it did at first.

Now consider the small minority of patients with the most severe reactions. Nowadays, doctors would generally recognise such symptoms as hallmarks of drug withdrawal, and therefore of dependence - and on this evidence, a doctor might simply decide that these patient were victims of an addictive drug. On the other hand, if a doctor was inclined to compare them with patients who didn't react at all, he might think otherwise. He might conclude instead that there was something about the individual patient which elicited that different response from the drug. The label "dependence-prone" implies that it is the patient who invokes these drug effects, rather than the drug that elicits some response from them.

That leaves the group of patients in between - the ones who experienced moderate anxiety and related symptoms when the active drug treatment was stopped. In these cases, accurate interpretations could be extremely difficult - because the less florid and distinctive symptoms of benzodiazepine withdrawal closely mimic the symptoms for which the drug was probably prescribed. Most benzodiazepines are prescribed for anxiety or insomnia, but anxiety and insomnia are also the most common symptoms of drug withdrawal.

When treatment with a benzodiazepine is stopped, moderate symptoms of anxiety might therefore be interpreted either as a recrudescence of the patient's original symptoms, or as evidence of drug dependence. The interpretation would be crucial because, if a doctor thought that anxiety following drug withdrawal was from an underlying condition, it would imply that the drug had been working all the time. Alternatively, a doctor might decide that dependence had developed, in which case there would be no clear evidence that the drug had been exerting a therapeutic effect.

By the 1950s, in the heyday of the barbiturates, some doctors did recognise the dangers of confusing symptoms of drug abstinence with symptoms of an underlying anxiety. But these lessons were quickly forgotten and the same mistakes were routinely repeated with benzodiazepines. For years, most doctors have assumed that benzodiazepines must have worked, because patients kept taking them - and many still believe it. If patients become distressed when benzodiazepines are withdrawn, this still indicates to many doctors that they need more treatment. Thus, dependence has been reinforced - as has the belief that these drugs can go on working for years.

Power and dependence

Dependence means many things. In this book, on the surface, it mainly means something to do with the relationship between patient and drug - including both the propensity of the drug to make someone want more of it, and the tendency of patients, for whatever reason, to seek out further supplies. Fundamental to the definition of dependence is "drug-seeking behaviour" by patients - but beyond this, the complexities and meanings of dependence are still poorly understood.

Over the years, different experts have argued that drug dependence either does or doesn't exist; that either the patient or the drug is responsible; and that it either does or does not matter. Is dependence necessarily unacceptable ? If benzodiazepines actually were effective in long-term use, and if the overall benefits outweighed the risks, dependence might be regarded as a price worth paying. It is not dependence as such that matters - but the balance that is struck between the medicinal power of the drug and its ability to subordinate the will.

Something analogous seems to apply in the relationship between consumers and the providers - the professional, commercial and government interests involved. Individual patients tend to be highly dependent on the providing system, trusting it to mean well and to do good, and to make progress by developing even better treatments and cures. On the other hand, as medicine develops as a system - in which power is increasingly held by organisations with mainly political and economic objectives - the greater the risks of abuse. Such power tends to extend and concentrate itself; to insist blindly that it is beneficial; to promote dependence and thrive off it; even to corrupt. The power of medicine can enable or disable: as with a drug, its effects are determined by how well it is understood and controlled.

Concern about the balance between power and dependence arises above all in relation to the availability of information about the real effects of medicines, and about how well the performance of medicine is controlled. Such information is power, and the lack of it produces dependence. It is one thing to protect people's feelings and their privacy, or to safeguard legitimate trade secrets - but the abuse of secrecy hides evidence of weakness and potential dangers, and obscures the need for reform.

Patients' rights to information about the risks they run with medical treatment are implied by the doctrine of "informed consent". In present practice, this generally means that patients who face clearly foreseeable and significant risks will be warned, and never normally be treated unless they agree. However, truly informed consent to treatment is still largely a myth. In practice, the average patient attending the average doctor for an average illness would stand a good chance of emerging with only a minimal understanding either of the nature or effects of the drugs prescribed, or of the true risks or benefits involved in taking them.

The usual explanation would be little time, and that many patients hardly understand. But another important reason may be that the average doctor can have only a limited understanding of a drug's full actions and effects - probably much less than the patient would hope for and the consumer might demand. The average doctor's understanding might well be influenced by high hopes and expectations - and then limited by uncertainties of diagnosis, lack of control over the patient's use of drugs, and an inability to monitor closely every patient's response. To this extent, doctors must depend heavily on pharmaceutical companies and government authorities to keep them out of real trouble - just as the patient relies on the doctor to do the same.

Just for their own sakes, consumers need to know about the performance of this system because, for all the benefits of drugs, there are also significant risks. Different experts vary passionately in their views about the extent of injury, but the coolest estimates suggest that people suffering "wholly or largely" from adverse drug reactions occupy between 3 and 5 per cent of hospital beds in the UK. [8]

In some cases, injury cannot possibly be foreseen; it may also result from risks knowingly and readily taken, when there seems no better alternative. Nevertheless, the evidence suggests that drug injury is often avoidable; that standards of drug treatment are often poor; and that the quality of care is sometimes bad. A consultant orthopaedic surgeon - with 25 years on the Council of the Medical Defence Union, which insures and provides legal representation for doctors - recently wrote to a national newspaper about this: "there are very many instances of carelessness, negligence and inhumanity on the part of medical practitioners". [9] But such outspokenness is rare.

The dangers of undue dependence on the health-care system arise not only for consumers, but for the providing system as whole. No public health-care system, however well endowed, can afford to stimulate demand - for this can only lead to inequitable or ineffective supply. But that would be only one of the reasons why the World Health Organisation has gone so far as to say that, without effective public participation, medicine cannot work.

" ... science and technology can contribute to the improvement of health standards only if the people themselves become full partners of the health care providers in safeguarding and promoting health ... people have not only the right to participate individually and collectively in the planning and implementation of health care programmes, but also a duty to do so."
[WHO, 1983]

The following case-history on sedative-hypnotic drugs will show that serious recognition of the consumer's role in medicine is a very recent development, still an idea ahead of its time. The story begins at around the time when medicine was starting to get organised - and the way in which the story unfolds also explains how powerful organisations within medicine began to emerge.

The medical profession itself became organised into roughly its present shape partly because doctors managed to get monopoly control over the distribution of opium. Through that process, which took place towards the end of the 19th century, doctors first defined themselves as professionals, to be clearly distinguished from traders in health. They achieved this notably by defining drug addiction (which they had done much to cause) not so much as a vice as a mental illness - which it was up to them to cure.

The drug industry, too, has strong roots in the supply of dependence-producing drugs; and the involvement of government in drug safety matters can also be traced through the story of sedative-hypnotic drugs. Even the drug control laws we have today resulted from the disaster with thalidomide, a sedative-hypnotic drug which was specifically marketed as safe for pregnant women.

As the benzodiazepine story unfolds, so the development of professional, commercial, government and patients' interests are discussed, to explain the parts they play in the system now. The moral of the story is that medicine can make real progress only if it is accountable, observing good scientific and social standards alike. Medicine makes progress not only by means of great discoveries and through the dedication of health-care professionals. Both are essential, but they are not enough on their own. The fact that doctors want to help and heal patients does not necessarily mean that the power of medicine will be used well. It was not enough to stop the benzodiazepines and other drugs of dependence being as badly prescribed as they were.

Medicine is still a long way from being as dedicated as government, drug companies and the medical profession would have everyone believe. The performance of the system needs much closer independent scrutiny than it now gets, and would benefit from it. In many respects, certainly compared with the past, pharmaceutical medicine is excellent. But to judge from the following case-history - and from the more general analysis of the safety of medicines in the final chapter of this book - it can surely be much improved.

1 Committee on Review of
Medicines, 1980
2 Drug & Ther Bull, 1985;
Ashton, 1987 (a)
3 Thomas, 1986
4 Wingate (Ed), 1985
5 Peterson, 1910

6 Observer, 1989-1990
7 Hollister 1972; McNair, 1973;
Waldron, 1977
8 Davies, 1981; Rawlins, 1981;
D'Arcy 1986; Dukes, 1988
9 Bonney, 1989

Chapter 2
MEDICINE OVERTAKES SIN

"There is no medical man now with a reputation to lose who would not venture an apology for the habitual use of more than a little alcohol, and this in a very diluted form. If there is any representative of that old race of convivial monsters who would imbibe three bottles of wine, or a score of glasses of punch or toddy, who thought no shame of falling under the dinner table and needing to have their cravat loosened and their neck ties be adjusted by the attendant page, let them know that their habits involve as great a violation of all sense and sciences as of manners and fashion."
[Lancet, 1862]

Medicinal alcohol

Alcohol was still quite widely prescribed on the National Health Service well into the mid-1980s, occasionally even as whisky or brandy - though mainly in "tonics", including one or two which were specifically marketed for infants and children. [1] But in 1984 the government decided, mainly for economic reasons, that these and other less useful medicines should no longer be reimbursed under the NHS, so alcohol is now hardly prescribed at all. Nowadays, the British Medical Association campaigns with increasing vigour about the addictive and otherwise serious consequences of anything exceeding modest consumption.

Alcohol had its heyday in medicine in the mid-19th century, mainly under the influence of Professor RB Todd of Kings College Hospital, London. According to the *Lancet*, the good professor even "found reason to give twenty or thirty ounces of brandy a day to young patients". [2] Such zeal may partly be explained by Todd's determination to prove the superiority of his theory of "alcohol stimulation" over the entirely contradictory theory of treatment which then prevailed. Doctors had previously thought that stimulation was the last thing a sick person needed, believing that the body should be "depleted", through blood-letting and other forms of purge. [3]

Alcohol stimulation duly became a craze. This was in spite of the efforts of the National Temperance League to promote more sober prescribing - and in defiance of some leading medical opinion that consumption had gone too far. During the 1860s, for example, The *Lancet* on several occasions ridiculed both the theory and practice of alcohol stimulation. "There is not a tittle of evidence that it can 'antagonise' any one disease", [4] said one editorial - yet it was prescribed "with lavish profusion in those numerous nervous afflictions to which weakly persons (more especially women) are prone". [5] The *Lancet* criticised the flimsy rationale for prescribing as well as the behaviour involved.

Naturally, many patients became addicted to alcohol but, just as naturally, the medical profession explained this away. In those days, doctors didn't think in terms of drugs having addictive effects; they tended to see drug-seeking behaviour as evidence of lack of willpower - or worse, if pleasure-seeking was involved. The notion of drug addiction did not exist until the late 19th century. Before then, it was rather assumed that people brought even habitual states of intoxication upon themselves.

Long after Todd's theories of alcohol stimulation had been discredited, the theory was that the person rather than the drug was to blame - and alcoholism was generally interpreted as a sign of genetic or social mishap, neither too far removed from sin. Partly for this reason, doctors refused to believe that they might have contributed to the problems they described. They flatly denied this reality, blaming their patients for dependence - especially patients with the temerity to try to blame them.

> "We now diagnose with confidence the existence of concealed drinking habits in thousands of cases which would have passed undetected not many years since. One of the most remarkable features of these secret drinkers is their inordinate propensity to tell lies, and their favourite falsehood, when they are detected, is to lay the blame of their evil habit on some apocryphal medical prescription of stimulants. Those observers, however, who have carefully studied the genesis of alco-

holic excesses are aware that the habit springs, in the immense majority of cases, from the temptation supplied by states of bodily or mental dejection and misery, and very often from a peculiar weakness of the nervous system which is inherited." [Anstie, 1965]

Such attitudes prompt questions about the origins of the often drastic and sometimes punitive treatment of the mentally ill - and specifically about the influence of a doctor's own prejudice and resentments. One does not need to look too far back, or too far from home, to see how readily dissident behaviour has been labelled as mental illness, and how cruel medical treatment can be. A number of examples are given in Chapter 3 of routine drug treatments of the mentally ill which by today's standards seem horrifying - but which in their day would have seemed quite unexceptional. To what extent might such ill-treatment reflect the professionals' sense of frustration, helplessness or pique; or the need to keep distanced from the mentally ill, to avoid becoming touched themselves? Evidence from around the world suggests that professional attitudes towards the mentally ill to some extent still reflect deep-seated notions of illness as an expression of personal fate, and of medical treatment as the next best thing to divine intervention.

That is certainly the way it was in the days when doctors routinely used alcohol as medicine, long after Todd's theories had been forgotten. Alcohol in fact retained a very significant place in therapeutics at least until World War II. The 1928 edition of Cushny's textbook on pharmacology and therapeutics noted that "it is difficult to prove that the moderate use of alcohol is injurious", and doctors were still taught that chronic alcoholism was "probably due to a mental defect". [6] In this most authoritative text, alcohol was recommended for the same conditions that tranquillisers would treat in their day.

"The action which lends alcohol its value in therapeutics is not its stimulant but its narcotic value, which allays the anxiety and distress of the patient, promotes rest and sleep, and thus aids toward healing, or at the worst renders illness more tolerable. Small quantities of other narcotics might be substituted for alcohol, but none of them perhaps excels it in producing that spirit of hopefulness and restful confidence that contributes so much to recovery." [Cushny, 1928]

This textbook advice would have been given to students who might have gone on practising medicine into the 1970s - which underlines the need for continuing medical education. This textbook also recommended doctors to try opium as a substitute drug when treating chronic alcoholism - though it did warn that the use of "opium and other narcotics may ... lead to a craving for these which is quite as serious as the original condition".

At the time, no-one knew that that there is no 'cross dependence' between alcohol and opiate drugs. The fundamental chemical differences between opium and alcohol mean that opium cannot satisfy a craving for alcohol. Alcohol addicts treated with opium therefore probably stayed dependent on alcohol and became dependent on opium as well: two crutches for the legless patient instead of one.

Opium

Until the 19th century, no distinction was made between drugs and spices; [7] and as late as 1850 opium could still be bought at the grocers along with the ginger beer. [8] Opium dissolved in alcohol was especially popular: it was known as laudanum.

As the 19th century wore on, opium was increasingly sold by druggists or apothecaries - the forerunners of today's chemists - though until early this century it remained quite freely available and was widely used. As supplies could readily be obtained, habitual users sustained their habit well enough to avoid the symptoms of withdrawal - so the main tell-tale sign of addiction was missing.

Thomas De Quincey was one of the first people to suggest that addiction was a problem, in *Confessions of an English Opium Eater* [1821]. De Quincey may have confessed, but he made a point of not apologising for his own habit on several grounds - including his obvious reverence for what he described as "just, subtle and mighty opium" ... "fascinating" and "divine". De Quincey also emphasised that he had started taking opium for medical reasons, noting that "infirmity and misery do not, of necessity, imply guilt". He also claimed to have succeeded very nearly in ending his addiction, where many others had failed: "I have struggled against this fascinating enthralment with a religious zeal, and have, at length, accomplished what I never yet heard attributed to any other man - have untwisted, almost to its final links, the accursed chain which fettered me".

Bad as he must have felt, De Quincey let it be known that he was no worse than many others, including some of the Great and Good. Tantalisingly, De Quincey said that it was really on their behalf he was confessing: "in consideration of the service which I may thereby render to the whole class of opium eaters".

> "But who are they ? Reader, I am sorry to say, a very
> numerous class indeed. Of this I became convinced some
> years ago, by computing at that time, the number of
> those in one small class of English society (the class of
> men distinguished for talents, or of eminent station),
> who were known to me, directly or indirectly, as opium
> eaters; such for instance as the eloquent and benevolent
> ——, the late dean of ——; Lord ——; Mr ——, the
> philosopher; a late under-secretary of state (who
> described to me the sensation which first drove him to
> the use of opium, in the very same words as the dean of
> ——, viz., 'that he felt as though rats were gnawing and
> abrading the coats of his stomach'); Mr. ——; and many
> others hardly less known, whom it would be tedious to
> mention ..."

Though he was in good company with his opium habit, De Quincey was clearly out on a limb in discussing it. Most people preferred to keep such matters private - as the writer, Sir Walter Scott, succeeded in doing for the best part of 150 years. Scott's own habit was revealed only by accident, through the discovery of a druggist's ledger in an attic in Scotland in the early 1960s. It recorded that between 1823 and 1825 Scott and his wife had been supplied with 22 quarts (5.5 gallons) of laudanum as well as 18 dozen opium lozenges and pills. [9]

By the 1820s, De Quincey describes the demand for opium as already "immense" in London, and spreading far beyond. De Quincey wrote, for example, that he had been told by several cotton manufacturers from Manchester that opium eating was rapidly becoming a habit among the work force:

> "so much so, that on a Saturday afternoon the counters of
> the druggists were strewed with pills of one, two or three
> grains in preparation for the known demand of the
> evening. The immediate occasion of this practice was the
> lowness of wages, which at that time would not allow
> them to indulge in ale or spirits."

In spite of the high consumption, for most of the 19th century, medical practitioners did not think or talk about the problem of opium in terms of addiction. Instead, they recognised two problems - one being the effects of opium on infants and children. By mid-century, it was said that many surgeons could immediately recognise an opium-eating baby: they appeared "shrank up like little old men" or "wizened like little monkeys". [10] The other main problem with opium was deaths through overdose. Some were accidents, others not; suicide remained a criminal offence until 1961.

Morphine

From around the middle of the 19th century, doctors began to use morphine in place of opium. As morphine was a refined and more potent form of opium, doctors might have suspected it too could intoxicate. Conceptually, there should have been no problem: the significance of potency would have been obvious, by comparing, say, the effects of a pint of ale and a pint of gin. But because less of it was needed to get a response, doctors somehow came to believe that morphine was actually safer than opium. Thus morphine began to replace opium and alcohol, and was used to treat states of chronic intoxication with these two.

The popularity of morphine, and belief in its superiority over opium, greatly increased with the invention of the hypodermic syringe in 1854. Doctors believed that an injection would cause less irritation in the gut, because the drug by-passed the stomach and went more directly into the bloodstream. [11] The early medical literature on subcutaneous injection of morphia "was unreservedly euphoric about its uses". [12] In 1868, an expert who advocated the use of hypodermic morphine for neuralgia (nerve pain) declared: "as to the question of danger, let me say, positively, that there is absolutely none". [13]

At first, hypodermic injections were given only by doctors; later, physicians taught patients how to inject themselves. [14] In time, both drug and syringes passed into the hands of patients and their servants and relatives; the habit spread as more and more people learned how to get morphine under their skin. [15]

Morphine also proved itself as one of the first (of many) sedative-hypnotic drugs used systematically by the military, probably first of all in the American Civil War [1861-5].

"Morphine was used during the Civil War without the least realization of its addictive potential. Addicted Civil War veterans, of whom there were presumably a good number, were diagnosed as having "Soldier's sickness". They were discharged with a supply of morphine and syringes as a form of aftercare. As a result, in the 19th century, many families had a morphinist as head of the household. In sharp contrast to the veterans of the Vietnam War, those veterans and war heroes were treated with tender civility." [Freedman, 1980]

The first warnings of a possible danger with morphine were published in 1870; in the meantime, the hypodermic habit had spread and become almost fashionable. The author of a celebrated 1887 report on Morphinomania warned that there were some society women who not only possessed "a regular arsenal of little injecting instruments" but who also dressed for the part.

"Ladies even, belonging to the most elegant classes of society, go so far as to show their good taste in the jewels which they order to conceal a little syringe and artistically made bottles, which are destined to hold the solution which enchants them. At the theatre, in society, they slip away for a moment, or even watch for a favourable opportunity of pretending to play with these trinkets, while giving themselves an injection of morphia in some part of the body which is exposed, or even hidden from view." [Sharkey, 1887]

By the 1880s, the medical profession and the general public had become alert to the problem of morphinism or "morphinomania" and there was even some alarm. However, there was no immediate official response, mainly because of the government's own interests in the trade in opium between British India and China. This business generated for the Exchequer about £2m a year, enough to pay for nearly half of the total cost of the civil service and crown. [16]

Later, Queen Victoria's government set up the Royal Commission on Opium, but it made little difference. In spite of the many submissions from doctors [17] - and a damning minority report and critique by Joseph Rowntree [18] - the Royal Commission concluded in 1895 that the moderate use of opium was "not attended by any injurious consequences." After two years of research both in Britain and India, the commissioners (bar one) found that opium was used intelligently as medicine and in moderation as a stimulant. They did not object to the colonial trade in opium, noting that "to deprive the natives of the drug would cause great suffering." [19]

Cocaine

Cocaine was first isolated from the coca plant in 1860, but South Americans had been getting cocaine into their bloodstream by chewing the leaves, for at least 2,000 years before. [20] At first, cocaine was used mainly in the US as a tonic: by the late 1870s, coca preparations were being advertised for "young persons afflicted with timidity in society" and as "a powerful nervous excitant". [21] Perhaps because it was sold in a dilute solution, and because it was widely available, no evidence of addiction was seen. On the contrary, once morphine addiction was defined as something to be treated, cocaine came into its own.

From the 1880s, cocaine was introduced into medicine in Europe, mainly as a cure for addiction to alcohol, opium and morphine. [22] The effective launch date was 1884, when Sigmund Freud published his monograph, *On Coca*. Freud himself used cocaine at this time, both to study and enjoy its effects: it was "a magical drug". He also used cocaine to treat patients, noting its great effectiveness in a variety of conditions, as well as its properties as a powerful aphrodisiac on some.

Young Freud specifically recommended cocaine as a cure for addiction, hoping to make his name. He staked its benefits partly on observations reported in two notably obscure American medical journals, partly on the manufacturers' claims. But his main authority for endorsing cocaine was personal experience: in his 1884 paper, Freud claimed that he personally knew of one case in which cocaine had been successfully used to treat morphine addiction. Freud was referring here to his own attempts to treat his close friend, Dr Fleishl. It was later established that the treatment, and then the friendship, entirely failed. [23]

When the American manufacturers, the Parke Davis Company, learnt of Freud's enthusiastic endorsement, they declared: "If these claims are substantiated ... [cocaine] will indeed be the most important therapeutic discovery of the age, the benefit of which to humanity will be incalculable." [24] Parke Davis and Merck were the two leading suppliers of cocaine at this time and they are the forerunners of two of the largest pharmaceutical companies operating today.

Notwithstanding this hype, the medical profession quite quickly recognised that cocaine addiction was no less a problem than the addictions it was meant to cure. It soon became clear that cocaine was associated with intense drug-seeking behaviour, and as a result Freud faced increasing criticism from his peers. One prominent doctor accused him of introducing, after alcohol and opium, "the third scourge of humanity." [25] In the face of this onslaught, Freud clung to his theories tenaciously, denying he had ever been wrong.

Because his life and thoughts have been so well documented, the basis of Freud's understanding of the nature of addiction is now fairly clear - and it is worth mentioning because of its relevance today. Freud was just one of many experts over the years to have insisted that the decisive element in drug dependence was the personality of the user, rather than the nature and effects of the drug. However, his advocacy for cocaine demonstrated such a marked capacity to deny hard evidence that it naturally prompts questions about the role of the unconscious in the medical professional's mind.

Freud had believed that his reputation and fortune depended on the great benefits of cocaine that he described in 1884 - so when his peers rounded on him a few years later, he was under great pressure to save face. In the circumstances, he could not simply admit that cocaine was an addictive drug, nor did he believe it, because he himself could stop. Nonetheless, he appeared to make some concessions to his critics. In a paper published three years on (1887), he agreed that some people did seem to get addicted to cocaine - but only because they had been previously addicted to morphine. This was not true, but it must have been quite persuasive, because the same line of argument has persisted. Well into the 1980s, the manufacturers of benzodiazepines claimed that their drugs were addicting only for established (or latent) addicts - people who would get addicted to almost anything, given half a chance.

Freud also claimed that the apparent addiction was not to do with the drug, but with the syringe. To assuage his colleagues, Freud argued this point with some nonsense about injections and variable rates of cerebral blood flow - though, according to his official biographer, this was not what he believed. Freud apparently condemned the hypodermic syringe rather than the drug because he understood that the syringe was unconsciously perceived as a threatening object, an obvious target for blame. This came to him from early experience with psychoanalysis: Freud believed that "patients who have an unwonted dread of it leave no doubt about its symbolic meaning to the unconscious mind." [26]

Whatever the psychological significance, Freud's condemnation of the hypodermic syringe wholly contradicted recommendations he had published two years before. In 1885, Freud had specifically recommended injecting cocaine; later, all he could do was deny it. His official biographer has noted how that earlier paper, like Freud's recollection of this episode, "seems to have been completely suppressed."[27]

Throughout his lifetime, Freud continued to insist that any addiction to cocaine "was not, as was commonly believed, the direct result of imbibing a noxious drug, but to some peculiarity in the patient". Freud had apparently been able to control his use of cocaine, yet he was severely addicted to tobacco for most of his life; apparently he saw no special significance in his own habit, though he acknowledged that smoking had probably caused cancer of his mouth and jaw. He underwent 33 operations for this condition in the last 16 years of his life but, until his death, he smoked "an endless series of cigars". Freud's experience underlines how patients may become scapegoats, especially if reputations are at stake; it also shows how even the greatest experts can be quite blind about themselves.

> "Freud died of cancer in 1939, at the age of eighty-three.
> His efforts over a forty-five-year period to stop smoking,
> his repeated inability to stop, his suffering when he tried
> to stop, and the persistence of his craving and suffering
> even after fourteen continuous months of abstinence - a '
> torture ... beyond human power to bear' - make him the
> tragic prototype of tobacco addiction." [Brecher, 1973]

Freud never renounced his view that addiction to cocaine was basically something that people brought on themselves - and long after he first advocated cocaine for morphinism, the problem remained.

> "Since the introduction of cocaine into general therapeutic use, numerous cases of the formation of a habit similar to that of opium or morphine, have been recorded. Some of these have been due to the attempt to substitute cocaine for morphine in the treatment of chronic mor-

phinism, the treatment often resulting in the development of an irresistible craving for both ...." [Cushny,
1903, 1928]

Doctors get it together

Probably without realising it, Thomas de Quincey witnessed some of
the earliest pressure to get the sale of opium controlled. De Quincey
wrote that he had been reliably informed by several "respectable"
druggists that they got into "daily troubles and disputes" in trying to
distinguish between opium eaters with a habit and those who wanted
the drug "with a view to suicide". Perhaps the point these druggists
were really making was that, unlike your average grocer, the professional could be relied on to tell the difference between someone who
was likely to remain a good customer, and someone who wasn't.

As the drug habit spread, there was increasing pressure from the
doctors for drug control - but for many years it was never achieved,
because of the great commercial and professional rivalries involved. [28]
For most of the 19th century, the doctors, the druggists and traders
were at odds with each other - while the medical profession was mostly at odds with itself. The result was a power vacuum which left
opium (and its derivatives) available to anyone who could afford it.
The earliest attempt to control it was the Pharmacy Act of 1868, which
required merely that drugs be labelled and dispensed only by qualified persons. But this law did not effectively restrict the sale of patent
medicines, many with opium among the ingredients. So, increasing
amounts of opium were sold over the counter, as the embryonic drug
industry began to grow.

The 1868 law was weak because the druggists and traders successfully resisted the doctors' attempts to control the supply of opium
themselves. This would have reduced their earnings, giving doctors
monopoly rights in a buoyant sellers' market. Control over opium
would have given doctors access to a large market of patients who
would have had to pay consultation fees for their drugs. It was quite
natural that the control of opiates should be central in professionalis-
ing medicine. Throughout the 19th century, opium and morphine
were among the very few effective drugs there were; they were used
copiously, as tranquillisers would be in their day.

It took until the turn of the 20th century to begin to control opium -
and it happened only because the different parts of the medical pro-

fession finally united and became organised. For most of the 19th century, medicine was dominated by factions. At the top of the profession were the university-educated Physicians; they considered themselves very superior indeed. After them came the Surgeons, descendants of the barber-surgeons of the middle ages. They became established as the Royal College of Surgeons in 1800 and, like the Physicians, tended to practise in hospitals and to treat only the wealthier classes, the "carriage trade". This left the Apothecaries to treat the masses: they dispensed medicines and often ran surgeries as well.

The deadlock which had helped to delay the introduction of controls over opium was finally broken in 1879, when the apothecaries joined forces with the surgeons, combining their entrance examinations. This left the physicians so isolated that they had to allow the apothecaries and surgeons to practise medicine with them. The following account explains how the medical profession developed from about 1880, and how it relates to general practice today.

> "At the bottom was the surgeon chemist. He did the work of a medical man and carried on the trade of a chemist, but it was this last he depended on - a shop with toothbrushes, soap, nail brushes, hair tonic and so on. Next came the surgeon-apothecary. They held open surgery signalled by a red lamp. They did no retail trading but would often dispense. They would charge a shilling or so for medicine and advice and visit for a weekly sum of from a penny to a shilling. Dispensing doctors have never entirely disappeared, but as he became grander, the surgeon-apothecary's surgery would go out of sight. Finally he would join the non-dispensing GP of the 1890s. His medicine would be made up by the chemist." [Gathorne-Hardy, 1980, after Rivington 1879]

By the beginning of the 20th century, the roles of doctor and chemist were well distinguished - though in some respects there was not a lot to choose between them. At this time, the basic training in therapeutics for medical students mainly involved memorising the drug list, *Materia Medica Pura*, and learning to write prescriptions in Latin. The Latin hieroglyphic on the prescription may not have helped the patient, but did help both to perpetuate the mysteries of medicine, and to keep chemists employed. The standard text of the day, *The*

Practice of Pharmacy, noted this.

> "One of the most important duties of the pharmacist is the unravelling of prescriptions, and upon his cleverness in accurately divining the intention of the physician will often depend his reputation for skill and ability."
> [Remington, 1905]

Latin survived on the prescription form until the 1970s, when there was an important change in the law. Shortly after the introduction of the first benzodiazepines, people in Britain for the first time became entitled to know the names of the drugs they were being prescribed. This change did not reflect a new awareness of patients' rights. It happened mainly because doctors treating emergency overdose cases needed to be able to identify the sedative-hypnotic or other drugs that victims had taken, so they could give the right antidote. [29]

Companies learn to depend on doctors

During the second half of the 19th century, the patent medicine market grew rapidly, and increasingly the doctors saw it as a threat to their trade, status and collective pride. The newly-emerging drug industry was trumpeting about guaranteed cures for everything, often boasting about patent medicines which would do far more for patients than any doctor possibly could. The manufacturers made claims for their products which ranged from cheeky to outrageous, and all cleverly exploited the magic and secrecy which was basic to the practice of medicine at that time. The doctors felt angry about all kinds of patent medicines - but they focused on products containing opiates, because there were good grounds for attack.

The gulf that existed between doctors and drug companies in the late 19th century is reflected, for example, in the code of ethics of the American Medical Association: "Equally derogatory to professional character is it, for a physician to hold a patent for any surgical instrument or medicine". [30] Nowadays, the patent system underpins pharmaceutical medicine - but around the turn of the 20th century, the newly-emerged doctors and the newly-emerging drug industry were poles apart.

The main issue between them was the control of opium, and in the end the doctors won. Victory came by vigorously publicising the dangers of the drug, at the same time prompting a series of prosecutions for drug supply by unqualified traders. By convincing the authorities that opium was safe(r) only if doctors controlled its use, the medical profession secured laws which forced many manufacturers of patent medicines to remove opium from their products.

This reform came just before the turn of the 19th century, but a few very popular medicines did manage to survive for a few years more - until the 1908 Poisons and Pharmacy Act finally put the lid on things. One of the last products to go was Mrs Winslow's Soothing Syrup, a morphine-based preparation for babies and infants which "contains no Poisonous Ingredient and may be used with Perfect Safety". The law barely controlled such lies. At the beginning of this century, the government's main concern would have been to sustain the 12.5 per cent stamp tax it collected on all patent medicine sales. [31]

The doctors' campaign against the patent medicines industry began with an attack on the most dangerous and popular brands, but continued for some years after the offending ingredients had been removed. The climax of the campaign was the publication by the British Medical Association of *Secret Remedies* in 1909 and *More Secret Remedies* in 1912. The preface to the first of these two classic and deliciously venomous books began with a diatribe on secrecy which all but suggested that the drug pedlars had invented it. It was as if the drug industry was trying to hijack the placebo effect and the doctors didn't like it at all.

"One of the reasons for the popularity of secret remedies is their secrecy ... To begin with, there is for the average man or woman a certain fascination in secrecy. The quack takes advantage of this common foible of human nature to impress his customers. But secrecy has other uses in his trade; it enables him to make use of cheap new or old fashioned drugs; and to claim that his product possesses virtues beyond the ken of the mere doctor; his herbs have been culled in some remote prairie in America, the secret of their virtues having been confided to him by some venerable chief; or again he would have us believe that his drug has been discovered by chemical research of such alchemical profundity, and is produced by processes so costly and elaborate that it can only be sold at a very high price." [BMA, 1909]

Though spurned by doctors, the infant pharmaceutical industry adapted to the market well enough to thrive. To the dismay of the medical profession, many patent medicine manufacturers simply reformulated their products and went on selling them as before. The makers of Mrs Winslow's Soothing Syrup responded to a series of prosecutions by removing the morphine and adding a sedative, potassium bromide, instead. The BMA fumed.

"Which of these two is the more unsuitable to giving to infants of a few weeks old is, for the moment, not the question: the alteration of the composition of a medicine which continues to be sold under the old name and with statements as to its having been made for sixty years, shows how utterly the public is at the mercy of the proprietors of such preparations, who are at liberty to omit or add ingredients or to alter the composition as they please." [BMA, 1912]

But in the meantime, the infant pharmaceutical industry was beginning to sort itself out. Companies assumed leading and lagging roles, and the leading companies increasingly sought and made contact with doctors. They needed doctors to prescribe and endorse the new and more potent compounds they were beginning to make; doctors in turn were pleased to have new treatments at their disposal. The claims made for these products were far from scrupulous - but perhaps they didn't appear so bad, because the old brashness was giving way to a more deferential tone. The big companies began to sweet-talk the doctors - and also gently began telling them what to do.

One of the first products a major drug company promoted specifically to the medical profession was diamorphine. It was developed by the German-based company, Bayer, in 1898, and sold under the brand name, Heroin. Bayer originally promoted it as a "non-addicting cough supressant" for infants, but before long it was used to treat addiction too.

Addiction defined, treatment unrefined

It took until 1913 for the first report of dependence on heroin to appear but, as so often happens, this first report spawned many more. And so, by the beginning of this century, a clear pattern of error and trial had emerged: doctors replaced one addictive drug with another, always ready to believe that the new drug was quite safe. This is how Cushny summed things up in the 1928 edition of his *Textbook on Pharmacology and Therapeutics*.

"The morphine habit has often been combated by the
substitution of other drugs, such as heroin or cocaine, but
the result generally has been that a new and even more
dangerous habit has been substituted for, or often merely
grafted on, the original. Numerous drugs have been proposed for the cure of morphinomania, but none of them
seems to have the slightest effect."

However, by the 1920s, the opiates were more effectively controlled
by law. To some extent this did acknowledge their strongly addictive
properties - though the prevailing view was still that the user was to
blame for addiction, as for much else that went wrong. And yet,
around the turn of this century, perhaps 10 per cent of doctors were
themselves addicted to cocaine and/or an opiate. [32] The overwhelming majority of patients treated for addiction came from the professional and middle classes as well. [33]

Addiction began to be defined as a condition requiring medical
treatment towards the end of the 19th century, as the medical profession began to get control of addictive drugs. The various theories of
addiction that had emerged by then "professed objectivity, but were
in fact closely linked to the 'vice' conceptualizations which prevailed
in anti-opium and temperance circles". [34] These defined the nub of the
problem as excess resulting from inadequate resistance to temptation.

But slowly there developed the concept of a drug as something
which could chemically bend and even overpower normal human
will. This realisation began to emerge from studies of the behaviour of
addicts cut off from their drugs. It was found that there was a definite
pattern of symptoms, a withdrawal syndrome which seemed distinct
from other forms of madness. This discovery began to temper more
extreme views, for example that addicts were "practically as moral
imbeciles, often addicted also to other forms of depravity". [35]

But until this understanding came, the withdrawal symptoms
which were later recognised as hallmarks of drug addiction were seen
as separate ailments - to be treated with laudanum and the like. [36] The
withdrawal syndrome was first clearly defined around 1880, notably
in a study of *Morbid Cravings for Morphia [Die Morphiumsucht]* by Dr
Eduard Levinstein of Berlin. [37] Levinstein's subjects were hospitalised
addicts who were abruptly taken off morphine and then observed and
nursed for several weeks until they were judged cured.

By the end of the 19th century, there were increasing numbers of medical experts and specialists on addiction, all with different ideas, but all agreeing that this was a condition which doctors should treat. Judging from the following recommendation for the treatment of acute opium intoxication, medical interventions could be very vigorous indeed.

"As the respiration begins to fail, it is to be encouraged by irritation of the skin, either by dashing cold water on it, by the electric current, or by flipping it with towels. The violent flagellation formerly advocated with the view of encouraging the respiration, served also usually to exhaust the nervous energy of both patient and attendant." [Cushny, 1903]

Medical experts recommended many different approaches to the treatment of addiction, but the main difference between them was in the timing of withdrawal. Later, the experts would advocate a progressive but gradual reduction of dose to reduce the chances of a violent reaction on withdrawal. But at first, the standard procedure was to withdraw people abruptly from their drugs, as Dr Levinstein had done. Abrupt withdrawal in fact became a medical speciality: it was so enthusiastically advocated and practised by doctors here that it was known internationally as The English Method. Later, people sometimes called it cold turkey - an allusion to the appearance of the withdrawn addict's skin, rather than to the country from which much opium came.

However, treatment for withdrawal was reserved mainly for the most wretched and conspicuous of addicts, or for patients who could afford clinic fees. Even at the turn of the 20th century, most people were not treated for addiction - other than with further supplies of drugs. Prescribing of opiates was still remarkably unrestrained, and there is little evidence that doctors felt they might be implicated in creating the very problems they claimed to be able to solve. Thus, until about 1880, it was still the custom at Kings College Hospital, London, to give patients morphine sometimes for weeks on end, and then abruptly discharge them. [38]

About 100 years later, many NHS hospitals were doing the same thing with benzodiazepines. [39] Well into the 1970s, hospitals would routinely prescribe benzodiazepines for in-patients, to keep them calm and help them sleep. It helped ward routines too: "Wake up Mr Smith: it's time for your sleeping pill". Over half of all hospital patients used to be given sleeping pills, [40] and once discharged from hospital, some would get further supplies from their GPs. Many people started a benzodiazepine habit in this way. [41]

1 Medawar, 1984 (a)
2 Lancet, 1865
3 Warner, 1980
4 Lancet, 1865
5 Lancet, 1870
6 Cushny, 1928
7 Wingate (Ed), 1985
8 Cit. Berridge, 1978
9 JAMA, 1963
10 Brockington, 1965
11 Peters, 1981
12 Parssinen and Kerner, 1980
13 Anstie, 1868
14 Peters, 1981
15 Parssinen and Kerner, 1980
16 Inglis, 1975
17 Peters, 1981
18 Inglis, 1975
19 Royal Commission, 1895
20 Connor, 1991
21 Caldwell, 1970

22 Grinspoon & Bakalar, 1981
23 Jones, 1953
24 Byck, 1974
25 Erlenmeyer, 1886
26 Jones, 1953
27 Jones, 1953.
28 Berridge, 1978
29 Drug & Ther Bull, 1972
30 Swann, 1988
31 BMA, 1909
32 Berridge, 1978
33 Berridge, 1978
34 Berridge, 1978
35 Movat, 1892
36 Musto, 1985
37 Levinstein, 1878
38 Berridge, 1978
39 Monopolies Commission, 1972
40 Wells, 1976
41 Clift, 1972

Chapter 3

MORE AND LESS HEROIC WAYS

"As an illustration of the persistence with which chloral is some-times given, in spite of evidence of the want of any benefit, and indeed of the positive harm done by it, I may mention a case of acute hysterical mania which I was asked to see once. Full doses of chloral had been given twice a day for weeks; and a larger dose at night. But the excitement had not been abated in the least, and the mental state was worse; moreover matters had reached the pass that it was impossible to get the young lady to take it by the mouth. The daily doses had perforce, therefore, been abandoned, and the nightly dose was administered by the rectum. But as there was great struggling, and much difficulty in doing it, the patient was every night rendered insensible by chloroform and the dose then injected. The treatment was discontinued for a few days but recurred to afterwards, I believe, and eventually, the patient died." [Maudsley, 1895]

Chloral

Back in the late 19th century - as alcohol, opiates and then cocaine began to lose favour - doctors looked to alternatives. One was chloral hydrate, a sedative-hypnotic in its own right which was also pre-scribed to treat addiction. Chloral is still sometimes prescribed as a sleeping draught, so it is worth asking how it survived so long. It was because of increased knowledge about how drugs work and the effects they have - and in spite of new trends and fashions in prescrib-ing.

When introduced in 1869, chloral was welcomed as "a new wonder drug" and "a sensational medicine". [1] Although it was not launched and promoted as drugs are today, there was an explosive demand for it: in the first 18 months after its introduction, around 50 million doses of chloral were used in England alone. Any potent novel medicine would have been welcomed at this time - because there were so few other medicines to choose from - but chloral had a very specific advantage. It was found to be less dangerous than opium in overdose and not nearly as popular for suicide. Chloral was increasingly adopted as a safer alternative to alcohol and the opiates, and later to cocaine. [2]

The first published reports of what would now be called "dependence" date from only a few years after chloral became available. By 1874, chloral eating was acknowledged to be a common problem; ten years later, Blyth's textbook, *Poisons*, recorded that "an enormous number of people habitually take chloral". But there was no great concern about this, partly because there were relatively few recorded fatalities, also because habitual use was relatively inconspicuous. Chloral does not cause euphoria to compare with opium or cocaine and it has a rather unpleasant taste. It could certainly cause dependence, but never emerged as a major drug of abuse.

By the end of the last century, the first official statistics on drug fatalities had begun to appear. Although they showed that many more people died from opium overdose, chloral did not get an entirely clean bill of health. It was quite soon recognised that the amount that would cause a fatal overdose was only about five times greater than the average amounts doctors then usually prescribed.

Today, doctors prescribe around half the dose usually given then - and doctors in those days were also much more inclined to prescribe very high doses for patients who didn't respond to less. When doctors used really high doses, they described their treatments as "heroic". They were not referring to the forebearance of patients upon whom such treatments were inflicted; the term rather implied that doctors were the heroes, because of their confidence in the drastic treatments they used.

Another important difference between chloral then and now is that doctors today are much more likely to recognise the importance of adjusting the dose of the drug to the response of the individual patient. One hundred years ago it was known that individual responses to chloral varied greatly: a report in *Chemist & Druggist* [1886] noted that some individuals were more affected by a lowish dose of chloral than others who could take five times that amount. But doctors did not realise this meant that they should generally start each patient on a lowish dose, working up to the dose that gave the best response. Instead, doctors tended to give big doses and then deliver firm opinions, one way or another, on the value of the drug - and, by extension, of themselves.

Partly because its effects seemed unpredictable, chloral had largely lost favour with doctors by the turn of the century - so why is it sometimes prescribed instead of benzodiazepines even today ? The short answer is that, although chloral acquired a bad name not long after it appeared, in time doctors learned to use it more effectively. The fact that chloral has survived underlines the important difference between how safe a drug can be if used properly, and how safe in practice it actually turns out to be.

Maudsley's uncommon sense

The pioneer psychiatrist, Henry Maudsley, discussed the use of chloral at some length in Pathology of Mind [1895] - and a century later some of his views about the place of drug treatment in psychiatric illness still seem ahead of their time. Maudsley had decided that the discovery of chloral "has been thus far, not a good, but an evil, to the human race". He preferred to use an opiate or bromide drug; better still, he looked to non-drug solutions instead. Although he took a dim view of chloral, Maudsley recognised that many other doctors did not - but then he reasoned that the most trustworthy doctors trusted chloral least.

> "Unhappily, experience speaks with directly contradictory voices: one physician of an asylum, after a full trial of the hydrate of chloral, endorses the description of it as 'crystallised hell', another considers it the most useful drug we have in the treatment of insanity: One physician declares most confidently that the one form of insanity in which opium or chloral is unquestionably pernicious is acute delirious mania; another physician boasts that he has never lost a case of acute delirious mania since he has freely used chloral hydrate in the treatment of it. Such are the contradictory voices of experience. One requires to know the character of the experimenter in order to decide which voice to trust; albeit one may feel pretty sure in a question of the action of a medical drug, that he who is least heroic in his use of it, and least confident in

his opinion of its powers, will be most likely, in virtue of
his mental temperament, to have observed accurately
and to have inferred soundly."

Maudsley was one of the first doctors to question the real benefit of
treatment which involved "putting the nerve cells of the patient's
brain into chemical restraint, so to speak" [3] - and to ask whether this
might promote and prolong mental illness rather than cure it. He was
also critical of methods of drug evaluation, and distinguished firmly
between drug efficacy and therapeutic effectiveness. Was it conceivable, he asked, that a drug like chloral could sedate as intended, while
harming the patient all along ? Such doubts led him to emphasise
repeatedly that chloral and similar drugs should be used very sparingly, if at all.

"And yet so little of this is considered that one frequently
hears the long-continued use of some sedative lauded
with naive exultation, and without a word being said, or
apparently without a thought being given, as to whether
patients recovered better, or recovered at all, by taking
it". " ... a single dose, or an occasional dose from time to
time, at the commencement or in the course of a mental
disorder, as a palliative, may certainly be useful, but its
habitual use is pernicious ... When that which may be
used fitly as a temporary help - whether it be stimulant
or narcotic - is resorted to as an abiding stay, the result
cannot fail to be disastrous."

Maudsley was one of the first to advocate what would now be
labelled a holistic approach:

"The wise physician will treat his patient, not an abstract
melancholic entity".

His views on drugs even led him to suggest that some of his colleagues themselves try a dose of their own medicine - for example a
strong mercurial purge to see how it made them feel. He proposed
many alternatives to drugs, including basics like attention to diet. The
melancholic, for example, was recommended to start the day with a
light breakfast, followed by something at about eleven o'clock, with
"oysters or a small quantity of meat at luncheon ... a dinner of not
more than two courses between one and two in the day, and a little
milk or arrowroot or beef tea before going to bed". Maudsley also
commended exercise in the treatment of mental disease.

"If one could persuade or compel a strong and turbulent
maniac to plough a field, or to row several hours a day,
or to walk twenty miles a day for a month ... the treatment would do him more good than he would get from
all the drugs of the Pharmacopoeia."

Underlying Maudsley's concerns was another idea that proved far
ahead of its time: he questioned whether sleep induced by drugs like
chloral did as much good as the real thing. The prevailing wisdom
was that chloral promoted 'natural' sleep - apparently on the grounds
that the sedated patient (unlike someone who was anaesthetised or
intoxicated) could be roused. Maudsley was most concerned that
everyone seemed to take for granted that drug-induced sleep was natural, just because they appeared to be the same.

"It really amounts to this - that it must be a benefit to get
sleep where there is sleeplessness, and that it is certainly
proper to extinguish a fire which is burning down a
house. But it is not considered, not even suspected
apparently, that natural sleep and narcotic-enforced
sleep may be two different conditions and ought not perhaps to be spoken of, without more discrimination, by
the common name of sleep ... Exact information with
respect to that point may be set down as entirely wanting: the chloral-produced state looks like sleep, and all
the rest has been assumed."

For all of these insights, Maudsley was less enlightened in some of
his views. He had weird ideas, for example, about the benefits of
wrapping mentally ill patients tightly in wet sheets; and his views on
masturbation appear extreme, even disturbed, [4] if generally in keeping with the times. Maudsley's views derived from a school which
held that masturbation was indulging the devil. His references to "the
miserable sinner whose mind suffers by reason of self abuse" and to
this "vicious habit", "utter moral perversion" and so on, underline the
closeness and confusion there still was between guilt, illness and sin.

"Physicians, the new guardians of morality, simply substituted new names for ancient evils: madness became
mental illness; drunkenness became alcoholism; and the
sin of Onan became masturbation. The old sins to be confronted and overcome were, by the late nineteenth century, diseases to be cured." [Parssinen & Kerner, 1980]

Ordeal by bromides

Kellogg's Cornflakes were introduced in 1898 specifically as an anti-masturbation food. [5] Masturbation was not only a sin; in the 19th century and for some time thereafter, doctors thought that it caused mental illness. Specifically they believed it was a cause of epilepsy - itself regarded as a hallmark of madness - and this partly explains how the bromides came to be used. Potassium bromide was first recommended in 1857 by the aptly named Sir Charles Lowcock. He had used it for epilepsy because he found it had a marked anti-aphrodisiac effect in 13 out of the 14 patients he had treated. [6] The bromides did indeed suppress the symptoms of epilepsy (but not by dulling desire) and before long they were established as a valuable class of drugs. There were many different kinds and mixtures to choose from, but potassium bromide emerged as the drug of choice.

The bromides came to be prescribed for many illnesses and for almost every seemingly abnormal state of mind, including drug addiction of all kinds. Bromides were generally used for conditions which would today be treated by tranquillisers and antidepressants, and were recommended for use in pregnancy and for children as well. As late as 1917, a correspondent to the *Lancet* suggested that: "A physician need have no hesitation in keeping an excitable or nervous child on a trifling dose of bromide throughout the greater part of his schooldays." [7] According to Seguin [1877] "the bromides are called for whenever there is excitement". Yet he also recommended them for depression - "a disease in which cerebral nutrition is quite surely lowered and perverted."

Along with a variety of other drugs, bromides also played their part in the defence of the realm. Some years after World War II, a prominent psychiatrist, Dr William Sargant, described how bromide and other sedatives had been used to encourage soldiers to face battle. They were used not only to restore shattered nerves, but also to prevent them shattering in the first place.

> "Millions of pounds in pensions were, for instance, saved in World War II simply because it was at last realised that immediate and heavy 'front line' sedation was generally more effective in the prevention of chronic neuroses, and of so-called 'malingering' reactions, than all the threats of shooting for cowardice and the verbal exhortations and moral punishments used instead as

treatments from time immemorial." [Sargant, 1958]

Even in the late 1950s, in the dying days of National Service (military conscription) in Britain, it was rumoured among soldiers that bromides were routinely used as anti-aphrodisiacs. But there may have been other explanations for the disgusting taste of army tea.

Early in their history, there was also some concern that bromides might cause permanent impotence, perhaps having "the power to absorb the testicle or other glandular structures" [8] - but the prevailing view was that the bromides were effective and safe, and one of the most valuable medicines available. It was claimed that: "there is not the slightest indication of impotency or anything disadvantageous resulting from long exhibition of the drug to counterbalance its beneficial effects". [9] Later, the potential dangers of overdosing and addiction were mentioned more, and an editorial in the *Lancet* (1889) emphasised that "every experienced practitioner ... must have noticed that the bromides are not as harmless as they were first thought to be".

The problem of bromide intoxication (bromism) was first noted in 1850; [10] not long afterwards there appeared reports which listed most of the symptoms of toxicity that are recognised today. But although it was known early on that bromides were only slowly excreted - and therefore tended to accumulate in the body - doctors did not appreciate the extent of illness this caused. The trouble was that patients were routinely prescribed higher doses of bromides than their bodies could excrete before the next dose was due - so the longer bromides were used, the more damaging their effects tended to be.

The nub of the problem was that the symptoms of bromide intoxication - "increased restlessness with disorientation followed by paranoid trends, hallucinations, and apprehension" [11] - in themselves suggested the need for treatment. A vicious cycle was therefore established: patients who behaved abnormally because of bromide intoxication were treated with more bromides, or perhaps with sedative-hypnotic drugs of other kinds. This phenomenon continued unnoticed for many years.

The beginnings of a breakthough came in 1927, when a simple test was developed for measuring the concentration of bromides in the blood - which could then be compared with levels that were known to be toxic. Some hospitals started using these tests right away, so that symptoms of bromide intoxication could more readily be distinguished from mental illness - but most doctors were very slow to react.

> "We do not wish to leave the impression that we consider bromide harmful or even useless as a therapeutic agent. Anyone who has had occasion to use bromides realises that it can be an effective and valuable sedative. We do believe however that the bromides are used much too indiscriminately and frequently produce harmful rather than beneficial effects. These harmful effects of bromide could be reduced to a minimum if physicians recognised the undesirable mental symptoms of bromide intoxication and were willing to use the simple method described by Wuth for determining the bromide concentration in the blood." [Wagner & Bunbury, 1930]

In spite of such advice, the bromides continued to be used on a phenomenal scale, and not just in hospitals: by 1930, bromides were included in four general practice prescriptions out of every ten. [12] Perhaps they did some good; they certainly also did much harm. Looking back, some 20 years after the event, Dr William Sargant described how patients he had seen in some institutions were kept in states of chronic bromide intoxication as if this were the norm.

> "My first locum appointment in a mental hospital, in 1934, showed me rows of patients sitting silently along benches with drooping heads and salivating mouths. You could generally tell the heavily drugged patients during a ward round because you could pat them on the backs of their heads while they were sitting in rows. This was because their relaxed heads fell so far forward on their chests. All these tranquillised patients were then using bromides in truly enormous doses." [Sargant, 1956]

But even as Dr Sargant was reminiscing about this grim past, there was still an appreciable amount of bromide intoxication. In his novel *The Ordeal of Gilbert Pinfold* [1957], Evelyn Waugh described his own experience of bromide intoxication and psychosis - though the medical implications of this went unnoticed for some time. Waugh's biographers recognised that Pinfold was an autobiographical account, but apparently never linked the ordeal described in the novel with Waugh's own use of bromides. The connection was first made in a report in *Clinical Neuropharmacology*, published 30 years on. [13]

> "The first signs of toxicity appear quite early in the book. Crimson blotches appear on his skin, he misspells words, his memory plays tricks on him, his body aches, and his complexion is muddy. He becomes clumsy, is irritable with his wife and is frightened by memory lapses. In this condition, he books passage on a ship bound for Ceylon [Sri Lanka] ... As he prepares to leave, Pinfold develops delusions and time distortions. He accuses his wife of giving some of his hairs to the neighbour to measure his life waves ... Arriving on the ship, Pinfold is unable to unpack and carries on a disjointed exchange with the steward:
>
> "I'm not very well. I wonder if you could unpack for me?"
> "Dinner seven-thirty o'clock, sir!"
> "I said, could you unpack for me?"
> "No sir, bar not open in port sir."

The wider significance of all this is how long it takes for medical practice to adapt, in spite of the clear need for change. Dr William Sargant and others had campaigned vigorously to restrict the use of bromides since the 1930s - and by the outbreak of War the dangers of these drugs should have been well known. The 1942 edition of Price's *Textbook of the Practice of Medicine* recommended, for example, that GPs prescribe bromides only for very severe anxiety. It warned that: "The symptoms of intoxication must be watched for with more than usual vigilance when bromide is being given, because if unrecognised as such they may lead to certification - for an avoidable drug-made psychosis".

Nevertheless, cases of bromism were reported in Britain at least until the 1970s [14]; and even today "despite the warnings on the dangers of bromides for over 50 years many preparations are still available in many countries ... and reports of iatrogenic bromism are still appearing in the world literature ... ". [15]

Years later, the same kind of mistakes would be made with the barbiturates, and later still with the benzodiazepines. Either through continuous use and/or after withdrawal, all of these drugs tend to produce symptoms which mimic mental illness - including, often, the very conditions for which they are usually prescribed. The bromides, the barbiturates, the benzodiazepines and many other similar drugs have all been extensively used in their day to treat the very symptoms of illness that they themselves have caused.

Drug and other treatment of the mentally ill

Though general practice prescriptions for bromides began to decline before World War II, specialists continued to use these and other drugs in a variety of drastic treatments. Around the 1940s, for example, psychiatrists treated schizophrenia with bromides to induce "continuous narcosis for nearly a fortnight". [16] Another treatment introduced in the 1930s, and used certainly into the 1970s, involved treatment with insulin to keep patients in a permanent state of coma: "a full course of therapy often entailed induction of one hundred or more comas, requiring hospitalisation for four to five months, even when treatments were given six times a week". [17] Equally hazardous were treatments in which drugs were used to induce convulsions. After the War, these gave way to electro-convulsive therapy (ECT) but both in those days carried substantial risks.

> "Both forms of convulsive therapy are frequently complicated by fractures and dislocations resulting from the sudden massive muscular contractions of the tonic seizure. Fractures of the bodies of the fourth to eighth dorsal vertebrae occur in about 20 per cent of the male patients and 5 per cent of the female patients. Such fractures may cause considerable pain and discomfort, but they are usually not disabling and do not, in the opinion of workers in the field, constitute a contraindication to further shock therapy." [Drill, 1958]

In the heyday of the bromides - around the end of the 1920s - some of the attitudes doctors held about the mentally ill seem by today's standards far from sane. By then the notion of mental illness as sin had largely given way to the belief that bad breeding was to blame - and that something should be done about it. Such views later found expression in the Third Reich, but they had some support in principle in Britain too. For example, a respected physician and historian of medicine, Dr Charles Singer, quite frankly proposed that ill-bred people should not be permitted to breed.

In his *Short History of Medicine* [1928], Singer asserted as a "medical principle" that: "Whatever view may be taken of the question of the artificial limitation of human fertility, it is almost impossible to imagine that the free breeding of these classes of defectives, epileptics and their congeners, will continue unchecked in any civilised community." He suggested that an important underlying cause of schizophrenia (then called dementia praecox) was poverty which itself was seen rather as sin/disease.

> "Much less hopeful is the outlook with those forms of insanity, especially common in the adolescent, which are of the nature of a perversion of development. Such is the large group known as 'Dementia Praecox'. These cases almost invariably originate from a mentally unsatisfactory stock ... It must be remembered that more than 90 per cent. of the insane in England and a similar percentage in other countries are paupers ..."

With hindsight, it seems that doctors did to some extent assert their authority by arousing anxiety and fear. At the same time, Dr Singer, and no doubt many of his colleagues, sincerely believed that "the general care and treatment of the insane has improved out of all knowledge during the last quarter of a century". Indeed, Singer asserted it was "probable that there is now no class of sick person who is more skilfully and considerately cared for".

There would have been little opportunity for patients to protest about their plight, let alone to identify ill-treatment as the cause. Since mental illness and drug dependence was believed to come from deep within the patient, complaining would have amounted to self-denunciation. If patients themselves were defined as the root cause of the problem, what could they possibly complain about and to whom? Even the experts who had been outspoken in criticising doctors for the indiscriminate and damaging use of bromides suggested that patients who suffered from bromism "consisted for the most part of that type of individual who is unable to make an adequate social adjustment and who resorts to alcohol and drugs as an escape from the situations in life which he considers intolerable." [18]

And yet there had been many improvements over earlier practices, even worse - and neither had Maudsley's views been forgotten 50 years on. The 1942 edition of Price's classic textbook, *The Practice of Medicine*, echoed his advice.

> " 'Mechanical restraint' and violence are now foreign to the treatment of insanity; the patient may be unre-

strained and violent, but his treatment may not ... force
must always be a last resort; and chemical substitutes for
it seem only little less of an evil. Drugs have their place in
the treatment of all kinds of mental disorder, but their
use easily turns to abuse ... Sedative drugs should not be
a short cut; neither should they be eschewed. They
should be given when other measures will not serve ..."

Nevertheless, it has been estimated that about 10 per cent of all
admissions to psychiatric institutions in the 1950s were the result of
bromism - so why was this earlier advice largely ignored ? Partly it
was because there seemed few alternatives to drug treatments. It is
not suprising that drugs proved indispensable if the alternative could
mean spending long and hard days in a tepid bath - paying meticulous attending to water temperature, presumably through ceaseless
manipulation of thermometer, bathplug and taps. This was one of the
suggestions Price made in 1942, as an alternative to drugs.

"Prolonged baths - for 8 or 10 hours daily at a constant
temperature of 96o to 98oF. - have much value in allaying
restlessness, whether of the manic or the anxious kind,
especially the former. They have the further merit of
diminishing angry contact with other people, permitting
fairly free movement and lessening dirtiness, besides
promoting sleep."

Some doctors must have been able to help patients by giving reas-
surance and advice instead of drugs. Yet there was never really any
serious competition between drug treatments and counselling by GPs,
in spite of myths to this effect. Not long after the War, for example, the
editors of *The Practitioner* (1953) lamented that the barbiturates had
become substitutes for former and better ways - which supposedly
involved "the careful search for the cause of the patient's insomnia
and worry which used to be the hallmark of the old family doctor."
But this seems fanciful. Price (1942) specifically warned GPs to leave
counselling to experts - suggesting that the directive advice doctors
were inclined to give often made things worse.

"Neurotic patients are often advised to get married,
especially if loneliness and sexual needs trouble them, as
though marriage were a panacea .... "
"Weary, depressed patients are often harmfully urged to
go to dances and lively seaside resorts where they must

try to look happy ..."
"Exhortations to 'pull yourself together' are as out of place as advice to take a voyage or an argument about delusions ..."
"It requires a close knowledge of the facts and psychiatric experience to give advice on matters that may wholly alter the course of a patient's life - advice, say, about separating from his wife, giving up his job, or emigrating to the Dominions."

1 Clarke, 1988
2 Olivieri et al, 1986
3 Maudsley, 1895
4 Turner, 1988
5 Observer magazine,
30 June 1991, 42
6 Goodman & Gilman, 1941;
Diethelm, 1930
7 Craig, 1917
8 Gibb, 1864
9 Wolfe, 1866
10 Diethelm, 1930 citing Huette, 1850
11 Wagner & Bunbury, 1930
12 Glatt, 1962
13 Hurst & Hurst, 1984
14 Carney, 1971
15 D'Arcy & Griffin, 1986
16 Price, 1942
17 Gulevich, 1977
18 Wagner & Bunbury, 1930

Chapter 4

THE BARBITURATE ERA

"On the appearance of any new drug an interesting cycle of events may often be observed. A trickle of favourable reports develops into a stream, and the drug then becomes fashionable. Then the stream of favourable reports dries up, and accidents claim attention. The drug falls into relative disrepute, and its use may even be abandoned ..." [British Medical Journal, 1956].

Drug companies change gear

By the 1930s - when the bromides were just starting to give way to the barbiturates - the classic drugs of dependence were quite strictly controlled by law. But there was an illegal trade in opiates - and the Swiss firm, Hoffman La Roche, was one of several drug companies involved. Roche later became the originators and leading suppliers of benzodiazepines, with products like Librium, Valium, and Mogadon.

The extent of Roche's activity in the illegal drug trade was mentioned in 1973 in the autobiography of Elmer Bobst, president of the US company until the end of World War II. He suggested that Roche had been involved in the supply of morphine to the underworld between the two wars. [1] However, the company's contact with the illegal drug trade had not gone unnoticed in its day. In 1927, after Roche had been involved in a succession of prosecutions for drug running, the Chairman of the British delegation to the Opium Advisory Committee of the League of Nations said he had "no doubt whatever that Hoffman La Roche and Company was not a firm to which a licence to deal with drugs should be given." [2]

The switch to the barbiturates partly determined how the pharmaceutical industry began to take its present shape. By the late 1930s, the industry had mastered the commercial basics of drug innovation, and had established some credibility with the medical profession. By then, the big companies were actively promoting their drugs to doctors - and systematically competing with each other, for the first time, through innovation of "me-too" products.

The barbiturates were among the earliest me-toos - drugs which are chemically and otherwise very similar to existing compounds and therefore usually superfluous to medical need. However, drug companies depend on me-toos both for their prosperity and survival; they have to, because real breakthroughs are very hard to come by and correspondingly rare. This is still the reality, though the industry does not like to admit it: in polite circles, me-toos have recently been renamed "innovative chemical extensions". [3]

Then as now, drug companies can hope to grow and to compete for fortunes between themselves only if they can make patentable products which are perceived as having distinct advantages over other drugs - whether or not they actually do. The patent system which underpins this style of competition gives manufacturers full monopoly rights on all sales, often for the best part of the drug's commercial life.

The commercial significance of the patent system is that it amply rewards innovation, its social purpose being to encourage the development of new products, and to promote health and economic growth. However, a disadvantage of the system is that it more or less compels manufacturers to promote their products as "different" and "best", even if they are not - ultimately because drug patents are granted on the basis of molecular uniqueness rather than therapeutic value. As a result, innovation in the pharmaceutical industry has been typified by the frenzied development and promotion of barely differentiated copies of the archetypes of successful drugs. There have been important, and occasionally very important drug innovations - but these have always been exceptions to the general rule.

The barbiturates are a case in point. By mid 20th century, some 2,500 different kinds had been synthesised, and many hundreds of different products containing one or more barbiturates were used. Leaving aside what was done to promote these products, there was not a lot to choose between them - though most doctors could clearly be persuaded there was. In the US, for example: "approximately 50 were marketed for clinical use. Today a dozen or so barbiturates are widely used; of these five or six would probably be sufficient to meet most therapeutic needs" [Goodman & Gilman, 1941].

The introduction of the barbiturates marks the beginning of the modern drug industry, and coincided with the start of two trends of much significance today. One is the rapidly growing concentration of power in the hands of a relatively small number of multinational companies: already the top 50 pharmaceutical companies control about two-thirds of all world trade, [4] and the number of major companies is declining fast. Secondly, most world markets today are saturated with me-too drugs: possibly as many as 70 per cent serve no really useful therapeutic purpose at all. [5]

The barbiturate drugs exemplify me-toos, in that they all do much the same thing, though they were promoted exactly as if they didn't. All barbiturates sedate or induce sleep, though there may be differences in their intensity and duration of action. These differences may be relevant in some drug treatments, but generally they are not - the similarities between members of this class being far greater than any differences between them. It was and is mainly for commercial reasons that the differences between products are stressed.

Safety claims and counter-claims

The first of the many barbiturates, Veronal, was developed by the Bayer company in Germany and introduced into Britain in 1903. It was advertised as "absolutely safe and without toxic effects", [6] but the first reports of fatal overdose appeared within a few years. By 1913, Veronal was one of the ten drugs most often implicated in fatal accidents and suicide. Quite early on, warnings were also sometimes given about the potential dangers of the barbiturate habit - though the risks seemed much lower than with drugs like morphine, which was still the gold standard of addiction in those days. By the end of the 1920s, what was still thought of as "chronic barbiturate poisoning" had become quite common, but addiction was simply not recognised at all. [7]

After Veronal came Luminal and then other barbiturates were introduced one by one - until, by the 1930s, the trickle had become a flood. All of these new products naturally had unblemished records, and the newly established pharmaceutical companies were getting better and better at persuading doctors that their products were best. This was the position in the US, just before World War II:

> "New barbiturates are constantly being introduced, usu-
> ally under confusing trade names, and claims are often

made that a particular compound is superior regarding potency, margin of safety or duration of action. At times it appears that the only goal in producing new barbiturates has been to obtain their exclusive sale by the manufacturer." [Goodman & Gilman, 1941]

During the 1930s, prescriptions for barbiturates tripled to make up for the loss of the bromides. However, as attention was increasingly focused on the barbiturates, so medical opinion began to divide more sharply about their safety in use. By the mid-1930s there were two vigorously opposed camps: one unreservedly critical of barbiturates, the other unreservedly not. The top man on the high ground was Sir William Willcox: he was in charge at St Mary's College Medical School in London, and consultant toxicologist to the Home Office.

As early as 1927, Willcox advised that barbiturates "should be given only on prescription, to be retained by the pharmacist, and the total number of doses ordered should not exceed six. The patient should be warned against daily use of the drug". The more this advice was ignored, the more passionately Willcox disapproved of barbiturates. By 1934, he was convinced they occupied "the foremost place among drugs of addiction" - but the medical profession as a whole was not aroused. Given the loss of confidence in the bromides, the restrictions on barbiturates that Willcox proposed met with a huge passive resistance. There was also active resistance to his rather obsessional and overbearing manner.

Willcox's ideas about warning patients of risks is still ahead of its time, but he was otherwise not too far out on a limb. Cushny's 1928 textbook, for example, also suggested restrictions, noting that that chronic barbiturate intoxication could and sometimes did result from normal therapeutic use. As with the bromides, Cushny linked the problem to the accumulation of the drug in the body - the solution was therefore to restrict the duration of treatment rather than to reduce the dose.

"Chronic poisoning with barbital is also not infrequently encountered in its therapeutic use as elimination of the drug is slow and cumulative effects as mental and bodily weakness, tremors and dizziness soon become manifest. For this reason the drug should not be given for longer than a week." [Cushny, 1928]

The opposition to such views was mainly led by two psychiatrists,

RD Gillespie [8] and M Craig. [9] Gillespie not only held strong opinions; he also had misleading statistics to support them. He said he had never once seen a case of barbiturate addiction, and argued that withdrawal was "not accompanied by the distressing subjective results and objective manifestations that accompany withdrawal of alcohol or morphine". Gillespie also reported that he had searched the world literature and found reports of only 157 fatalities from barbiturates before 1932. He emphasised that barbiturates accounted for only 1 in every 400 suicides, a proportion "remarkably small".

Looking back on this era, a 1947 *Lancet* editorial commented: "Perhaps the attack on [the barbiturates] was too intemperate; certainly the defence seems to have been successful". Indeed, the barbiturates were increasingly prescribed during Willcox's lifetime; and remained the most widely used sedatives for at least 25 years after his death in 1941.

In the US today, barbiturates are still sometimes used as sedative-hypnotic drugs; in Britain hardly at all. In the UK, barbiturates are no longer allowed to be promoted as sedatives, and are otherwise reserved for cases of "severe intractable insomnia". Reading between the lines, this means that barbiturates should be prescribed as sleeping pills only for people already severely dependent on them. This official form of words, "severe intractable insomnia", seems to be a euphemism for well-established dependence; it also obscures the now well-established fact that the hypnotic effects of barbiturates wear off after about a couple of weeks of continuous use. The main justification for prescribing them for longer would be to prevent a crisis for the patient if the drug were withdrawn.

Addiction redefined

The controversy about the safety of barbiturates rumbled on and on, but it was the overdose problem, rather than addiction, that was the main focus of concern. As an editorial in the *British Medical Journal* noted in 1954: "the sinister potentialities of the barbiturate hypnotics has been a perennial subject of debate in the medical press for the past thirty years". But nothing much was resolved, in spite of the marked increase in accidental deaths and suicides. There were over 400 recorded fatalities a year by 1950, and twice as many ten years on - but barbiturates were increasingly prescribed. [10]

By the late 1950s, there was marked concern in some quarters about

the use of barbiturates, also some fierce criticism of the medical profession, from within. One report concluded that there was "no doubt ..
that the barbiturates are misused on a vast scale" [11]; another argued they were grossly overprescribed, "almost as a placebo, often to assuage the doctors' anxieties". [12] By now, there was concern about the problems of addiction, as well as the risk of overdose. By the end of the 1950s, it was suggested that "there must be few general practices without a case of barbiturate addiction". [13]

But at the same time, it was also credibly claimed that there was little true addiction around. Even in the mid-1970s, the organisers of a campaign to reduce barbiturate prescribing said addiction was an essentially invisible problem: "most practitioners never or only rarely see an easily recognisable case of gross barbiturate abuse and it is difficult to realise what a national problem this has become". [14] Why did some doctors think addiction was rare, while others thought it common ? It was mainly because the meaning of addiction had never been properly defined, and meant different things. In particular, while most doctors emphasised the differences between "addiction" and "habituation" - others began to see the connection between the two.

Until well after the arrival of the first benzodiazepines in the early 1960s, there was real confusion among doctors about what addiction actually was. Partly this was because addiction was implictly defined in terms of the effects of opiates: as they were then effectively under control, almost by definition, addiction was hardly ever seen. By the 1950s, doctors read or heard about serious addicts, but would rarely come across them. Not among their own patients at least.

Doctors believed there was no "true" addiction to the barbiturates, so even if they had come across major withdrawal symptoms, they would have been inclined to seek other explanations for them. For example, a major withdrawal symptom such as convulsions might have been interpreted as evidence of latent epilepsy - or as some investigators in the 1930s called it, an unusual "complication" of treatment. [15] Because doctors didn't think in terms of true addiction to barbiturates, they tended not to see it. Nor would they have been inclined to report such cases, when the most trusted authorities denied that such a condition could really exist.

> "Addiction to the barbiturates, in the strict sense of the
> word, probably does not occur. Habituation, in contrast,
> is not infrequent and certain patients may experience

craving and psychic disturbances after the barbiturate is withdrawn. This phenomenon is, however, rather characteristic of the sedative-hypnotic group of drugs." [Goodman & Gilman, 1941]

This distinction between the so-called physical and psychic symptoms of drug addiction and withdrawal again emphasised that it was the personality, rather than drug effects, which was the root cause of dependence. Doctors believed until the 1950s that true drugs of addiction would cause physical symptoms on withdrawal - whereas psychic symptoms signalled personal inadequacy rather than the direct effect of a drug. There is an echo of this fallacy in the present-day belief that cocaine withdrawal precipitates only psychological symptoms, and that it does not produce a physical syndrome on withdrawal. Given the intensity of drug-seeking behaviour associated with this drug, it may well be that the relevant experts do not yet understand enough about the biochemistry of behaviour to be able to say that a physical withdrawal syndrome actually exists. At tissue level, it surely does.

This unfortunate distinction has reinforced the tendency, over the years, to presume that a drug is innocent unless and until it is proved guilty - to high standards of proof. This meant that patients tended to be blamed for dependence until that proof was found. But to prove anything, someone first had to buck the trend and ask the question: can the drug cause addiction ? Then there had to be some scientific investigation to establish the answer beyond reasonable doubt. And then doctors had to translate the answer into professional action, which meant discarding past practices and beliefs. This all took time - with the barbiturates, nearly 50 years.

Though doctors assumed that patients themselves were basically responsible if they became "habituated" to barbiturates, of course they didn't actually round on their patients. Probably many doctors felt that their patients needed to feel dependent, because of their circumstances and the kind of people they were. But whatever doctors thought, drug habituation did tend to be seen as the result of something done by the user, rather than by the drug - and to some extent still is.

Partly because of the low opinions they held of patients, and partly because of the high opinions they held of themselves, doctors and drug companies constantly stressed the differences between "addiction" and "habituation". If attention had been focused instead on how these two phenomena could be related to each other, the experts might have recognised mainly differences of degree. Using the woolly criteria of those days, one could not have clearly distinguished, for example, between a relatively mild addiction and a severe habituation. Until well after the 1960s, the main similarities and differences were these:

• Above all, addiction implied that, if a drug were suddenly withdrawn, there would be a full-blown withdrawal syndrome - a characteristic collection of severe symptoms, (eg convulsions, delirium). Habituation was associated with fewer and less severe symptoms on withdrawal - though they included some of the same symptoms as in full-blown withdrawal (eg anxiety, insomnia, tremors, disorientation).

• Addiction implied that the user took very much more than a normal therapeutic dose. Habituation suggested consumption at levels close to the therapeutic dose, if somewhat above it. If the patient rapidly escalated the dose, that was characteristic of addiction - whereas habituation was associated with a more gradual increase of dose, if any at all.

• Addiction implied that the original drug effects soon wore off - ie that the same dose of drug had a rapidly diminishing effect, if used without a break. This is the phenomenon of drug tolerance. Its relevance to dependence is that it may urge the patient to take more of the drug, to try to restore the original drug effects. With habituation, tolerance was commonly seen, but it appeared to be much less marked: some drug effects might soon disappear, but did not usually cause patients to take higher doses of the drug.

• Finally, addictive drugs were associated with euphoric effects, and therefore linked to pleasure-seeking. Euphoria strongly reinforced compulsive drug taking, because these initial effects quite quickly wore off, and could be sustained only by increasing the dosage. Euphoria and pleasure-seeking were not associated with habituation, which was regarded as unfortunate rather than reprehensible.

But the main reason why it took so long for addiction and habituation to be recognised as part of the same phenomenon was that the hallmark of addiction was a severe withdrawal syndrome - whereas repeat prescribing was the hallmark of habituation. Patients deemed to be merely habituated tended to stay on their drugs, so there was little evidence of the effects of withdrawal. As long as patients were reasonably compliant, they got their drugs. Thus, habituation was not perceived as much of a problem: as the extent of dependence could be defined only if and when drugs were withdrawn, the true picture was never revealed.

In this climate, doctors did not know what was happening because literally they did not know what they were talking about. The terms "addiction" and "habituation" were quite freely used, but in practice meant both different and similar things. Eventually, the World Health Organisation set up an Expert Committee to sort things out. The WHO Committee concluded that things had become so confusing that the words "habituation" and "addiction" should be altogether abandoned. Instead, the term "dependence" should be used - always referring to the type of dependence involved.

In a widely reported statement, the WHO in 1964 defined in detail what it meant by "dependence of the barbiturate type". It was characterised by "a strong desire or need to continue taking the drug" and "a tendency to increase the dose" as well as psychic and physical dependence on the drug - with characteristic symptoms on withdrawal.

> "The complex of symptoms which constitute the abstinence syndrome, in approximate order of appearance, are: anxiety, involuntary twitching muscles, tremor of hands and fingers, progressive weakness, dizziness, distortion in visual perception, nausea, vomiting, insomnia, weight loss, and a precipitous drop in blood pressure on standing; convulsions of a grand mal type and/or a delirium resembling alcoholic delirium tremens may occur." [WH0, 1964]

Dependence of the barbiturate type

It took until 1950 to establish beyond doubt that the barbiturates were "true" drugs of addiction, thus correcting "the erroneous impression, which has been widely held in both the United States and England, that abstinence symptoms did not follow the abrupt withdrawal of barbiturates from chronically intoxicated persons". The reality was established by Dr Harris Isbell and associates at the US Public Heath Service Hospital in Lexington, Kentucky. Working under strict experimental conditions, this team had given five volunteers doses of barbiturates "sufficiently large to induce continuous mild to severe intoxi-

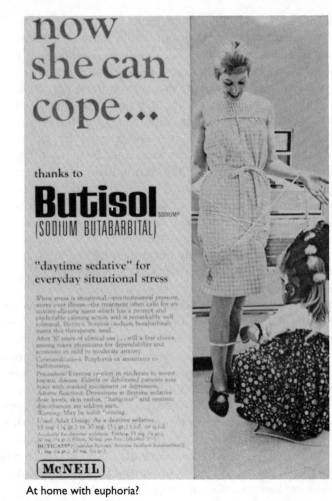

now
she can
cope...

thanks to

Butisol SODIUM®
(SODIUM BUTABARBITAL)

"daytime sedative" for
everyday situational stress

When stress is situational—environmental pressure,
worry over illness—the treatment often calls for an
anxiety-allaying agent which has a prompt and
predictable calming action and is remarkably well
tolerated. Butisol Sodium (sodium butabarbital)
meets this therapeutic need.

After 30 years of clinical use . . . still a first choice
among many physicians for dependability and
economy in mild to moderate anxiety.

Contraindications: Porphyria or sensitivity to
barbiturates.

Precautions: Exercise caution in moderate to severe
hepatic disease. Elderly or debilitated patients may
react with marked excitement or depression.

Adverse Reactions: Drowsiness at daytime sedative
dose levels, skin rashes, "hangover" and systemic
disturbances are seldom seen.

Warning: May be habit forming.

Usual Adult Dosage: As a daytime sedative,
15 mg. (¼ gr.) to 30 mg. (½ gr.) t.i.d. or q.i.d.
Available for daytime sedation, Tablets, 15 mg. (¼ gr.),
30 mg. (½ gr.); Elixir, 30 mg. per 5cc. (alcohol 7%);
BUTICAPS® Capsules Butisol Sodium (sodium butabarbital)
15 mg. (¼ gr.), 30 mg. (½ gr.).

[McNEIL]

At home with euphoria?

Advertisement in Journal of the American Medical Association, 24 March 1969

cation" for 3-5 months - before abruptly withdrawing the drug and
observing the response. They concluded that "in fact, addiction to
barbiturates is far more serious than is morphine addiction".

"In the first 12 to 16 hours after abrupt discontinuation of
medication, the patients appear to improve. Their thinking and mental status become clearer and most of the
neurological signs of intoxication disappear. As the signs

of intoxication decline, the patients become apprehensive and so weak that they can hardly stand ... Anxiety, tremor and weakness continue to increase [until] usually about the thirtieth hour, one or more grand mal convulsions which are indistinguishable from those occurring in idiopathic epilepsy, occur ... Generally, patients have no more than three major convulsions but numerous minor episodes, which are characterized by clonic twitching without loss of consciousness, or by writhing athenoid movements of the extremities, may occur before, between, or after the major convulsions ... Whether or not convulsions occur, barbiturate addicts are likely to become delirious, usually between the third and seventh days of abstinence The onset of the psychosis is often heralded by insomnia of 24 to 48 hours duration after which the patients begin to experience hallucinations and delusions..." [Isbell et al, 1950]

This study broke new ground, but only slowly began to change old ways. Although its main conclusion was accepted, the study was otherwise so perversely interpreted that its most important implications were missed. As a result of this study, it became accepted in principle that barbiturates were true drugs of addiction - but it was also assumed that barbiturates could cause addiction only after long exposure to huge doses. The volunteers had been kept in a state approximating to drunkeness for several months, as Isbell's team steadily increased the dose of barbiturates to the highest possible level - a pattern of dosing that was needed to counteract the effects of drug tolerance. The men involved in this bizarre ordeal took their first dose on rising and were kept in a state of intoxication all day.

"The neurologic signs were usually detectable, but minimal in degree, before the 9am dose. They increased in intensity throughout the day and were maximal after the 11pm dose. At this time, all patients would be staggering and unable to walk except by sliding along the walls. In spite of close supervision, they occasionally fell and were injured. Subject 1 broke two ribs by falling on a chair and lost a fingernail which was caught in a door. Patient 4 fell and incurred a laceration over his left eyebrow." [Isbell et al, 1950]

The extreme conditions in which this study was done reinforced the view that barbiturates would be safe in therapeutic use. This was emphasised in leading medical journals: four years after the Isbell study, the *Lancet* reported: "Thus 'addiction' occurs only with habitual ingestion of 'far above therapeutic doses', and as tolerance is relatively small, mainly psychologically abnormal people are likely to increase the doses so far" [16]. At least until the 1960s, it was generally believed "that barbiturate addiction is rare except in fundamentally very disturbed individuals". [17]

What doctors really needed to know was whether there was some threshold above which abstinence symptoms could be expected to reinforce drug taking - and one of the first people to throw light on this was a neuropsychiatrist at the Henry Ford Hospital in Detroit. In 1951, Dr EJ Alexander published a prominent review of clinical and animal studies, as well as data from his own clinical practice, to try to define what was what. Dr Alexander specialised in a treatment which involved putting patients on barbiturates to keep them asleep for about 16 hours a day, for a week or so - and then abruptly stopping the drugs. One of the purposes of his treatment was actually to precipitate withdrawal symptoms which, for some reason, were considered to have a beneficial therapeutic effect.

Dr Alexander reported that, even after only a week of treatment at high therapeutic doses, his patients experienced withdrawal symptoms which included marked irritability and insomnia, tremor, hallucinations and sometimes convulsions - and he concluded from this that some physical symptoms of dependence would definitely result from dosages used in ordinary clinical practice. He also made the all-important point that doctors in general practice might be prescribing barbiturates in effect to ward off symptoms of drug withdrawal. Later in the 1950s, others came to the same conclusion, expressing concern that doctors might thereby be contributing to illness. Notable among them was Dr Richard Hunter, a psychiatrist at Guy's Hospital in London. He suggested that dependence could set in after only a few weeks of regular treatment with barbiturates.

> "Once it has developed, not only do the patient's symptoms for which barbiturates were in the first place prescribed, return in full force when a dose wears off, which might but for drug-taking have subsided without treatment - but they are reinforced by the symptoms of barbi-

turate abstinence. These are depression, anxiety with
sweating, tremor, palpitation and disturbed sleep. From
then, the drug is no longer taken for the original symptoms, but simply to ward off increasingly distressing
abstinence symptoms. The cause of this exacerbation
may not be recognised by doctor or patient - both may
think his original illness has got worse. This may lead to
yet further increase in barbiturate dosage with the result
that not only do abstinence symptoms become severer,
but the symptoms of barbiturate intoxication are added
as well. These are similar to all chronic intoxications of
the nervous system and therefore further worsen the
patients' mental state. Thus a mild psychiatric distur-
bance, in all likelihood amenable to one or two sympathetic interviews, becomes converted into a serious and
perhaps protracted illness." [Hunter, 1957]

Dr William Sargant came to share these views. In 1958, long after
his campaign against the bromides, Dr Sargant began to reflect how
"fashion and authority in drug prescribing may certainly change in
the most startling way". Sargant was by then wondering if he had not
in the past gone too far in recommending the routine use of barbiturates - speculating that this might have been "in rebellion at some of
the absurdities of my St Mary's teaching on sedatives". He was referring here to his student days, under Sir William Willcox, when "the
giving of any barbiturates was considered a major therapeutic crime".
But, one generation later, the physician who had earlier been shocked
by the sight of patients drugged with bromides was seeing some of
the most severe effects of barbiturate intoxication. The saddest cases
Sargant described were patients who had undergone brain surgery
because their doctors had not realised that it was the barbiturates that
made them so ill:

" ... in 1944, I made the statement that these barbiturates,
in moderate doses, did not cause addiction in the true
sense of that word, nor severe symptoms on withdrawal.
But I think that this statement has now to be modified.
For I, with others, have come to realise that patients with
chronic tension states may continue to remain tense and
anxious for many years, because they are, in fact, suffering more from a self-induced or doctor-induced chronic

barbiturate tension state than from a persisting anxiety neurosis per se. I am now seeing patients who have had one, two or even three leucotomies performed for a chronic persisting tension and who have then turned out to be, probably, cases of chronic barbiturate addiction" [Sargant, 1958]

But such warnings did not have the desired effect any more than the warnings from Willcox had done. Barbiturate consumption doubled during the 1950s and continued to rise well into the next decade. In 1964, an editorial on The Barbiturate Problem in *The Practitioner* asked if "this fantastic amount" of barbiturates was really necessary - "or is it that too many doctors - general practitioners and consultants - are taking the line of least resistance and prescribing barbiturates as a blunderbuss remedy for all the anxieties and stresses to which mankind is heir ?"

Questions to this effect were also asked in Parliament, but the Minister of Health was not moved: "I have no evidence that harmful effects or dependence occur at all frequently in relation to the number of prescriptions." [18] Later, and perhaps with some irony, Sir Derrick Dunlop said he thought that such ill-effects were "remarkably rare in Britain considering the prodigal amounts that are prescribed." [19] Sir Derrick was the first head of the Committee on Safety of Drugs, the forerunner of the Committee on Safety of Medicines, the mainstay of the drug control system which operates today.

1 Braithwaite, 1983
2 Cit. Braithwaite, 1983
3 OHE, 1990
4 Chetley, 1990
5 Management Sciences for Health, 1981
6 Wills, 1906
7 Cushny, 1928
8 Gillespie, 1934
9 Craig, 1934
10 Glatt, 1962.
11 Locket, 1957
12 Hunter, 1957
13 Batchelor, 1960
14 Bennett, 1977
15 Palmer & Paine, 1932;
Palmer & Braceland, 1937
16 Lancet, 1954
17 Brit Med J, 1958
18 Robinson, 1964
19 Dunlop, 1967

Chapter 5

A DOSE OF REGULATION

"Perhaps nearly 10% of the patients in our general hospitals are suffering to a greater or lesser extent from our efforts to treat them - from iatrogenic diseases as they are called, or more optimistically but somewhat ironically, from diseases due to medical progress. Many of us had become somewhat complacent about the toxic effects of the formidable agents we were using, and in Europe it took the emotional reaction to the thalidomide disaster, which you ...[Americans] ... were fortunate to avoid, to galvanise us from our somewhat laissez faire attitude. After that disaster public and medical opinion demanded that an organisation independent of the manufacturers, who in Britain had hitherto borne almost the sole responsibility for the safety of their products, should be established to assess the safety of new drugs in relation to the purpose for which they were to be used." [Dunlop, 1969]

Alternatives to barbiturates - meprobamate

The barbiturates first began to face serious competition in the sedative-hypnotic market in the mid-1950s, following the introduction of several new drugs not chemically classified as barbiturates, but otherwise very like them. In spite of safety claims, there was no good evidence that these drugs offered real therapeutic advantages over true barbiturates; [1] nor any sound reason to believe they would cause less drug dependence. In 1957, the relevant WHO Expert Committee published a report which concluded that, in terms of dependence, these new drugs "resemble the barbiturates and should be subjected to national control." [2]

The first and best known of these barbiturate-like drugs was meprobamate, which was introduced into the UK in 1954. There were two leading brands - Equanil, made by the US company, John Wyeth

& Brother; and Miltown, made by another American firm, Carter-Wallace. Inevitably, they were promoted as much safer than barbiturates - both in overdose and in relation to addiction. One of the many investigators who attested to the safety of this new drug was an American university-based psychiatrist, Dr Frederick Lemere.

In a 1955 paper, Lemere said he thought meprobamate was safe enough, but in the following year he published a retraction. Lemere was the first to report a dependence problem, and did so partly because meprobamate was being so extravagently promoted and prescribed. Miltown and Equanil were being advertised as non habit-forming and were massively prescribed - and there was even talk of selling them off-prescription. In the light of this, Lemere felt there would be a significant problem with the drug.

"I would like to modify a preliminary report in which I said that meprobamate was not habit-forming. Further clinical experience has convinced me that this is by no means always the case and that a few patients do form a harmful habit for this drug ... I have had 13 cases among over 600 patients for whom I have prescribed meprobamate in which the drug had to be discontinued because of excessive self-medication ... [and] ... I have had nine patients report that it took increasing doses of meprobamate to obtain the same effects. Apparently, a few patients do have a build up of tolerance to this drug ... Withdrawal symptoms are sometimes experienced ... One patient who had been taking large doses (6.4gm daily for one month and no other medication or alcohol) had a convulsion (the only one he had ever had) 10 hours after discontinuing this medication." [Lemere, 1956]

These conclusions were soon confirmed in several controlled studies. [3] Among them was a 1958 report by Thomas Haizlip and John Ewing, a medical student and consultant psychiatrist respectively. Their report was of particular interest, because it set out to define the thresholds of dosage and/or duration of treatment at which significant withdrawal symptoms would appear. The two investigators broadly followed the design of Isbell's study with barbiturates, but used much lower doses of meprobamate and for much less time (about 2 - 4 times the normal dose, for 40 days). They reported that although most patients experienced only "mild" withdrawal symptoms (including "vomiting, tremors, muscle twitching and overt anxiety") nearly all patients experienced a withdrawal reaction of some kind.

> "At the end of forty days, all patients were switched surreptitiously to placebo. Clinical observation revealed objective evidence of an abstinence syndrome in 44 out of 47 patients who were previously on meprobamate. The typical withdrawal syndrome included various degrees of insomnia, vomiting, tremors, muscle twitching, overt anxiety, anorexia and ataxia [staggering, uncoordinated movement]. Eight patients showed a picture of hallucinosis with marked anxiety and tremors much resembling delirium tremens. In three patients grandmal seizures developed."

In spite of this and other reports, meprobamate was massively promoted and prescribed, notably between 1955 and 1965. According to the American Medical Association [1965], the popularity of meprobamate and other barbiturate-like drugs was partly due to doctors switching patients "from barbiturates to the newer sedatives in the mistaken belief of safety from abuse". The AMA warned that: "The increasing number of patients heavily dependent on the substitute drugs attests to the danger of this practice".

Why were these early warnings about dependence largely ignored? The main answer seems to be that the few critical reports about meprobamate were far outweighed by the number of favourable ones, though most of the latter "were so poorly conducted that no valid conclusions can be drawn from their data". That was the conclusion in a 1958 review of nearly 100 early reports on meprobamate, conducted by two doctors from Johns Hopkins University in the US. [4] A reliable US source [Medical Letter, 1959] concluded that: "the available evidence ... leaves no doubt that addiction can be induced with meprobamate".

The tendency to point the finger at the patient was another factor in under-estimating the risk of dependence with meprobamate; and it was powerfully reinforced by messages from the manufacturers. Here, by way of an extreme example, is an investigative journalist's account of the views held by the originator of meprobamate, Dr Frank Berger. He was testifying at 1966 hearings on drug addiction by the US Food & Drug Administration (FDA):

"The star witness for Carter-Wallace's entire case was Dr Frank Berger. His creation of meprobamate had turned the sleepy little company into a pharmaceutical wonder-house overnight and Berger was tenaciously trying to keep his legend alive ... Berger disputed the whole FDA case and much evidence that had piled up against meprobamate over the past ten years. He said the only type of person who would abuse meprobamate would be a 'psychopath'; according to him, meprobamate produced no euphoria, 'no kick', as he called it. He was struck, he said, by the very low number of dependence problems with meprobamate and told of the many 'unsolicited' letters he had received from patients who took meprobamate for years without any problems ... Berger estimated that 500 million prescriptions for meprobamate had been written since he developed it. He said meprobamate had a highly selective action on the brain and could not be compared with barbiturates .... He said the reason for abuse of meprobamate was the same as abuse of aspirin, Coca Cola or anything else. 'There are certain abnormal individuals who will abuse almost anything and some of them will abuse meprobamate ...'."
[Pekannen, 1973]

But Dr Berger failed to sway the US authorities, and meprobamate was scheduled under drug abuse laws in 1967. Basically this meant that prescriptions had to be in the doctor's own handwriting, and that repeat prescriptions were no longer allowed. In the UK, meprobamate was finally scheduled as a "controlled drug" much later (along with the barbiturates and other barbiturate-like drugs) under the Misuse of Drugs Regulations, 1985. Doctors wrote over 150,000 prescriptions for Equanil in 1984; although it can no longer be prescribed on the NHS, it is still available in the UK.

The sleeping pill that changed the law
The 1960s began with a drug disaster involving another barbiturate-like drug. Thalidomide was sold in the UK by the Distillers Company under the name of Distaval. It was marketed as a sleeping pill, advertised as "completely safe" [5] and specifically promoted for use by pregnant women. Thalidomide was first used in the UK in 1958 and was

withdrawn in December 1961. Worldwide, an estimated 10,000 severely deformed babies were born before August 1962.

The thalidomide catastrophe marked another important turning point in the history of medicine. It ended the age of innocence, and led to the opening up of parts of the health-care system to a degree of public scrutiny and control never known before. As a result of the thalidomide disaster, Parliament and the public "suddenly woke up to the fact that any drug manufacturer could market any product, however inadequately tested, however dangerous, without having to satisfy any independent body as to its efficacy or safety". Those were the words of the opposition spokesman on health, Richard Crossman, in 1963. As Minister of Health in 1967-68, Crossman was responsible for introducing the Medicines Act, the main law on the safety of medicines today.

In the UK, it took until the early 1970s to set up the machinery of drug control, about ten years later than in the US. In America, there had been basic drug safety laws since the 1930s, and they helped to keep thalidomide out - though credit was due mainly to the FDA official responsible for reviewing the drug. From 1962, the so-called "Kefauver-Harris amendment" required the Food & Drug Administration to obtain satisfactory evidence of drug efficacy as well as safety before a drug could be licensed for sale. An estimated 60 per cent of drug products on the market were believed effective for at least one claimed indication, though only about one in eight products could fully satisfy the requirements of the new law. [6]

In the UK, the most authorititive estimate suggested that about two-thirds of all drugs on the market were therapeutically effective, and the rest "undesirable". [7] That estimate was made by two panels of experts advising the Committee of Enquiry into the Relationship of the Pharmaceutical Industry with the National Health Service. This Committee, chaired by Lord Sainsbury [1967], was set up by the government, three years after the thalidomide disaster. The Sainsbury report gives quite a strong flavour of the state of pharmaceutical medicine in the mid-1960s. The report identified many deficiencies, and proposed new law.

> "Much evidence was submitted to us which was critical
> of the literature sent to doctors. For example, the Royal
> College of General Practitioners described much of the
> literature as 'bad - seemingly in the form of cheap public-

ity, with inaccurate claims, lack of contraindications and good references, lack of price ...' The British Medical Association told us that the main disadvantage to doctors was the absence of any 'independent medical control or scrutiny over the literature'. From the hospital authorities we received complaints of 'repetitive and uninformative literature' and of literature 'which does not contribute to existing knowledge of a product', and of 'highly coloured advertising matter reminiscent of detergent propaganda, which advocates use of the drug but gives little or no information on dosage, action and reaction'. [p 67]

"We believe that it is wrong that doctors should be influenced in any aspect of the practice of their profession by mere advertising techniques. Nor should they be informed, as they are to some extent at present, by persons with little or no relevant training. Eventually postgraduate education in therapeutics should make it unnecessary for doctors to lean so heavily on the firms for information about medicines ... In our opinion it is unsatisfactory that so large a part of the information on medicines available to practitioners should come from the industry selling them". [pp 94, 97]

"We consider that some limitation on the freedom of marketing of medicines is now essential" [p 93] ... "There is an urgent need to set up a new body to deal with these matters and to advise the Government in the whole field of medicines ... We propose that it should be known as the Medicines Commission ..." [p 92] "It is our aim that the Commission should become in due course the accepted source of information on all matters concerning the use of medicines ..." [p 97]

Although the Sainsbury report produced much evidence of weakness in the system, many of its recommendations were not acted on. The Medicines Commission was set up, however, and later emerged as a committee of doctors, academics and representatives of the pharmaceutical industry. The main independent element in today's drug control sytem - the Committee on Safety of Medicines (CSM) - was set up by the Medicines Commission, and answers to it still.

The promise of self-regulation

The thalidomide catastrophe of couse put pressure on the pharmaceutical companies, but they responded in kind. Through their trade body, the Association of the British Pharmaceutical Industry (ABPI), companies emphasised that they could be trusted to play a leading part in making drugs effective and safe. Central to the ABPI's commitment to high standards was its Code of Pharmaceutical Marketing Practice. The ABPI Code acknowledged that doctors depended on the industry, especially for information about the effects of drugs, and it emphasised that: "The manufacturer has the double responsibility, therefore, of offering at the same time the product itself and information on its character, action and uses". [8] The Code required member companies to observe specific provisions relating to the quality of drug information supplied.

> "Information furnished to the medical profession about a medical speciality product must be accurate and balanced and must not be misleading, either directly or by implication"
> "Claims for the usefulness of a product must be based on an up-to-date evaluation of all the evidence and must reflect this evidence accurately and clearly"
> "Communications on medical specialities must reflect an attitude of caution.
> "Methods of marketing must never be such as to bring discredit upon the pharmaceutical industry"

The earliest versions of the ABPI Code also required member firms to describe "clearly and concisely" the properties and uses of drug products in all promotional materials and other communications with the medical profession. However, the ABPI never intended to enforce the Code strictly itself: the then chairman of the ABPI [1967] explained that individual companies would naturally observe high standards, because it was overwhelmingly in their interests to do so.

> "Putting aside all considerations of ethics and humanity, every company in simple self-interest would obviously wish to market only products that are both effective and safe ... "It has not been found necessary to apply sanctions to secure compliance because members of the association are anxious to ensure that their marketing activities conform to the highest standard."

The Medicines Act was passed in 1968 and implemented from about 1972 - but the pharmaceutical industry did to some extent succeed in softening the impact of legislation. The companies argued they could be relied on to observe high standards in promoting their products - and that self-regulation was actually the only effective way of achieving this. [9] The industry has always emphasised this and, by and large, the government has always taken it at its word. Nowadays, the industry is responsible even for enforcement of some of the drug laws - in the performance of which duties it has not always impressed.

> "In the 18 years 1972-88 the Medicines Act was breached over 1200 times. Health ministers, by not enforcing the regulations concerning promotion, have abrogated their responsibility to the ABPI, but the evidence suggests that the code has failed to deter promotional excesses. The ABPI's wish to secure compliance with the code seems weaker than its wish to pre-empt outside criticism and action: its self-regulation seems to be a service to itself rather than to the public. It is suggested that the code of practice committee should become publicly accountable, that the majority of its members should represent the health professions and the public, and that effective sanctions are needed." [Herxheimer and Collier, 1990]

Introduction of data sheets

Central to the control of drug promotion in the 1968 Medicines Act is the requirement that manufacturers distribute to all doctors a data sheet, to include formally approved information about the properties and uses of a drug. This had been proposed by the Sainsbury Committee as one of the bedrocks of its system. The data sheet was intended not only to spell out the facts for doctors; it was also meant to define what should and should not be claimed in promoting the drug. Claims made for a drug - whether by sales representatives, in advertising or otherwise - had to be "not inconsistent" with what the data sheet said.

Some idea of the standards actually attained in data sheets following the introduction of the Medicines Act may be appreciated by briefly looking at what happened to the main barbiturate-like drugs, other than meprobamate. [10] None of them survived in the UK, though not because their data sheets deterred prescribers by warning of serious risks. The data sheets made these drugs appear much safer than they really were.

Methyprylon was introduced by Roche as Noludar in 1955. The first case of dependence was reported in 1960, and Roche first warned of this risk in the data sheet 25 years later. Until 1984 the data sheet said "Noludar has a wide safety margin" and made no reference to any problem of dependence. The following year, the data sheet warned that "Noludar has a high addiction potential". In 1989, the drug was withdrawn.

Ethchlorvynol was sold as Placidyl and Serensil and made by the US firm, Abbott Laboratories. The drug was introduced in 1955; the first report of dependence dates from 1959, with several others in 1964. Serensil was withdrawn in the UK around 1978 - at which date there was no warning in the data sheet about any risk of dependence. However, there was a warning in the US equivalent of the data sheet at that time: "Severe withdrawal symptoms similar to those seen during barbiturate and alcohol withdrawal have been reported following abrupt discontinuance of prolonged use ...". The US warnings also emphasised "Prolonged use may result in tolerance and psychological and physical dependence. Prolonged administration of the drug is not recommended." [11]

Glutethimide was sold as Doriden and introduced in 1955. The first case of dependence was reported in 1957 but, ten years on, the manufacturers claimed that: "Doriden is well tolerated, enjoys a wide margin of safety and freedom from toxic effects at recommended dosage. In a small minority of patients a rash may occur". [12] A gentle warning about dependence was later introduced by the Swiss manufacturers, Ciba-Geigy, before they withdrew Doriden in 1983.

Another barbiturate-like product, Mandrax, is also worth mentioning, if only because it received the warmest of recommendations from Dr William Sargant [1973]. Mandrax was a combination of two drugs [methaqualone + diphenhydramine], sold in the UK from 1955 by the then French-owned firm, Roussel. It was eventually withdrawn from the UK market following a rash of reports of overdose, dependence and abuse from the mid 1960s on.

All of these drugs were largely replaced by the benzodiazepines, starting in 1960. That was just before thalidomide came off the market: in those days there was no drug licensing system and no Committee on the Safety of Medicines, meant to ensure fair play. When the first benzodiazepine was introduced, self-regulation by the drug companies was all there was. The doctors by then had become very largely dependent on the industry for drug information and prescribing advice. Until 1972, there were no effective legal controls over drugs at all.

1 Lasagna, 1956; Medical Letter, 1959

2 WHO, 1957

3 Stough, 1958; Medical Letter, 1959

4 Laties & Weiss, 1958

5 Sunday Times, 1979

6 Temple, 1984

7 Sainsbury, 1967

8 ABPI, 1967

9 Lumley, 1968

10 Olivieri et al, 1986

11 Physicians Desk Reference, 1977

12 British Encyclopedia of Medical Practice, 1967

Chapter 6
INTRODUCING THE BENZODIAZEPINES

"In biology, and in medicine in particular, if a problem looks simple, it is because of ignorance. All problems are complicated and they look simple only because the complications have not been discovered. For this reason one can say that the first results of research are to replace ignorance by confusion. We always hope that the next stage will make things clear, but it always takes longer than expected." [Hamilton, 1967]

The discovery

The first of the benzodiazepines was chlordiazepoxide - Librium. It was introduced in the US in 1959 and into Britain a year later. Chlordiazepoxide was developed by the American branch of the Swiss-based company, Hoffman La Roche, and has since been sold by Roche subsidiaries all over the world. It was discovered partly by chance and nearly never made it, but it turned out to be one of the biggest selling drugs of all time.

In strictly chemical terms, chlordiazepoxide was quite different from any drug previously used in a pharmaceutical product - though it was derived from the parent compound of some of the more potent "major" tranquillisers introduced in the 1950s (eg chlorpromazine, brand name Largactil). This parent compound had first been synthesised in Germany in 1891. Forty years on, two chemists at the University of Cracow did some further work on it - and later one of those chemists went to work for Roche. In 1955, some 20 years after his university research, Leo Sternbach discovered that nothing more had been written about this parent compound, so he decided to investigate further. [1]

Sternbach's account of his research at Roche describes how he and his colleagues set out, in effect, to tinker creatively with the original molecule, to make other compounds fairly like it - in the hope that these derivatives would have some therapeutic effect. Most drug innovation proceeds in much the same way today. It involves cleverly modifying bits of molecules which are already known to have clinical and commercial value, and then screening the new compounds for toxicity and therapeutic effect. This style of innovation involves some element of "suck it and see".

> "Our interest in tranquillisers started in the mid-1950s, shortly after the first representatives of this group of drugs proved to be of remarkable clinical value. Since we were chemists at heart, we planned to attack this problem completely empirically, considering mainly the chemically attractive features of such an approach. We decided to select a relatively unexplored class of compounds and to prepare novel members belonging to this group, in the hope that some of these products might exhibit the desired pharmacological properties." [Sternbach, 1973]

When new compounds are produced in this way, the most promising ones are then screened in basic animal tests. In the UK, in 1988, nearly 1.2 million laboratory animals were used in preliminary screening of possible medical products, accounting for about one-third of all animals used in licensed experiments. In the same year, another half a million animals were used in more refined tests on the much smaller number of compounds which did well in the original screening. These follow-up experiments typically involve longer-term studies of therapeutic effectiveness and safety; and also aim to establish how a drug works, how it is broken down in the body and what range of effects it has.

As it happened, the small batch of chlordiazepoxide made at Roche in 1955 lay around on a laboratory bench for two years, because Sternbach and his colleagues had been distracted by other tasks. But eventually this supply of chlordiazepoxide was found in a huge laboratory clean up. It was then submitted for preliminary screening, pretty much as a precaution before throwing it out.

> "During this clean-up operation, my co-worker, Mr Earl Reader, drew my attention to a few hundred milligrams of two products ... [which] had been prepared in 1955 ... The products were not submitted for pharmacological

testing at that time because of our involvement with other problems [but] ... we submitted in 1957 the water soluble salt for pharmacological evaluation. We were quite prepared for a negative result and considered this the end of our work with quinalozoline 3-oxides ..." [2]

Within a few days of submitting this new compound for prelimi-nary screening, Sternbach got an enthusiastic telephone call from Roche's head of pharmacology, Dr Lowell Randall. In a battery of six tests, the new compound had done well when compared with a barbi-turate (pentobarbitone), a barbiturate-like drug (meprobamate) and a "major" tranquilliser (chlorpromazine). Two tests, on mice, indicat-ed muscle relaxation, and sedative and taming effects. Another showed muscle relaxation in cats; and the last three demonstrated anticonvulsant and sedative effects, again in mice.

With an eye to marketing, further tests were then done, notably on "vicious, agitated monkeys, dingo dogs and other wild animals" [3] in captivity in the San Diego and Boston zoos. [4] The climax of the pro-gramme involved a filmed demonstration of a lion tranquillised with chlordiazepoxide behaving beautifully in the company of a lamb. Under the influence of the drug, the lion appeared unaggressive yet awake [5] - and Librium was launched soon afterwards partly on the strength of it. [6] Although it had to compete in a market now replete with different sedative-hypnotics, Librium rapidly caught on: "few drugs have had so enthusiastic reception in both lay and medical press." [7]

First clinical trials

Following the studies in animals, Roche asked a number of doctors in the US to try the new drug on their patients. Soon afterwards, these investigators reported that chlordiazepoxide was also very effective in humans. Their published reports all praised the new drug and most conveyed real excitement about its effects. Chlordiazepoxide seemed a potent and potentially very useful drug, apparently a real improve-ment on the barbiturates and barbiturate-like tranquillisers then in vogue.

Taken at face value, these and many other reports suggested that Librium was everything a tranquilliser should be. These early reports of clinical experience involved over 800 doctors and some 16,000 patients; and there was a clear consensus in the very small proportion

of these reports which seem to have been published that chlordiazepoxide really was very good.

"The effect of Librium on the symptoms of excessive
withdrawal and tension (excessive control) is remarkable, and may be illustrated by the description by one
patient, a teacher: 'I think it is miraculous. I was feeling
outgoing. The effect was so liberating I felt very excited
and very outgoing ... I would walk into the class completely unprepared and end up well."[Toll, 1960]

"Without exception, Librium produced improved control
through a pure 'relief from strain', with no sedative effect
and with the patient maintaining total contact." [English,
1960]

There were, however, two problems. One was that all of the published reports about Librium were from uncontrolled studies: they
didn't compare chlordiazepoxide with anything else - another drug
or placebo. [8] And none of these early trials was conducted "blind", so
investigators as well as patients knew they were testing an exciting
new drug. This introduced a high bias in favour of chlordiazepoxide,
as everyone would have been expecting good results. For these and
other reasons, the results obtained in these trials might have been
quite unrepresentative of the drug's performance in any larger population. Roche and its investigators had failed "to observe any of the
established disciplines of the controlled clinical trial". [9]

The other problem seems paradoxical - yet, from Roche's point of
view, the great enthusiasm conveyed in the investigators' reports
must have seemed something of a mixed blessing. On the one hand,
reports did suggest there would be a great demand for Librium. On
the other hand, Roche knew that any drug which could relieve anxiety in such a spectacular fashion, and make miserable patients feel so
good, might also prove to be a drug of addiction. This might explain
why the Roche reviews of all these investigations on Librium conveyed none of the excitement that the drug seemed to have produced
in investigators and patients alike. In the main review produced by
Roche in the US, the author attributed what he called good "patient
acceptance" to the superiority of chlordiazepoxide over previous
medications. [10] Similarly, Dr John Marks, the reviewer from Roche
Products Ltd in the UK, favoured low-key terms such as "beneficial
effect" or "favourable response". [11] Neither review acknowledged -

as several investigators had reported - that Librium sometimes made patients feel euphoric.

> "On Sept. 21st 1959, she was started on Librium 25mg t.i.d. [three times a day]. By October 5th the patient had shown marked improvement. She is now euphoric, working hard, and no longer gets upset by anyone." [Farb, 1960]

> "The drug's antidepressant and euphoriant action made unnecessary in many cases the addition of other drugs aimed at the target symptom of depression ... When they feel better they are advised to reduce their pills ... and then gradually to discontinue it altogether. Obviously to convert an anxiety state into an addiction is poor therapy and a euphoriant drug that eases anxiety might easily become one of addiction." [Bowes, 1960]

> "Patients often reported a sense of well-being which was considered by some of our investigators to be a mild euphoria-like syndrome." [Tobin et al, 1960]

> "The ready acceptance of the medication by all the patients may in part be accounted for by the prompt relief of anxiety, the lack of serious side effects and to the definite although mild euphoria." [Toll, 1960]

For whatever reasons, direct references to euphoria in the literature seemed to stop completely from the mid-1960s - and soon afterwards Roche began to deny that its products actually caused such effects. A charitable explanation would be that Roche was concerned that hard-core addicts might be alerted if attention were drawn to the drug's pleasurable effects. Two major reviews of clinical experience with chlordiazepoxide, published by Roche in the late 1960s, suggested that euphoria was either extremely rare [12] or that it did not happen at all. [13] The alleged lack of euphoriant effect was also suggested by Roche as one of the reasons why dependence on chlordiazepoxide was not a problem.

> "The rare occurrence of psychic dependence is probably due to the fact that the presently available benzodi-azepines have a relatively slow onset of action, do not produce euphoria and cause ataxia at higher doses, a side effect which is unpleasant and embarrassing." [Zbinden et al, 1967]

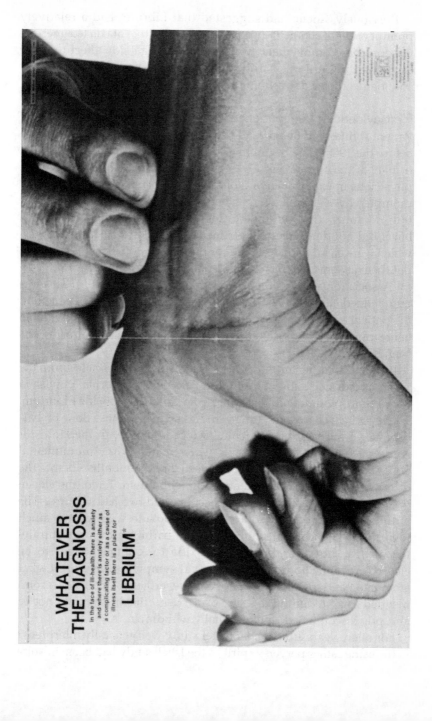

Previously, Roche had suggested that Librium had a relatively prompt onset of action. [14] In addition, the idea that ataxia (staggering, uncoordinated movement) was a nasty enough side effect to deter excessive drug use was hardly supported by experience with alcohol and many other sedative-hypnotic drugs.

First evidence of dependence risk

Patient rights, as they are understood today, were barely developed before the 1960s. The beginnings of reform date from the publication in 1949 of the Nuremberg Code: it made recommendations to guide physicians in experiments involving human subjects, and had been prompted by revulsion over the behaviour of doctors in Nazi concentration camps. The Nuremberg Code said many of the right things, but it did not deter many experiments of the kind Isbell had done - which were clearly not designed for the benefit of patients, and which put them at some risk. The turning point came when the World Medical Association adopted the Declaration of Helsinki in 1964. This further defined clinical investigation and treatment in terms of benefit to the patient - stating, for example, that "clinical research on a human being cannot be undertaken without his free consent, after he has been fully informed". [15]

Just a little earlier, in 1961, Dr Leo Hollister and associates from the Veterans Administration Hospital in Palo Alto, California, published their report, Withdrawal Reactions from Chlordiazepoxide - Librium. The report was based on human studies similar to those done on barbiturates by Isbell and his team, a decade before. In the Hollister study, 11 psychiatric in-patients were treated with "monumental doses" of chlordiazepoxide for between 2 and 6 months - before the drug was surreptitiously and abruptly withdrawn. Ten of the eleven patients had marked withdrawal reactions and two had seizures. The withdrawal symptoms from chlordiazepoxide were pretty much identical to withdrawal symptoms from barbiturate or barbiturate-like drugs. However, chlordiazepoxide took much longer to be cleared from the body - so withdrawal symptoms were somewhat attenuated and took longer to appear. Nevertheless, Hollister recommended as a precaution that, in normal use, "the drug should not be abruptly discontinued", but gradually withdrawn. [16]

For many years after, the Hollister study was generally interpreted in the same rather perverse spirit as the Isbell study had been. In spite of what was known by the early 1960s about the dependence liability of the barbiturates and similar drugs, it was taken for granted that chlordiazepoxide would cause dependence problems only after prolonged treatment at very excessive dosages.

Ethical considerations may well have influenced the design of another Hollister study, reported in 1963, which involved a new benzodiazepine called diazepam. The general design of the study was similar to the earlier one - although this time patients were given much lower doses and there were shorter treatment periods than before. The 13 patients on diazepam were given only up to about twice the usual maximum dose and were treated only for six weeks before the drug was withdrawn. Even with this much lower exposure, Hollister found that: "Clinical signs of withdrawal reactions were apparent in 6, one of whom had a major seizure on the eighth day following withdrawal". [17]

It was not noted at the time, but this study was also important in demonstrating that diazepam could exert profoundly different effects on different individuals, which could not be explained by the dosage or duration of treatment. As all his patients were considered schizophrenic, ill enough to need hospital treatment, their very different responses to diazepam could hardly be attributed to different degrees of psychic susceptibility to dependence. This makes it all the harder to accept that people get into trouble with drugs like diazepam because of personality traits which make them "dependence prone".

Hoffman La Roche called their new drug Valium and launched it in 1963. Diazepam was later to emerge as the most popular of all benzodiazepines, and the archetype of the whole class - though, for most clinical purposes, the differences between chlordiazepoxide and diazepam are slight. However, Roche naturally emphasised all the differences between the two - even the fact that diazepam was more potent (per milligram), though this hardly mattered at all. Valium was launched as Librium had been. As before, Roche asked a number of selected doctors to test the new drug; later, enthusiastic endorsements were published in medical journals.

> "Before Valium was marketed early last year, it had been exposed to perhaps the most rigorous testing of any psychotropic drug in history. Over 30,000 cases had been assessed by some of the finest researchers in this country." [Bowes, 1965]

But the way in which these trials were conducted again left much to be desired. This was the comment made in the Prescribers' Journal [1964] - a guide to better drug use, sponsored by the Department of Health and sent free to all doctors in the UK.

"Unfortunately, there do not seem to be any satisfactory controlled clinical reports available to assess the value of diazepam ... Further studies on all aspects of the use of diazepam are required before its proper place as a therapeutic agent can be assessed."

Several early reports on diazepam at least indirectly hinted at the possibility of dependence problems. One, for example, reported that 3 out of 16 healthy adult volunteers "became slightly euphoric" on high therapeutic doses; [18] and there were also references to patients feeling quite high - eg "The patient states she feels 'wonderful' as long as she takes the medication." [19]

Another investigator, who had attempted a more systematic analysis of patients' comments about diazepam, noted that "remarks made by patients in ... order of frequency referred to the experienced tranquillising effect, stimulation and euphoria, release of inhibitions and side effects ..." This investigator also reported that one of his 45 patients had a major withdrawal reaction. She had twice upped her own dose and then stopped the drug altogether: typical *grand mal* seizures resulted on each occasion. [20]

One of the few investigators invited by Roche to test both chlordiazepoxide and diazepam was Dr H Angus Bowes, Director of the Institute of Neurology and Psychological Medicine in Grand Forks, North Dakota (population 39,008 in 1970). Dr Bowes wrote enthusiastic reports on both drugs, but preferred diazepam: "Valium ... in my considered opinion is the first drug of choice in the treatment of neurotic illness". However, in the course of treating many patients with diazepam, Bowes had also observed that one or two had staggered along to see him.

"Addiction. Five of my five hundred patients have become overtly dependent on Valium and presented themselves for examination with slurred speech, ataxia, a dry mouth and dilated pupils. They were all addictive personalities, exploiting the thesis that if one pill did so much good, four would do much better. Gradual withdrawal of the drug under Taractan [a major tranquilliser] and Librium while in the hospital was accomplished without any convulsive phenomena." [Bowes, 1965]

Bowes did not discuss the possibility that other patients might have been staggering around in their own homes. In those days, patients had to flaunt the evidence of their dependence, and behave in an unseemly fashion, to be noticed at all. Once identified, they would usually be labelled "addictive personalities" or "dependence prone".

First use of the law

The World Health Organisation's Expert Committee on Dependence-Producing Drugs in 1964 identified chlordiazepoxide as one of a range of non-barbiturates capable of producing "dependence of the barbiturate type". Although relatively little was known about chlordiazepoxide at that time, it was classified with barbiturates on two main grounds. One was that Hollister had shown it could produce the classic symptoms of barbiturate withdrawal; the other was "cross-dependence" between benzodiazepines, alcohol and barbiturates.

For some years, it had been recognised that if an addiction to one drug could be sustained by another, then both caused dependence of the same general kind. So, patients dependent on a barbiturate could be switched to chlordiazepoxide and experience no symptoms of withdrawal, because their dependence had transferred to the benzodiazepine. The WHO Expert Committee had drawn attention to the significance of cross-dependence in one of its earliest reports.

"The Committee wished to emphasise that all available evidence at the present time indicates that any substance which will sustain an established addiction - ie will adequately replace the drug which has produced the addiction - must be considered as also capable of producing an addiction." [WHO, 1950]

In its 1964 report, WHO did not classify diazepam as liable to produce dependence of the barbiturate type, but only because it was too new. Diazepam clearly belonged with the rest. Hollister and his team had by then demonstrated a barbiturate-like withdrawal syndrome for diazepam; and cross-dependence was recognised between diazepam and the other sedative-hypnotics, including alcohol. By the mid-1960s, there was good reason to think that any benzodiazepine would be liable to cause dependence of the barbiturate type.

The main significance of the WHO recommendations - which were well publicised in the UK and US [21] - was that they implied that the risk of dependence with benzodiazepines was comparable to the risk with barbiturates. The WHO committee chairman - also a consultant to Roche in the US - reportedly "said he felt Librium and Valium should be classified with the barbiturates and had told Roche this."[22]

A weakness of the WHO report was that it implied that dependence would prove to be a real problem only when benzodiazepines or barbiturates were used well above recommended doses and for long periods of time. It also made the mistake of defining the problem in terms of the severity of withdrawal symptoms, when the wider problem was that people went on taking these drugs for years.

WHO did not really address this question, though there were certainly grounds for concern about the barbiturates in therapeutic use. The amounts of barbiturates prescribed at that time indicated demand far in excess of therapeutic need: in Britain every tenth night of sleep was drug induced. [23] [24] Nor did the WHO report discuss the adverse effects of barbiturates on patients' mood and mental performance. Nor did it mention that doctors might possibly be feeding drug dependence - by mistaking symptoms of drug withdrawal (eg anxiety, insomnia) as evidence of a continuing need for medication. [25]

The WHO committee was probably more concerned about the explosive increase in recreational and self-destructive drug abuse in the 1960s, and perhaps this helped it to underestimate the problem of therapeutic dependence. Even so, this frank abuse did prompt questions about the relationship between medicinal and unsupervised use of the same drugs. As evidence grew of the more destructive effects of these drugs, through the behaviour of "addicts" in public, naturally there was more reason to question the safety of these medicines - just as had happened with opium and many other addictive drugs, years before. Whatever the differences between ostentatious abuse by a few thousand, and determined use by millions, the fact was that neither seemed to be able to function without regular use of their drugs.

Nevertheless, the UK Department of Health decided that there was no sizable problem in relation to the amounts of drugs prescribed. The DoH claimed that there were only 200-300 barbiturate addicts at this time - and that the so-called drug problem was as much as anything the result of unwarranted and extensive coverage by the news media. [26] In the US, by contrast, the scale of prescription-drug abuse was known to be enormous. The Food & Drug Administration (FDA) had estimated its extent by comparing the amounts of certain drugs manufactured, with the amounts legitimately prescribed. By 1965, the FDA suspected "that approximately half the 9,000,000,000 barbiturate and amphetamine capsules and tablets manufactured annually in this country are diverted to illegal use". [27] Either some companies were supplying wholesalers with grossly excessive amounts of drugs - or the medical profession was over-prescribing to an extent which was not only keeping patients topped up, but supporting nationwide drug abuse as well. Or both.

The US government responded to this problem by scheduling barbiturates and amphetamines under the Drug Abuse Control Amendments of 1965. This law required manufacturers to keep accurate records and documentation to show what quantities of scheduled drugs they made and where they were distributed. The law also gave government the right to add to the list of scheduled compounds any drugs which "after an opportunity for a public hearing had been officially determined to have a potential for abuse" [28] This was of great commercial significance. It reduced the likelihood that companies would supply illicit markets through business intermediaries. It meant that drugs might be prescribed less because of the stigma attached to them. And it also threatened to limit drastically the opportunities available to Roche for differentiating their benzodiazepines from other sedative-hypnotic drugs.

The US hearings on Librium and Valium ended in November 1966 and led to a recommendation in April 1967 to schedule both drugs under the Drug Abuse Control Amendments. By this time, the barbiturates, meprobamate and other sedative-hypnotics had already been scheduled - but Roche decided to resist.

Roche argued that the benzodiazepines were absolutely not in the same league as the barbiturates, and that it would be "unjustified and unwise" to schedule them. They claimed that there was far less evidence of a dependence liability with their drugs than with the others - and there was some truth in this if only because Librium and Valium had not been on the market for nearly as long as the rest. Although the law was essentially concerned with "potential for abuse" (ie evidence of risk, rather than proof of harm) Roche apparently felt threatened by "the libel of comparing Librium and Valium with barbiturates which would come when they were all included in the same law". [29]

The company mounted successive appeals and lobbied intensively against the US government's proposal - and was aided by a fair amount of bureaucratic paralysis in the FDA and other US federal agencies. The long story of how Roche kept the US government at bay for eight years has been well reported elsewhere, but the flavour of the affair is well enough conveyed by the following account:

"On March 28, 1973, the Third US District Court of Appeals in Philadelphia issued a forty-four page decision on the Librium and Valium case. In it, the court noted the evidence that Valium and Librium produce euphoria, tolerance, withdrawal and paradoxical rage, that they are diverted illegally and have a substantial potential for significant abuse, was ample. But the Court said, at the very beginning of the FDA hearing in 1966, FDA Counsel James Phelps did not submit to Roche Laboratories the report of the FDA Advisory Committee which included mention of Librium and Valium. The report did not contain information which would have materially changed the case, but the appeals court said the denial of the report to Roche Labs was a denial of due process, and it therefore reversed the hearing examiner's ruling against Librium and Valium. So, after hearings, lobbying battles and court proceedings lasting about eight years, Librium and Valium succeeded in escaping regulation. 'We won everything but the case', a government lawyer remarked on the appeals court decision." [30]

1 Sternbach, 1973, 1980, 1983

2 Sternbach, 1980

3 Hines, 1960

4 Harris, 1960

5 JAMA, 1960

6 Ingram and Timbury, 1960

7 Medical Letter, 1960

8 Medical Letter, 1960

9 Medical Letter, 1960

10 Hines, 1960

11 Marks, 1960

12 Svenson & Hamilton, 1966

13 Zbinden et al, 1967

14 Hines, 1960

15 Smith, 1980

16 Hollister et al, 1961

17 Hollister et al., 1963

18 Towler, 1962

19 Vilkin & Lomas, 1962

20 Aivazian, 1964

21 BMJ, 1964; JAMA, 1965

22 Pekkanen, 1973

23 Practitioner, 1964

24 Fort, 1964

25 Hunter, 1957; Sargant, 1958

26 Parish, 1971

27 N Eng J Med, 1965

28 N Eng J Med, 1965

29 Pekkanen, 1973

30 Pekkanen, 1973

Chapter 7

BENZODIAZEPINES WITH THE LIGHT OFF

"Does a doctor think differently about a medicine that he calls a tranquilliser than one he calls a sedative - or an anti-anxiety agent or an anti-psychotic agent ? The American Medical Association Council on Drugs thinks that he does, and that settling for a less precise name can lead to less precise understanding and to uncertain use of these agents. For that reason, the Council has discarded the term "tranquilliser" as a drug category in the 1967 edition of its publication New Drugs ..." [JAMA, 1967]

The third benzodiazepine

Roche's promotion of Librium and Valium had helped to persuade many doctors that there was a real difference between "sedatives" and "tranquillisers" - when in fact their similarities mattered much more. For most practical purposes, a sedative is a tranquilliser - and vice versa - and they are basically defined in identical terms as "drugs which produce a calming effect, relieving anxiety and tension". [1]

The main difference between them was that "tranquillisers" were to a great extent promoted and perceived as non-sedating sedatives - seemingly a contradiction, but not in marketing terms. The uniqueness of Librium and Valium was established first, by emphasising the differences between them and the barbiturates; secondly, by idealising what they could do for people – including the doctors who prescribed them. Prescribers of Roche tranquillisers were characterised as concerned, understanding and resourceful physicians. They were persuaded that these drugs would create real calm in patients; it was not euphoria they produced, but a sense of well-being appropriate to coping with the harsher demands of life.

Roche did not want to emphasise the potential of Librium and Valium as sleeping pills - though either would have been effective as a hypnotic if doctors had prescribed them in rather higher doses for use at night. It would have confused the message to tell doctors that these drugs were effective not only as non-sedating tranquillisers, but also as sleeping pills. Instead, Roche tended to advise doctors how to minimise unwanted side effects such as drowsiness - either by reducing the dose, or by waiting a few days until the effects wore off. Roche didn't mention that the drowsiness quickly wore off because patients had developed some tolerance to the drug.

Then in 1965, Roche introduced a third benzodiazepine, nitrazepam. They called it Mogadon and promoted it exclusively for insomnia - though at lower doses, nitrazepam could have been used for anxiety about as well. Following precedent, there was little reliable evidence of the therapeutic value of nitrazepam: reports of trials "appeared in relatively inaccessible journals and are mainly of poor quality". [2] Before long, Mogadon became the most prescribed hypnotic in the UK. Mogadon was promoted extremely effectively. It was differentiated entirely from its major competitors, the barbiturates - and from the other two benzodiazepines as well. Seven years after Mogadon was launched, Dr William Sargant told a symposium that he had always understood that there were important differences between diazepam and nitrazepam - and that he was shocked to learn there were not. Sargant said that he had learned for the first time at the symposium that these were essentially similar drugs, but used at different doses. The other main difference was that Mogadon was promoted as a sleeping pill, and Librium and Valium as tranquillisers.

> "I have only just learned that 'Valium' and 'Mogadon'
> are similar. Here is a supposed expert being led up the
> garden path by this situation. I hope that this conference
> will in some way make a strong resolution that in the
> future drugs with similar action and effects are grouped
> together. Because of advertising, doctors are going from
> one drug to another quite unscientifically"
> [Sargant, 1972]

But although nitrazepam and other benzodiazepines were essentially similar, there was one decisive difference between them and the barbiturates. The benzodiazepines had been found relatively safe in overdose, whereas the barbiturates were increasingly implicated in suicides and fatal poisoning cases. In 1970, there were over 20,000 emergency hospital admissions for barbiturate poisoning, including around 2,000 deaths. The barbiturates were implicated far more than any other drug. [3]

Roche pressed this advantage for all it was worth: it ran a powerful advertising campaign, in effect warning doctors to switch patients from barbiturates to Mogadon, to avoid a death on their hands. "Mogadon: far safer, far better", the company claimed.

The switch to Mogadon

Throughout the 1970s, the campaign against the barbiturates was increasingly run from within the medical profession. Reports in medical journals confirmed not only that benzodiazepines were much safer than barbiturates in overdose, but also suggested that they were less liable to interact harmfully with other drugs, and less likely to cause dependence. A prime mover in this campaign was an Ipswich GP, Dr Frank Wells. In an influential report, published in 1973, he described how he and his colleagues had achieved in their group practice a comprehensive change-over from barbiturates to nitrazepam (Mogadon).

Wells and his colleagues had identified 116 patients (1.5% of the practice) who were taking barbiturate sleeping pills. About half had taken them for over 5 years, the longest for 26 years. All patients agreed to the switch to nitrazepam, and within three months had all achieved it. But as Wells emphasised, that was not the end point of this exercise: "At the end of the first three months, all that had happened was the substitution of a cheap, effective, hazardous, and toxic hypnotic, by an expensive, effective, safer alternative". The objective was to try to reduce prescribing of hypnotics in the practice, and to get patients off sleeping pills altogether.

> "One of the first and most important points to consider when initiating treatment with hypnotics is the length of time for which these drugs are going to be prescribed."
> [Wells, 1973]

For one year after the switch-over, the 116 patients on nitrazepam were actively supported and encouraged to reduce their consumption and, if possible, to stop. By the end of the year, about half the patients had stopped, and about a quarter had succeeded in reducing the dosage. This was an important initiative, and ahead of its time - but it also had important limitations.

The study had been so conceived and designed as to reinforce belief in one of its own premises, which happened to be false. Wells and his colleagues had set up their initiative believing that nitrazepam was not a drug of dependence - and had interpreted their results accordingly. As Wells said: "One of the objects in doing this exercise was to substitute a known habit-forming drug by one which was known not to produce dependence ..."

The investigators therefore assumed that there was no cross-dependence between barbiturates and benzodiazepines - so they prolonged the switch to nitrazepam over an average 7-8 weeks. Assuming sensitive adjustment of dosage, it would have been quite feasible to switch patients to nitrazepam without delay; as it was, the benzodiazepine was gradually substituted for the barbiturate only when patients were felt to be ready for it: "patients who experienced no withdrawal symptoms and who slept well on nitrazepam were able to have their programme accelerated, while on the other hand those who developed nightmares or became insomniac for whatever cause had their substitution programme lengthened accordingly."

What this exercise really amounted to was drug withdrawal, achieved though the inadvertent use of highly effective double-blind placebo techniques. The results achieved reflected the careful attention given to patients and active encouragement to participate. The doctors would have conveyed to patients their mistaken belief that a non-habit-forming drug had replaced the barbiturate, reassuring all concerned. Many of the patients who managed to stop taking barbiturates quite easily probably had no chemical need for nitrazepam at all.

The results of this study did not in fact support the conclusion that nitrazepam was free from risk of dependence: on the contrary, if the drugs had been switched the other way round, the barbiturates would have emerged looking just as good. What the study did show was that doctors could take very useful steps to reduce the risk of dependence on sleeping pills. With encouragement, many people could be withdrawn from sleeping pills without much difficulty - although, most important, a hard core of patients apparently could not.

If the Wells study had been interpreted upside-down, its main conclusion would have been that about one-quarter of the patients could not reduce their dependence on sleeping pills after one year. But partly because of the emphasis on the success the experiment, the report defied such an interpretation. It did not discuss in any detail why some patients succeeded while others failed; nor did it explain whether continuing dependence on sleeping pills was related either to dosage or duration of use.

The campaign against barbiturates

The campaign to substitute benzodiazepines for barbiturates was fuelled mainly by concern about suicides and accidental deaths - but Mogadon was also recommended on the grounds that it carried less risk of dependence. For example, in a 1973 promotional pamphlet, Roche claimed that Mogadon had a clear advantage over barbiturates and Mandrax: "since addicts attending the treatment centres often urgently demand barbiturates or methaqualone/diphenhydramine [Mandrax] and are not keen on Mogadon". [4]

One message here was that "dependence of the barbiturate type" was something else. Another was that the dependence problem was essentially to do with small numbers of hard addicts - rather than with very large numbers of patients. But the relevance of the Roche claim was in any case dubious, since a report published three years earlier in the US had specifically noted that alcoholic patients often urgently asked for Librium by name.

> "Patients in whom chlordiazepoxide is used successfully
> to subdue the symptoms of withdrawal from alcohol,
> may experience an abstinence ... when deprived of chlor-
> diazepoxide as long as four weeks after sobriety ... Fre-
> quent and intense pleading for chlordiazepoxide in this
> population, when inebriated or sober, has been so
> notable that habituation should be called to the attention
> of physicians ... They do not simply request relief of dis-
> tress but plead for chlordiazepoxide by its trade name."
> [Finer, 1970]

But the important question was what happened in general practice. Several studies threw light on this and they all agreed on one main thing - that most patients on barbiturates appeared to present no problems at all. They tended to take their pills as prescribed - as most patients on benzodiazepines did then, and still do today. As William Sargant observed in 1956, patients on barbiturates "generally stick carefully to the prescribed dose, and, though they become anxious if they are taken off them, they do not get into trouble because of their barbiturate-taking". [5] Even after years of use, most patients did not increase the amounts of barbiturates they took, above the dosage originally prescribed. [6] There was nonetheless every reason to believe that they were dependent on them.

Adams and associates gave a more detailed picture in their 1966 report on Patients receiving Barbiturates in an Urban General Practice. This practice was ahead of its time, having a policy of prescribing for no more than a month at a time - but in other ways appears representative of practice elsewhere. Of about 10,000 patients, 407 were on barbiturates, mainly for anxiety; most were women and over half had been taking them for at least a year. There was evidence of some dose escalation in only 47 patients - characterised as "frequent attenders at the surgery [who] complained of symptoms which defied accepted treatment [such] that the family doctor felt impotent in dealing with them".

Comparable findings were reported by Drs John Johnson and Anthony Clift in 1968 - and were followed up with an important report on Factors leading to Dependence on Hypnotic Drugs which Clift published in 1972. The findings in this later report put into clearer perspective the conclusions of the switch-over study reported by Dr Frank Wells in 1973.

Clift's study involved about 150 patients attending his Manchester general practice, all of whom had complained of insomnia for the first time. These patients were divided randomly into two groups. In the main group, 100 patients were prescribed either nitrazepam (Mogadon) or amylobarbitone (a barbiturate) - and were specifically encouraged to try to manage without sleeping pills as soon as they could, a message that was reinforced in regular follow-up interviews. The remaining patients were prescribed nitrazepam (or in one or two cases a similar drug) and "they were not given any special advice about drug dependence and received repeat prescriptions as they felt they required them".

A year later, one in every three patients in this second group was still requesting prescriptions for nitrazepam - compared with only one in every 12 of those encouraged to stop. Sixteen of the 50 patients in the unexhorted group stayed on nitrazepam - compared with 5 on nitrazepam and 3 on amylobarbitone, in the main group of 100. Clift concluded that: "One of the most important factors in the prevention of drug dependence seems to be frequent review by the doctor after the first prescription and his cautionary advice to the patient". His study showed that the doctor's approach was a far more important predictor of drug dependence than the kind of drug used: "no difference was found in the development of dependence on amylobarbitone and nitrazepam".

This important message went largely unheeded. There was a rush in the 1970s to switch patients from barbiturates to nitrazepam - but much less emphasis on getting patients off sleeping pills altogether, as Drs Clift and Wells had done. Another active campaigner for rational prescribing, Dr Peter Parish, noted that Roche gave detailed instructions in its sales literature for converting patients from barbiturates to Mogadon, but "there is no mention of subsequently reducing or stopping Mogadon therapy". [7] Essentially the same was true of the Campaign on the Use and Restriction of Barbiturates (CURB). This was a pressure group set up in 1975 "to acquaint doctors to the contemporary problems concerning the use and abuse of barbiturates" - but the campaign went no further than that.

CURB was funded by the DoH and set up by the medical profession, not only to improve prescribing standards, but also to "keep its own house in order, without interference from outside". Public criticism of the medical profession's contribution to the barbiturate problem was then recognised by some doctors as a threat to their "clinical freedom" - ie the right that doctors had traditionally claimed to prescribe as they know best. The chairman of CURB emphasised that, if the profession was to resist outside intervention, it had to demonstrate that it could control its own affairs through self-regulation: "the medical profession, although almost uniquely self-critical, is of course a proud and sensitive body", he said. [8]

Soon after it was set up, CURB organised a seminar to review the barbiturate problem. To judge from published reports on the meeting, the focus of the campaign was exclusively on problems with barbiturates. There was little emphasis on the limitations and dangers of sleeping pills and anti-anxiety drug, as such - though this did concern some of the more prescient doctors there.

> " ... some doctors at the seminar were worried that a similar conference would have to be called in ten years' time to discuss the problems of habituation and misuse associated with the benzodiazepines." [Goldsmith, 1975]

When CURB was wound up in 1977, it was because the organisers of the campaign felt the job was done. In the same year benzodiazepine consumption reached its highest peak, around 30 million prescriptions a year.

Laboratory study of sleep

Serious studies of the effects of drugs on sleep date from the mid-1960s, around the time Mogadon was launched in the UK. These studies broke new ground, producing objective evidence to suggest that hypnotics gradually ceased to work after only a few weeks of continuous use. They also began to explain how dependence on drugs like nitrazepam could be created and sustained.

Sleep studies can in some ways measure very precisely the effects of drugs on insomnia and sleep - and, most important, they can achieve far greater precision than is possible when testing the effects of drugs on anxiety. When a volunteer or patient is tucked up and wired up in a bedroom-like sleep laboratory, it is straightforward enough to get basic measures, such as how long it takes to fall asleep and how long the sleep goes on.

By contrast, it has always proved extremely difficult to measure the effects of drugs on anxiety, especially in long-term studies. Levels of anxiety fluctuate greatly, and they rise or fall because of many factors other than drugs. Nor is it easy to define how severe an anxiety is, when so much depends on the patient's own assessment and on the doctor's style of interpretation. Anxiety comes in many guises, and different people see it and feel it in different ways.

Some of the earliest studies of the effects of drugs on sleep were carried out by Dr Ian Oswald and his colleagues in the Department of Psychiatry at the Royal Edinburgh Hospital. They were among the first to use measurements from electroencephalograms (EEGs): volunteers were wired up all night so that the EEG could record electrical messages from different parts of the brain. The EEG not only registered major activity in the brain; it could also little murmurs and signs of dreams and nightmares too.

The basic routine in a sleep laboratory drug study involved measuring the duration and other parameters of sleep at three different stages. Stage one covered the first few nights of sleep in the laboratory, the period before the volunteer took the test drug. This pre-drug stage gave subjects a chance to settle in. It also allowed research workers to make baseline measurements - to allow before-and-after comparisons to be made. Stage two was the period on-drug; and stage three the period of withdrawal and beyond.

Using these techniques, Oswald and his colleagues were able to demonstrate the physiological characteristics of different kinds of sleep. One was rapid eye movement (REM) sleep - periods of sleep which signalled dreaming time. Oswald established that hypnotic drugs tended to reduce periods of REM sleep - also that there was a marked increase in REM sleep above baseline, once the drug was withdrawn. This explained why patients often had nightmares, even when stopping a drug after only a few days.

By 1964, Oswald and his colleagues strongly suspected that, when someone stopped taking a sleeping pill like nitrazepam, a backlash effect made the insomnia worse than it had been, even before the drug treatment began. This "rebound" effect was soon confirmed in the sleep laboratory, and was shown to exist when drugs were stopped even after very short courses of treatment.

Oswald's work again prompted the question which others had raised during the 1950s: did patients go on taking sedative-hypnotics mainly to avoid the withdrawal effects ? And were doctors and patients tending to misinterpret the symptoms of drug withdrawal as a recrudescence of their original symptoms ? [9] Even before the launch of Mogadon, Oswald had realised that what had always previously been dismissed as a psychological dependence on hypnotics might actually be a physical dependence after all. He suggested that something intensely and intimately physical might be happening when sleeping pills were withdrawn - even if it was not obvious to the doctor and could barely be measured at all.

> "We see so many patients, whom we would not call bar-
> biturate addicts, who just take a couple of sleeping pills
> each night, and who are extremely resistant to any sug-
> gestion that they should give them up. We learn from
> them that these pills were started, often in hospital, 5 or
> 10 years ago and have never been stopped. 'I've tried to
> stop them, doctor, but I just can't sleep properly without
> them.' And so it goes on year after year, and 10 per cent
> of all NHS general practitioner prescriptions are for
> sleeping pills. Five hundred million sleeping pills a year
> in England & Wales - excluding hospital and private pre-
> scribing. One wonders how many prescriptions are
> given at private consultations because the regular NHS

practitioner refuses to accede to further requests for the
beloved sleeping pills.   Is it solely a psychological
dependence, has the patient merely learned that swal-
lowing the pills opens a quick avenue to oblivion ? Or
has her physiology been changed, so that the drug is
now woven inextricably into her brain chemistry so that,
if the drug were suddenly lacking, a violent chemical
perturbation would arise ?" [Oswald, 1964]

In 1965, Drs Oswald and Priest published the research on which
these comments were based, in their report Five Weeks to Escape the
Sleeping-pill Habit. In two experiments, volunteers were given either
nitrazepam or a barbiturate, each night for up to 18 nights, and then
the drug was withdrawn. Sleep patterns were studied throughout the
night and recorded on over 35 miles of paper produced by the EEG.
The authors' summary of their main findings said: "Nightmares
occurred at first after stopping the drug, and a number of measurable
neurophysiological functions took over five weeks to return to normal. Attention is drawn to the difficulty experienced by some patients
in renouncing the use of sleeping pills". Later, Oswald suggested
another most important conclusion - how much more there was to
learn.

"Recent research using EEG techniques has shown that
hypnotics do not induce natural sleep, and have made
plain how ignorant we formerly were about their effect
on sleep, and how much more ignorant we shall appear
to have been when new techniques become available in
future." [Oswald, 1968]

Hypnotics soon stop working

From the mid-1960s onwards, sleep studies gave more and more
objective evidence of the limitations of benzodiazepine and other
hypnotics. It became increasingly clear that there was a problem with
tolerance - ie that the drug's original effects usually lasted no more
than a few days - and there were problems on withdrawal as well. [10]

Further reports from Edinburgh introduced the idea that hypnotic
drugs, in effect, allowed sleep to be "borrowed" - leaving an increasing debt to be repaid at the time of withdrawal. This in turn underlined the recommendation "that patients should be supported while
they are being withdrawn". [11] These findings were discussed shortly

afterwards in an editorial - Sleep Now, Pay Later - in the *Journal of the American Medical Association*. It commented: "Small wonder that patients whose use of sleeping pills is loosely supervised find it almost impossible to kick the habit". [12] Later reports prompted similar comments in the UK. [13] [14] In particular, the *British Medical Journal* emphasised the need for short courses of treatment and close supervision of patients on sleeping pills.

> "... when the patient's insomnia is a symptom of a life-long anxious temperament, or an endless succession of emotional crises and interpersonal disharmonies, a hypnotic may do no more than satisfy the doctor's own desire to appear helpful in the face of a daunting therapeutic prospect ... A patient who is subject to the presence of noise, discomfort, and natural fears will find a hypnotic of great comfort, but the routine prescription of such drugs merits renewed and critical scrutiny." [*British Medical Journal*, 1970(a)]

Around 1970, there was also increasing concern that dependence on hypnotics was largely an iatrogenic disease - "a condition created and maintained by doctors". [15] This was recognised in the clearest and most painful terms in the following commentary in *Prescribers Journal*, by a Suffolk GP:

> "In 20 years of practice, I am unaware of ever having helped a patient by prescribing a hypnotic, but I have written many such prescriptions and continue to do so. By prescribing hypnotics, I have caused much misery and harm and prevented many people, including myself, from taking a more positive attitude to a common symptom. I have no doubt caused dependency and habituation on a wide scale ... Experience has taught me, very slowly, much that my clinical teachers did not. I can think of no subject worse taught to medical students or to hospital residents than that of the management of sleeplessness ... I was taught by example how easy and laudable it was to start such drugs. No-one ever discussed the difficulties of stopping them. It is understandable that such ignorance continues to be widespread. Only a general practitioner watching his patients over a long period of time can possibly be aware of the mischief

caused by hypnotics. By the time he becomes fully aware of the natural history of hypnotic users many years of habituation will have ossified a pattern of prescribing. To change this will cost both the patients and doctor super-human effort." [Stevens, 1973]

In the meantime, the techniques established in Edinburgh had been extended in the US, notably by a team working under Dr Anthony Kales. In 1974, Kales confirmed and further defined the phenomenon of rebound after drug withdrawal. His work also established that sleeping pills became increasingly less effective after short periods of continuous use. Usually within two weeks, tolerance to the effects of sleeping pills had developed to such an extent that duration of sleep on-drug was no greater than it had been before the drug had been started.

Kales was particularly struck by the finding that insomniac patients continued to sleep badly, in spite of taking hypnotic drugs. In turn, this underlined a major deficiency in drug evaluation procedures: "studies of hypnotic-drug effectiveness under [the] conditions of chronic use are virtually non-existent, yet these drugs are often administered for periods ranging from months to years in an attempt to manage and treat insomnia". The evidence that sleeping pills soon became ineffective directly contradicted what many doctors had believed for years.

The fact that these drugs stopped producing a hypnotic effect did not mean that they had no effect at all. By the mid-1970s, much evidence suggested they could cause dependence. It was also known that chronic use of hypnotic drugs had a continuing effect on sleep patterns - though the significance of the differences between drug-induced and natural sleep were not at all well understood.

Neither is the significance of dreaming and dream suppression at all clear. The definition of "dream" in the *Penguin Dictionary of Psychology* underlines how much more there is to learn:

"Dream - A lot of people have wrestled with this one; let's define it simply as 'imagery during sleep'. Dreaming appears to occur in many organisms and is intimately related to rapid-eye-movement (REM) sleep."
[Reber, 1985]

Many other questions remain unanswered. For example, to what extent will the effects of a drug differ if it is used either to induce sleep or to reduce anxiety ? Would diazepam, for example, stop working as a hypnotic, but go on working as an anxiolytic ? Such are the difficulties of testing the effects of drugs on anxiety, it seems impossible to be sure.

1 Martin (Ed), 1985
2 Smith, 1966
3 Smith, 1972
4 Roche, 1973
5 Sargant, 1956
6 Fraser, 1958; Johnson & Clift, 1968
7 Parish, 1971
8 Bennett, 1977
9 Alexander, 1951; Hunter, 1957
10 Kales, 1974; Institute of Medicine 1979; Committee on the Review of Medicines, 1980

11 Evans et al, 1968
12 JAMA, 1969
13 Evans et al, 1970
14 Kales et al., 1969; Oswald, 1968
15 Lewis, 1970; Fisher, 1970; Oswald, 1970; Whitlock, 1970; Abrahams et al., 1970; Parish, 1971

Chapter 8

WHATEVER THE DIAGNOSIS ...

"Almost two decades of laisser faire research [into diazepam, chlordiazepoxide and meprobamate] have yielded no adequate, systematic data base for meaningful inferences. About all one can safely and tritely conclude is that all these drugs affects performance under some conditions. There simply is no reasonable basis for generalising about either the specific or the comparative effect of these drugs. Surely this deplorable net result of undirected and misdirected science and pseudo-science suggests that some routine should be established to provide a comparable data base for evaluating the effects on performance of any anti-anxiety drug marketed for administration to humans." [McNair, 1973].

The old versus the new

Re-enter Dr Leo Hollister from the Veterans Administration Hospital in Palo Alto, California. Ten years have passed since the early 1960s, when Hollister found that the first benzodiazepines produced barbiturate-type withdrawal symptoms when hefty and lengthy treatments were suddenly stopped. Towards the end of the 1970s, Hollister will enter the story again, helping Roche to defend the benzodiazepines when they later come under attack. But back in 1972 - in a paper on the prudent use of anti-anxiety drugs - Hollister raised fundamental doubts about their usefulness, and about how they were being prescribed.

He began by asking whether the benzodiazepines and similar drugs were actually effective in treating anxiety. He seemed almost to apologise for raising this at all, since it questioned the judgement and practice of most of his colleagues. Nevertheless, he considered it a live issue. It was indeed very difficult to design clinical trials to demonstrate that anti-anxiety drugs did work, and hard evidence of their effectiveness was lacking. Hollister said it was "generally accepted" by doctors that these drugs could relieve symptoms of anxiety - but because of this lack of evidence, "many doubt that the benefits of drug therapy are very great".

"Considering the widespread and continuing use of these drugs, it may seem impertinent to question their efficacy. Yet a number of well-designed controlled studies have failed to elicit consistent differences between drug and placebo therapy of anxiety ..."

"In a study that has become something of a classic, meprobamate was compared with placebo in anxious patients, using all the customary criteria of a double-blind controlled study, but adding the variable of having two different physicians doing the prescribing. One physician was trained to take a 'therapeutic' stance; he was generally supportive and sympathetic and had great confidence in the treatment. The other took an 'experimental' stance, with somewhat opposite attitudes. The difference between drug and placebo was significant in the group of patients treated by the first physician, but not in those patients treated by the second". The moral is clear: If you are going to prescribe these drugs, at least try to work up some enthusiasm for them and try to communicate it to your patients." [Hollister, 1972]

Hollister's point was that benzodiazepines and other anti-anxiety drugs would be effective if believed to be effective - and that the doctor's confidence in the drug was an essential part of the treatment. Whatever the drug did for the symptoms of anxiety, the placebo effect was also strong: the chemistry of the relationship between patient and doctor might be just as effective as the chemistry of the drug.

Next, Hollister asked how effective and safe the various anti-anxiety drugs were in relation to each other. Again, he almost apologised for producing "at best contentious estimates". But he suggested it was still not clear whether there were significant differences between the various benzodiazepines - and he also thought that the differences between benzodiazepines and other anti-anxiety drugs were not all that clear.

"One is inclined to rank the benzodiazepines ahead of meprobamate and phenobarbital and them, in turn, ahead of placebo. Nevertheless, some might question whether the rank order can be that clearly defined ..."

Hollister believed that benzodiazepines had the advantage because of reduced risk with overdose - but not in respect of tolerance, drug habituation or physical dependence. He thought there seemed little or nothing to distinguish between the benzodiazepines and pheno-barbitone (a widely-used long-acting barbiturate), though both seemed safer than meprobamate. The major difference he saw between the benzodiazepines and phenobarbitone was that the former were much less likely to be used for suicide.

Then Hollister asked how well these drugs were used. He concluded that "anti-anxiety drugs are used widely but not necessarily well", recommending that drugs "should be considered no more than symptomatic adjunctive treatment". Hollister emphasised in particular that anxiety was often episodic, and therefore that drug treatment should be intermittent too: "Such episodes of treatment might be limited to a week ... By limiting treatment to short courses, problems of tolerance with loss of efficacy, or increased doses with the risk of physical dependence, are avoided." For much the same reasons, Willcox had suggested a one-week limit for barbiturates, 40 years before.

Hollister also emphasised the importance of adjusting the dose to the individual's requirements - pointing out that if one gave a group of patients the same dose of diazepam, some ended up with much higher concentrations of drug in the body than others. Then he suggested that the traditional several-times-a-day dose schedules made little sense with drugs like diazepam or chlordiazepoxide - which remained in the body at therapeutic concentrations easily long enough for the patient to manage with one dose a day. Hollister didn't say so, but this made no more sense than filling up the petrol tank of a car after every 50 miles or so. Frequent dosing might also have reinforced the drug habit.

Too many brands, too many diagnoses

There was no hard evidence at this time of important differences between benzodiazepines - though there was also no shortage of opinions about the uniqueness of each member of this class of drugs. The manufacturers constantly emphasised these differences, often by publicising the views of selected experts. The medical literature of this period encouraged prescribers to be quite fanciful in their choice of one kind of drug over another. One US expert even related drug choice to class.

> "In other words diazepam seemed to be best suited for the sicker, middle-class, psychiatric practice patients and phenobarbitone sodium for the less sick, low socioeconomic class, clinic patients, while both drugs appeared to be equally effective clinically in general practice." [Rickels, 1968]

The early 1970s provided ample space for new drugs, and there were always new corners of the market to fill. If the promotional material was to be believed, anxiety was everywhere: at work, in human relationships and in organic illness of all kinds. Wherever there was anxiety, there too was Valium - for infants, the elderly and everyone in between. [1] "Valium Roche", as they began to call it, was advertised not just for anxiety - but for "the neurotic skin", "the anxious heart" and the like. [2] Librium, in the meantime, was available whatever the diagnosis - and according to one advertisement was even making its own signal contribution to world peace.

> "The Sixties. It is ten years since Librium became available. Ten anxious years of aggravation and demonstration, Cuba and Vietnam, assassination and devaluation, Biafra and Czechoslovakia. Ten turbulent years in which the world-wide climate of anxiety and aggression has given Librium - with its specific calming action and its remarkable safety margin - a unique and still growing role in helping mankind meet the challenge of a changing world." [Roche, 1970]

By the mid 1970s, several new benzodiazepines had come on to the market and other companies had begun to compete with Roche. The major contender was John Wyeth & Brother, a subsidiary of the American Home Products corporation. Wyeth had introduced oxazepam in 1966, under the brand name Serenid-D. Then in 1972, they launched lorazepam, better known as Ativan. Wyeth promoted both for anxiety, but specifically recommended oxazepam for elderly patients, though there was little evidence then that it was better for this. [3] Now there is more. [4]

Altogether, there were seven benzodiazepines on the market in 1974, when the *Drug & Therapeutics Bulletin (DTB)* published the review: Benzodiazepines - too many similar compounds? The *DTB* is an authoritative, independent newsletter for the medical profession, published by the Consumers' Association in the UK; its drug evaluations (like those of the *Medical Letter* in the US) reflect the consensus view of specialists in different branches of medicine. The *DTB* review complained that there were already more than enough benzodiazepines on the market. These were the drugs already available - all but Mogadon for anxiety.

Drug	Main brand	Manufacturer
Chlordiazepoxide	Librium	Roche
Diazepam	Valium	Roche
Nitrazepam	Mogadon	Roche
Oxazepam	Serenid-D	Wyeth
Medazepam	Nobrium	Roche
Lorazepam	Ativan	Wyeth
Clorazepate	Tranxene	Boehringer-Ingelheim

The *DTB* concluded that the differences between these benzodiazepines were too small to justify the introduction of these seven (let alone the many more in the pipeline). Although each was promoted as if it was significantly different from its rivals, this was unwarranted. "The only pharmacological activity which differentiates the benzodiazepines to any extent is the anticonvulsant action", but this was of little clinical significance. As sedatives and hypnotics, there was virtually nothing to distinguish between different benzodiazepines. Thus, "to single out nitrazepam for use as a hypnotic is irrational" - and its widespread use as a sleeping pill reflected marketing policy rather than the pharmacology of the drug. If taken in a single dose at night, diazepam, chlordiazepoxide or lorazepam would all be just as effective as nitrazepam in promoting sleep.

One reason there was so little to distinguish the pharmacological effects of different benzodiazepines was that they were chemically so closely related. They were not only structurally similar. They also shared many active metabolites - breakdown products. For example, diazepam, clorazepate and chlordiazepoxide all break down in the body to the same metabolite (desmethyldiazepam) which in turn is metabolised to oxazepam. In other words, the different benzodiazepines generally acted in the same way because they were more or less the same thing.

With so many similar products, the manufacturers felt they needed to promote them on a grand scale, so that doctors could tell them apart - though from a therapeutic perspective, the extent of promotion was absurd. Roche led the way: sales of Librium and Valium alone accounted for about 70% of its turnover in 1970. In that year, Roche spent 44% of its promotion budget on sales representatives, who were making over 1,000 visits a week to doctors; 16% of the budget went on some 500 whole-page advertisements in 25 different medical journals; and they mailed out 97 separate promotional items for their two main drugs. [5] Doctors received overwhelmingly more information about drugs from the manufacturers than from independent sources [6] - just as they do today.

The bogus differentiation of benzodiazepines created some serious problems. For example, doctors who did not realise that different benzodiazepines belonged to the same class of drugs sometimes prescribed two or three at a time. Many patients had their dosages and their dependence increased because doctors did not realise that the effects of benzodiazepines were additive: two drugs at the regular dosage have the same effect as either drug at double the regular dose.

Another, deeper problem was caused by having all these products. The apparent variety of drugs tended to reinforce in doctors the belief that there was a pill for every ill - and to some extent, an ill for every pill. The benzodiazepines were promoted for use in so many manifestations of anxiety and stress that this was almost inevitable. Doctors were in effect encouraged to make diagnoses, and to customise their prescribing, not just from clinical symptoms - but by matching the symptoms they perceived in their patients with the images and impressions they got from advertisements. This was the point made at an important 1972 symposium, sponsored by the Department of Health.

"What I wish to draw to your attention is a fundamental weakness that I see in the reliability of so much diagnosis in formal psychiatry. The argument which I wish to advance is that the doctor prescribes psychotropic drugs in order to be able to make psychiatric diagnoses.

" 'Well Mrs Smith, I have listened to your story and examined you, and it seems to me that you are a case of diazepam. You had better have some anxiety'. It seems to me that whether or not our patients are hooked on the drugs, the doctors are certainly hooked on the diagnoses. Now we can ask a question that I regard as perhaps more rewarding than 'Why do general practitioners prescribe psychotropic drugs ?' - that is the question 'Why do general practitioners prescribe psychiatric diagnoses' ?" [Marinker, 1972].

Government regulation begins

The Department of Health's decision to sponsor the 1972 symposium had been influenced by the publication in late 1971 of a major study by Dr Peter Parish on the prescribing of psychotropic drugs in general practice. His study drew attention to what seemed an increasingly serious problem of over-prescribing of benzodiazepines and other sedative-hypnotic drugs. The symposium was about problems - though its title was bland, The Medical Use of Psychotropic Drugs. As fate would have it, Drs Clift and Wells attended the symposium; and Dr William Sargant was in the chair. This was where Sargant first learned that nitrazepam and diazepam were not much different, but much the same.

However, the problems discussed at the symposium were not really what concerned the DoH: they mainly cared about the effect of all the prescribing on the NHS drugs bill. The DoH has always tried to avoid doing anything which might be interpreted as telling doctors what to prescribe, or how. It has also been careful not to offend the industry - let alone enrage it by suggesting that companies might produce fewer drugs of the same kind. Apart from the occasional drug disaster - and problems of dependence with implications for law and order - government's main concern about drugs has always been to do with their cost.

The first government initiative to affect the benzodiazepines had nothing directly to do with their performance as medicines. By the early 1970s, the government had become concerned about evidence of uncompetitive practice and profiteering by Roche Products Ltd. This prompted a Monopolies Commission enquiry and the publication in 1973 of a highly critical report. Its main conclusion was that Roche's prices for chlordiazepoxide and diazepam had for some years "been manifestly too high", earning a return on capital of over 70%. [7] Later the company agreed to repay several £ millions to the government, and to stop certain kinds of promotion.

The fuss began after two smaller drug companies obtained legal rights to market their own versions of chlordiazepoxide and diazepam - in advance of the expiry of Roche's patents in 1975 and 1976. These two companies were required under the terms of their licences to pay Roche a royalty of about 15 times the cost of the basic drug ingredients - yet both had managed to undercut substantially Roche's price on the finished product. Roche had responded by trying to put the squeeze on these companies in a variety of ways.

For one thing, Roche had been supplying hospitals with Valium and Librium, free of charge. This not only blocked the competition; it also contributed to dependence - but in response to the Monopolies Commission enquiry, Roche ceased this practice in 1972. In the same year, Dr Anthony Clift published his seminal report on hypnotic drug dependence, in which he estimated that about one in five of his patients had started their hypnotic habit in hospital.

By this time, government had also set up the machinery of the Medicines Act, 1968. Under the new law, companies with drugs already on the market were given automatic rights to continue selling their products. These older products, such as Librium and Valium, were given Licences of Right, later subject to review - but all new products had to have a full Product Licence from the start. The basic features of the drug control system introduced in 1972 are the same as those today.

• Before testing a new drug in humans, companies have to provide satisfactory evidence of pre-clinical testing in order to obtain a Clinical Trial Certificate, or an exemption from it.

• On the basis of animal, human and other studies, companies must submit satisfactory evidence of the safety, efficacy and quality of their drugs to get a Product Licence.

• The Product Licence is granted subject to formal and important terms - eg undertaking to inform the authorities about problems. The terms relating to safe and effective prescribing have to be spelt out in a data sheet.

• A drug must not be "actively promoted", unless prescribers have been supplied with the current copy of the data sheet. This should include all of the basic information a doctor would need to prescribe the drug appropriately - and no form of drug promotion should be inconsistent with the advice in these instructions for use.

• The Committee on Safety of Medicines (CSM) should advise the drug licensing authority (the DoH) on safety matters - and to this end, it organises a voluntary adverse drug reaction reporting system. Doctors who suspect that a patient has become ill though taking a medicine are asked to use a special Yellow Card to report details to the CSM.

This new system was outlined at the 1972 symposium on The Medical Use of Psychotropic drugs by the DoH's lone representative. He told participants that drug safety was the important thing - but then he hedged rather, emphasising the need to avoid delaying the introduction of important new medicines, as well. This was not too relevant because, as the Monopolies Commission had noted: "really outstanding drugs are still very few in number and if a firm makes one major advance in 10 - 20 years it is doing very well".

More to the point, the Department's representative said he wasn't sure how much help they could give in screening drugs like benzodiazepines - mainly because of the difficulties involved in measuring the effects of anti-anxiety drugs. Another factor was that the official scrutiny of Product Licence applications was in those days handled by a professional staff of just ten. [8]

Wyeth's warnings on dependence

The effects of the licensing laws on drug safety have always been hard to assess. From the outset, in 1972, the only information the DoH has regularly provided about the licensing process has been how long it takes, on average, to process the applications it receives - and the numbers of applications that pass and fail. No information has ever been given about specific licence applications, including the reasons why individual products were either approved or turned down. To disclose such information would be an offence under section 118 of the Medicines Act.

From the outside, perhaps the best way of estimating how the licensing authority has assessed a particular risk is to look at the data sheet - to see how the warnings given compare with published information about the drug. It also helps to compare UK data sheet warnings with equivalent warnings in other countries, notably the US. Here, for example, is the warning for clorazepate (Tranxene) issued in the US in 1973 - more than a decade before any warning of dependence risk appeared in the drug's UK data sheet. The following appeared in the American equivalent of the data sheet - the drug "label" - published in the *Physician's Desk Reference*, an annual compendium of drug information, sent to all doctors in the US.

> "Physical and psychological dependence: Withdrawal symptoms (similar in character to those noted with barbiturates and alcohol) have occured following abrupt discontinuation of clorazepate. Symptoms of nervousness, insomnia, irritability, diarrhea, muscle aches and memory impairment have followed withdrawal after long-term use of high dosage ... Evidence of drug dependence has been observed in dogs and rabbits which was characterized by convulsive seizures when the drug was abruptly withdrawn or the dose was reduced ..."

In the UK, in 1973, there were only two data sheets for benzodiazepines which mentioned dependence risk, though neither said much. Wyeth's data sheet for oxazepam (Serenid-D) advised prescribers to take care when treating known drug abusers, but also claimed that no cases of dependence or habituation had been reported. At least two suspected cases had in fact been reported by then. [9] And as the WHO's Expert Committee on drug dependence had warned in 1970, the dependence potential of oxazepam should be assumed equivalent to that of other benzodiazepines, as presenting a significant risk to public health. [10]

Why did Wyeth not refer to published reports of dependence on oxazepam? One reason was that the company believed that clinicians who thought they had seen dependent patients were mistaken. Roche shared this view and, like Wyeth, responded to published reports of benzodiazepine withdrawal symptoms, with rejoinders suggesting doctors were probably describing symptoms of the patient's underlying illness. [11] When a case of oxazepam (Serenid D) dependence was published in the *British Journal of Psychiatry* in 1972, [12] Wyeth's spokesman was adamant in defending his company's product - though he had apparently not seen the patient involved.

> "The quoted withdrawal signs are evidence of the anxiety accompanying the patient's depressive illness, allowed to burst forth once the oxazepam was discontinued ... In my view there is no evidence of dependence produced by oxazepam in this case." [Harry, 1972]

At this time, the only other benzodiazepine product which carried a warning was Ativan, the Wyeth brand of lorazepam. However, the data sheet didn't mention the word dependence. It also overlooked a serious problem with lorazepam, first noticed in 1972.

The problem was originally revealed to Dr Rene De Buck. He was a consultant psychiatrist at a university hospital in Belgium, and one of the first people to study lorazepam in a controlled clinical trial. De Buck presented his results initially at a 1972 symposium on lorazepam, sponsored by Wyeth; a year later, his paper was published in a special journal supplement about the drug.

De Buck's trial involved 30 anxious patients on high therapeutic doses of lorazepam for less than one month. The study apparently made no effort to investigate what happened when the drug was withdrawn at the end of the trial. Nothing was said about the outcome for 28 of the 30 patients - but the other two took themselves off lorazepam before the end of the trial, and both then had convulsions. One clearly had a convulsion because of stopping lorazepam. The other patient's convulsion De Buck attributed, not to lorazepam, but to withdrawal from an antidepressant drug the patient was taking at the same time. She shouldn't have been: "Patients who had taken another psychoactive drug previously were asked to discontinue it for 15 days before entering the study". By taking the antidepressant as well, this patient violated the trial protocol, invalidating some results.

These were obviously very important findings: a major withdrawal reaction (or two) to a new benzodiazepine, after only a few weeks' controlled use on therapeutic doses. Such events had never been reported before. They were certainly the most significant findings in the study, but they were not mentioned in the all-important part of the paper, the summary.

"The summary is the article's most important part. Many will only read the summary and it may be reproduced throughout the world. It should be brief and clear with just the essential points." [Hawkins, 1976]

De Buck's account of the two patients who had convulsions appeared in his paper in the detailed section about side-effects. There was no warning even in the conclusions - which said "the side effects reported above are only very rarely encountered and it is thus concluded that lorazepam is a very safe drug". Rather as an afterthought, De Buck added: "it is perhaps wise not to discontinue medication abruptly."

Partly because of this, crucial information about the dependence risk was overlooked - and it was forgotten for the next eight years. During most of this time, the UK data sheet for Ativan carried this warning:

> "It is advisable to avoid abrupt discontinuation of Ativan as some sleep disturbances may result. This applies especially when high doses have been given for prolonged periods."

In 1978, Wyeth organised another symposium on Ativan - this time to help launch it in the US. And on this occasion, the noises made about dependence were all reassuring. In his review of the papers presented at the US symposium, the Wyeth representative repeatedly emphasised that there was no problem with the drug. He didn't actually say that there was no evidence of any dependence problem, but he conveyed just that. In his review, he managed to make the point on five separate occasions, using this particular form of words:

> " ... with no indication of any tolerance to efficacy" ... " ... and there was no evidence of the development of tolerance to efficacy" ... "... there was no evidence of the development of tolerance to efficacy" ... "...with no evidence of the development of tolerance to efficacy" ... "This extensive clinical evidence indicates that lorazepam ... gives statistically and clinically significant relief of the associated anxiety, with no evidence of the development of tolerance to efficacy." [Richards, 1978]

The meanings of "tolerance"

When Wyeth claimed there was "no evidence of tolerance to efficacy" with lorazepam, two things might have been inferred. One was that the drug kept on working. The other was that patients would not escalate the dosage: there would be no reason to if the effects of the drug did not wear off. However, just as there was widespread uncertainty about the meaning of "addiction", "habituation" and "dependence", so there was much confusion about the meaning of "tolerance" - as there is still is today.

It is therefore hard to be quite sure what Wyeth meant, or how this word tolerance would have been understood. When Roche and Wyeth used the word in data sheets, they generally meant it in a positive way. They said that there was good tolerance of their products or that they were well tolerated - and what they meant was that most

patients wouldn't experience side effects. But in another sense, tolerance meant something that doctors knew was bad - the tendency of
drugs to lose their original effectiveness, which could lead to patients'
increasing the dose to try to regain the lost effect. So doctors may well
have inferred that "...with no evidence of the development of tolerance to efficacy" meant no need to worry about addiction.

However, it was not safe to assume that there was "no evidence of
tolerance to efficacy", just because patients in clinical trials had not
increased their dose. Tolerance can equally well result in a diminished response to the drug - ie loss of drug effectiveness - as the WHO
had been saying for years.

> "... an adaptive state characterised by diminished
> response to the same quantity of a drug or requiring a
> larger dose to produce the same pharmacodynamic
> effect." [WHO, 1964].

Despite this, doctors were generally encouraged to believe that,
without escalation of dosage, there was no development of tolerance,
no loss of drug effectiveness and therefore no risk of dependence. At
that time, there would have been no obvious reason for doctors to be
concerned about something called "tolerance" which wasn't associated with dosage escalation. Why should anyone have worried about
diminished drug effectiveness when the benzodiazepines were in
constant demand ? The climate in the mid-1970s was such that
nobody was really sure what tolerance meant, nor greatly minded.
But whatever it was, there seemed to be a lot of it about.

> "What do we mean by tolerance ? In its broadest sense it
> seems to me that the pharmacologic effect of a single
> dose is different from the pharmacologic effect of chronic
> doses. If we interpret tolerance in that way, probably
> everybody who takes diazepam on a chronic basis devel-
> ops some degree of tolerance; they almost have to. For
> example, after a single 10mg dose, the peak blood level is
> about five times less than is observed after two weeks of
> 10mg daily. Despite this steady-state level, these people
> are not walking around sedated or sleepy after they have
> been taking the drugs for two weeks or more. There
> almost has to be some kind of adaptation of the central
> nervous system to the presence of the drug" [Greenblatt,
> 1977].

This was what tolerance meant to a widely-known US expert in this field, a benzodiazepine enthusiast, Dr David Greenblatt. On his definition, there would not have been much to distinguish between the tolerance that developed to either barbiturates or benzodiazepines. If the effects of diazepam diminished, or remained unchanged, after two weeks - in spite of a five-fold increase in the concentration of the drug in the body - there had to be tolerance to the drug's effects.

Nevertheless, doctors tended to believe that there was no problem without escalation of dosage - a phenomenon relatively rarely reported or seen. Once the benzodiazepines became established, doctors lost sight of the fact that barbiturate type dependence was generally insidious and often undiagnosed. The WHO's 1964 advice, that benzodiazepines and barbiturates caused the same kind of dependence, was largely forgotten - as was the fact barbiturates had been used extensively for 50 years before it was first recognised that they were true drugs of dependence all along.

1 Roche, 1968
2 Roche, 1970
3 American Medical Association, 1966
4 Wolfe et al, 1988
5 Monopolies Commission, 1973
6 Parish, 1971
7 Monopolies Commission, 1973

8 Mansell-Jones, 1972
9 Selig, 1966; Hanna, 1972
10 Isbell & Chruschiel, 1970;
WHO, 1970
11 Fyfe, 1966; Medd, 1975
12 Hanna, 1972

Chapter 9

NEVER GOOD TO BRING BAD NEWS?

"Given the widespread extent of benzodiazepine use, the issue of benzodiazepine misuse is of considerable medical and social importance. Unfortunately, achievement of a rational clinical perspective of this problem has been made nearly impossible by a barrage of irresponsible and sensationalistic journalism by popular newspapers, periodicals, and television." [Greenblatt & Shader, 1978]

Consensus and other views

In the second half of the 1970s, views about dependence on benzodiazepines seemed increasingly to polarise - especially in the US. The orthodox view was that the risks of dependence were minimal; and many doctors thought it disturbing that the press and media should exaggerate the problem so greatly, because this made patients worry even more. Dr David Greenblatt was one of several prolific writers on the benzodiazepines who was outspoken in such views.

Greenblatt had been explaining his views on tolerance to the benzodiazepines at a small roundtable discussion, held in Chicago in late 1976. Nine experts from all over the US discussed Valium: A Discussion of Current Issues, and the verbatim (but presumably edited) text of the proceedings was later published as a brochure and used for promotion. The roundtable was sponsored by Roche, and Dr Leo Hollister was in the chair.

Much of the roundtable discussion dealt with the question of what the participants referred to as "dependence" - which Dr Greenblatt and other participants clearly understood to mean full-blown addiction. An acknowledged expert on the benzodiazepines, Greenblatt confessed "I have never seen a case of benzodiazepine dependence". He said he thought it "an astonishingly unusual event" in relation to the amounts prescribed, and "unusual enough to be a medical curiosity worthy of a medical case report or of being picked up by the press." [1]

Hollister confirmed that in day-to-day practice one would rarely if ever come across cases such as he had seen in his withdrawal studies in the early 1960s. He also emphasised that benzodiazepine withdrawal symptoms were attenuated: because the drug and its active metabolites generally took several days to clear the body, there was a "built-in tapering of drug effect" after withdrawal. Hollister explained that, after his earlier studies on chlordiazepoxide and diazepam, he had been expecting "a flood of reports of withdrawal reactions". But it had never come.

> "The probable reason is that patients abort these reactions early on because they think their original symptoms are returning, and they get back on the drug. So we rarely see the full-blown picture."

No-one at the roundtable picked up this point, though it clearly suggested the possibility of widespread dependence. But the participants appeared to believe that the real problem with dependence was that patients worried about it too much. Patients had become scared because of exaggerated publicity about a few hardcore addicts, the kind who abused any drug they could find - including many different tranquillisers, all of which tended to be called "Valium". Everyone agreed how important it was to distinguish clearly between patients and addicts.

> "It is important for physicians to know that the recommended doses of Valium cannot produce anything resembling addiction. It is only with extraordinarily high doses over a long period of time that we see tolerance and withdrawal effects. I am more concerned these days about the patient on prescribed amounts of Valium who becomes upset after reading some less than accurate article. The fear of being 'hooked' is added to his other anxieties. He needs information and reassurance about the safety of the drug." [2]

The consensus at the roundtable was that diazepam was a versatile and very useful drug which in Western countries was, on the whole, conservatively prescribed. They decided that physical dependence was rarely a problem in therapeutic use, though doctors did need to be on the look-out for vulnerable patients and the "addiction-prone". Participants felt that "abuse of diazepam has been grossly over-reported", allegedly because of media misunderstanding.

The roundtable apparently agreed that the main reason the benzo-diazepines seemed to be implicated in abuse was that they were slow-ly metabolised and therefore remained in the body for longer than other drugs. The participants believed this meant that, when blood samples from addicts or overdose victims were analysed, benzo-azepines were much more likely to be identified than other drugs. In their view, that was "largely" why the benzodiazepines were singled out for criticism.

But benzodiazepines were probably less likely to be detected than older drugs. Blood tests for tranquillisers in multiple drug abusers were not routine, [3] and techniques for identifying benzodiazepines in the blood were still at an early stage of development. Until about the mid-1970s, the screening methods generally used were not sensitive enough to detect therapeutic concentrations of diazepam and metabo-lites in the blood. [4] What seems to have been the first major study of overdose cases based on chemical analysis was not published until 1976 - the year of the roundtable - and this identified diazepam as the drug most implicated (after alcohol) in a series of over 1,500 overdose cases. [5]

This broadly confirmed an earlier report - based not on chemical analysis but on carefully researched drug histories - from the Mayo Clinic in Minnesota. [6] By the mid-1970s, the benzodiazepines and bar-biturates were about equally likely to be implicated in overdose cases. The benzodiazepines, in themselves, did less harm - though there was growing concern that they increased the danger of overdose from bar-biturates and similar drugs.

Clinical evidence also suggested similarities between barbiturate and benzodiazepine abuse. One of the first studies was published by two Norwegian doctors in 1969. They analysed the drugs taken in one year by all 565 patients seen at the psychiatric clinic in the Oslo Uni-versity hospital. They found that 1 in 12 patients had abused chlor-diazepoxide or diazepam by taking excessive amounts; and conclud-ed "that there were no certain differences between the benzodi-azepines and barbiturates" in this respect. [7]

And in the following year, the directors of two university psychi-atric clinics in Germany reported eight cases of dependence on diazepam. The authors emphasised that they could not reconcile what they were seeing in their clinics with the conventional wisdom that the benzodiazepines were safe. Their paper was in German; its summary was translated and directly to the point:

> "Drug dependence of minor tranquillisers, which belong to the benzodiazepine derivates, especially of diazepam is said to be a rare complication. Hitherto only isolated cases have been published. This impression seems to be in contrast to the steadily growing practical experiences. In a relatively short time 8 patients being dependent on diazepam could be observed ... In all cases there was a drug dependence of barbiturate-alcohol type according to the definition of WHO expert committee on addiction producting drugs (1964) ... The drug-dependence shows all classical criteria of addiction, including a tendency of increasing the dose, psychic and physical dependency with withdrawal symptoms." [Peters & Boeters, 1970]

In a later report, two surgeons from Lexington, Kentucky briefly described the cases of five patients admitted to hospital for non-psychiatric conditions between 1973 and 1976. All patients had been taking diazepam at recommended doses, most for at least two years. On admission to hospital, all medications had been withdrawn before surgery and anaesthesia, and these patients had experienced hallucinations and related symptoms apparently as a result. [8] Also in 1976, a detailed report on 30 consecutive cases of withdrawal psychosis seen in the psychiatric department of a Danish university hospital, implicated about equally benzodiazepines, barbiturates and barbiturate-like drugs. [9]

Under-reporting of dependence

Critical reports were, nevertheless, still few and far between, certainly in relation to the amounts of benzodiazepines prescribed. Adverse reports were also far outweighed by favourable ones, and overwhelmed by the volume of promotion. In the world literature, only around 100 reports of dependence on benzodiazepines were published in the first 15 years of their use. Yet by then, "some 10 to 20% of ambulatory adults in the United States and other Western nations ingest benzodiazepine derivatives on a regular basis due to anxiety, tension or insomnia". [10] By the mid-1970s prescriptions for benzodiazepines in Britain were approaching 30 million a year.

The main reason why there were relatively few published reports was presumably the one mentioned by Hollister at the roundtable discussion in Chicago. Hollister's view was that "the frequency and severity of withdrawal reactions from benzodiazepines has been for many years remarkably low" [11] - because patients aborted withdrawal symptoms by continuing to take their drugs. These patients were thereby reinforcing their dependence on benzodiazepines - disguising it at the same time - as they had done with the barbiturates for many years before.

An element of fear may also have played some part in inhibiting publication of reports about drug risks. With the manufacturers ready to pounce (and with intense interest from the media and press), many doctors would have hesitated before blowing the whistle on a drug - as well they might today. And in this atmosphere, doctors might have been more inclined to dismiss complaints from patients who said they were hooked - though probably patients didn't complain, unless cut off from their drugs.

Since those days, bits and pieces of information have emerged about the extent of professional intimidation and its effects. [12] Very unexpectedly, the problem was referred to in a 1987 letter to the BMJ by two doctors at the Department of Health, quoting their former colleague, Dr John Griffin. By then, Griffin had become Director of the Association of the British Pharmaceutical Industry (ABPI) - in which capacity he reportedly said this:

> "Within the last three months, I have had complaints
> from physicians giving me letters that have been sent to
> them from member companies which have been harass-
> ing them. Harassment does occur. We are fooling our-
> selves if we believe that it does not." [Jones and Mann,
> 1987]

This outspoken revelation was the DoH's way of being adamant, in the face of nagging from the ABPI, that it was not prepared to release to companies the names of doctors who reported details of adverse reactions to the Committee on Safety of Medicines. To this day, the CSM guarantees anonymity to doctors to doctors who report suspected adverse drug reactions under the Yellow Card scheme.

But despite this guarantee of confidentiality, there is still massive under-reporting of adverse drug reactions - which suggests that professional intimidation may not be such an important issue. In spite of encouragement, only about one in six doctors has ever sent in a Yellow Card; and the organisers of the scheme acknowledge to this day that the great majority of adverse reactions are never reported at all. The main reasons were suggested by Dr Bill Inman, the man who set up the scheme. He identified these "seven deadly sins":

"*Complacency*, the mistaken belief than only safe drugs are allowed on the market. *Fear* of involvement in litigation, a lesser problem perhaps in the United Kingdom than in the USA. *Guilt* because harm to the patient has been caused by the treatment the doctor has prescribed. *Ambition* to collect and publish a personal series of cases, a common human failing that may lead to serious delays in recognition of a hazard. *Ignorance* of the requirements for reporting, perhaps as a result of failure in communication between the reporting centre and the professions *Diffidence* about reporting mere suspicions which might perhaps lead to ridicule And finally, *lethargy* - an amalgam of procrastination, lack of interest or 'time'; inability to find report cards and other excuses." [Inman, 1976]

The Yellow Card scheme was set up after thalidomide, in 1963. During the first 13 years of its operation, doctors sent in just 8 Yellow Cards about dependence on benzodiazepines - of the order of one report for every 10 million prescriptions. In one important respect, though, these data were extremely revealing: there were equally few reports about barbiturates and barbiturate-like drugs. So, whatever the risk with benzodiazepines actually was, the available evidence suggested that it was about the same for sedative and hypnotic drugs of different kinds. That point was missed.

Though some undercurrent of concern about dependence seems to have emerged by the mid-1970s, there were few outspoken voices at this time - and the impression is of critics feeling isolated from mainstream medical opinion. This came across quite strongly in a letter published in the *Journal of the American Medical Association* in 1974. It had been prompted by a rather bland editorial in that journal; [13] and is reproduced here in full:

"Your Editorial, 'Drugs for Anxiety' prompts an uneasy feeling that has been growing for some time. Diazepam is cited as a safe drug not particularly subject to abuse when prescribed on an as-needed basis with a cover statement that some psychic distress should not be alarming. This is floridly at variance with my uncollated experience; in fact, so much so that I regard it virtually as a 'once on, never off' preparation. I have long prescribed it only for stressful circumstances of clearly brief duration. Despite this precaution, I never prescribe it without a heartfelt sigh, knowing how frequently the initial prescription will be followed not by the requested visits for discussion, but by calls from the pharmacist relaying ever more frequent requests for refills, and then psychotherapy-by-telephone as the patient attempts to justify his need for the drug in three minutes rather than come in to discuss problems. Am I alone in the woods, or is there a silent plurality out there whose misgivings are not reflected in the usual recommendations published for psychotropics ?" [Cochran, 1974]

One of the few published responses to this letter came from a doctor at a Boston teaching hospital, who had seen several patients on the psychiatric ward experiencing barbiturate-type withdrawal symptoms, even after low doses of diazepam taken for four to six months. [14] This tallied with the findings of two earlier, formal studies which demonstrated abstinence symptoms when patients were abruptly withdrawn from therapeutic doses of chlordiazepoxide after 4 months. [15] The US authorities were persuaded by these earlier studies to require manufacturers to warn that the efficacy of benzodiazepines for anxiety was doubtful after 4 months of continuous use. Much later, the UK authorities adopted this 4-month efficacy standard (2 - 4 weeks for hypnotics) as well. [16]

Perceptions of dependence

In the 1970s, barbiturates were defined as the main problem in Britain - although there was some concern about repeat prescribing of benzodiazepines and other psychotropic drugs. In Britain, most patients got their benzodiazepines on repeat prescriptions: often this meant the doctor's receptionist signed the prescription form, and that the patients would not see the doctor for months on end, occasionally for years. [17]

A survey reported in 1980 that about three-quarters of all psychotropic medicines were supplied on repeat prescription, and that over one half had been prescribed for at least a year. [18] This confirmed earlier reports: "The more frequently the same item had been prescribed, the less likely the patient was to see the doctor"; [19] and "there appeared to be a relationship between duration of therapy and the entry of repeat prescription details by ancillary staff". [20]

Another problem was lack of basic and continuing medical education - and the growing dependence of doctors on companies for drug information. Many doctors would have left medical school by 1960 when the first benzodiazepine arrived. In any case, pharmacology and therapeutics were in those days a neglected part of a doctor's training - as they still tend to be. In the mid-1960s, one American scholar reported: "No country has produced so many wise reports on the improvements of medical education as Great Britain, and no country has done so little about it". [21] The stream of wise reports has continued ever since, but medical students still learn relatively little about drugs. [22]

At the 1972 DoH symposium, it so happens there was a medical student - from St Mary's Hospital Medical School in London, where Drs Willcox and Sargant had been 40 before. This is what he said about his training in drug use:

> "Several contributors have proposed education as a possible solution to these problems and, as a medical student, I am only too aware of the present deficiencies of educational facilities. In the whole of a five year course, many students can expect to receive as little as ten weeks' pharmacological training in which time it is necessary to gain a working knowledge of some 3,000 products and a critical evaluation of the £23m promotional machine with which they will later be confronted." [Robson, 1972]

This is not to say that most qualified doctors actually felt overwhelmed by all the benzodiazepines and the lack of hard information about them. Collectively, doctors may well have felt encouraged to have so many different and promising tools at their disposal - and pleased that there were always new benzodiazepines to try, because new drugs always gave new hope. In any case, the doctors cherished their "clinical freedom", their right to prescribe as they pleased. On those grounds alone, they would have strenuously resisted any attempt by government to limit the numbers of benzodiazepines available to them - as later they did.

General standards of prescribing in the 1970s did cause some concern; routine and uncritical prescribing of benzodiazepines in the 1970s was known about and tolerated, if frowned on. Overwhelmingly, therefore, the dependence problem was masked by continuing drug use - and by doctors not seeing things too clearly and tending to look the other way. Around the mid-1970s, probably many doctors were actually incapable of diagnosing dependence on diazepam.

The direct evidence for this is slight but sweet. It came from the heart of a report by two US physicians, published in 1976. Barry M Maletzky and James Klotter set the tone of their review by saying they had scrutinised 28 published scientific reports, all confidently stating that benzodiazepines were not addicting drugs - and found that none of them could be relied on. They were uninformative, inadequately controlled, confused or otherwise flawed. Maletzky and Klotter were quite polite about it, but this is what they seemed to mean.

Significantly, Maletzky & Klotter called their report Addiction to Diazepam, and it was published in *The International Journal of the Addictions*. Twelve years had passed since the WHO Expert Committee had defined "dependence of the barbiturate type" - suggesting that the term "addiction" was confusing and should no longer be used. But even if they helped to perpetuate the confusion over terms, Maletzky & Klotter were aware of the need for definition. They themselves drew attention to the confusion there seemed to be over the word addiction - for example, by citing one early report which had said: "there appears to be no addiction to chlordiazepoxide, though there is a tendency to develop dependency on it". [23]

Maletzky & Klotter then neatly demonstrated how difficult doctors could find it to accept that there was addiction to (or dependence on ?) diazepam. They illustrated the gulf that existed between true and unconsciously biased observations - at the same time revealing the whole point of having blind and properly controlled trials.

A panel of 14 doctors was asked to read the case notes of 50 patients on diazepam, some of whom showed well-known signs of drug dependence. The symptoms were described in some detail, though the drug in question was not identified. When they had read the notes on a particular case, the physicians were asked to rank each one according to the severity of the drug dependence there appeared to be. In their ratings, in some cases, they recognised a serious drug problem:

None	Slight	Moderate	Great	Severe
19	11	11	6	3

After recording these ratings, panel members were informed that the drug in question was diazepam; they were then asked to reassess the severity of dependence in each case. At this point, the physicians opened their eyes but closed their minds. Their collective judgement, in line with the conventional wisdom, was that diazepam did not cause anything like addiction. They now described what they previously thought was a serious problem as a minor one:

None	Slight	Moderate	Great	Severe
36	9	5	0	0

The difference between these "blind" and "open" assessments might be compared by analogy to a judge who, having reviewed the case of Mr X, concludes on the facts that he clearly did commit some offence - only to reverse the decision when it is later revealed that Mr X is none other than Mr Y. The image of the benzodiazepines as safe drugs was by this time well ingrained: the drugs weren't to blame, so rogue patients and the odd rogue doctor tended to be blamed instead.

Could dependence be benign ?

By the mid-1970s, the benzodiazepines were riding so high in Britain that there was even serious talk of making them available without prescription. The key figure behind this proposal was George Teeling-Smith, Director of the Office of Health Economics, an offshoot of the ABPI. Teeling-Smith had also attended the 1972 symposium on The Medical Use of Psychotropic Drugs - and it was there he first raised the question: Is drug dependency sometimes acceptable? He acknowledged there was some dependence, but suggested that the time had come to reconsider the moral questions involved, in the light of society's more liberal views on other drugs.

"Should we accept that some patients ought to be
allowed to become dependent on psychotropic drugs -
although we would obviously accept that this is 'second

best' to tackling the underlying problem ? Most of us
would accept that it is inevitable, even perhaps desirable,
that one should accept alcohol as a socially acceptable
drug. Our attitude towards the use of marihuana is liber-
alising steadily - and in this climate we have to reconsider the morality of dependence on prescribed medicines."
[Teeling-Smith, 1972]

Teeling-Smith's ideas were developed in an unsigned 1975 report
from the Office of Health Economics (OHE), which proposed that the
prescription laws for benzodiazepines and similar drugs should be
relaxed - or at least that paramedics (eg health visitors) be given
authority to prescribe them too. This report no longer argued that
drug dependence was a price worth paying: on the contrary, the independence of the consumer was said to be at stake. The OHE now suggested that benzodiazepines probably presented no greater risk of
"addiction" than many freely available alternatives.

"It may be suggested that currently available tranquillisers such as the benzodiazepines should be regarded as
suitable for use in the area of self-medication, at least in
as far as this would place them in an intermediate position between 'medical' and 'social' drugs and so tend to
preserve the independence of the user and to protect him
or her from the social side effects of medicalisation ...
Current evidence indicates that they may in the final
analysis prove to be significantly safer and less addictive
than the social drugs or some medicines currently on free
sale." [OHE, 1975]

Here was the industry proposing to liberate consumers by letting
the benzodiazepines go free - while the WHO still ranked them with
meprobamate, methyprylon and phenobarbitone, as drugs presenting
"a significant risk to public health". [24] Although benzodiazepines
were considered less hazardous than most barbiturates, the WHO had
in 1970 recommended an expiry date on all prescriptions, with limits
on the amount prescribed and on the number of repeats.

The nature and scale of risk

The OHE's proposals for deregulation made no headway, [25] and soon
the moment passed - as further information surfaced about the benzodiazepines' dependence risk. First, there was a report from Dr Ian

Oswald's sleep research team in Edinburgh of increased levels of anxiety and insomnia following abrupt withdrawal from short-term, normal-dose use of a new benzodiazepine. The subjects in this study did not know that placebo had been substituted for the active drug after three weeks - but they reported a marked increase in anxiety after the switchover. Again, this suggested that habitual use was reinforced by the failure to recognise withdrawal symptoms for what they were.

> "There was a trend towards daytime anxiety reduction while on the drug but there was a prolonged and striking increase of anxiety following withdrawal. To this anxiety may presumably be attributed the poor daytime concentration and sense of subjective impairment on rising in the morning that were present following withdrawal ... one must suppose that the prolonged anxiety and other effects we have seen following withdrawal from fosazepam would be no less likely after intake of benzodiazepines such as diazepam. If this is true, it would point to a self-perpetuating feature in the clinical consumption of benzodiazepines in that they are taken to relieve anxiety but are responsible for enhanced anxiety as soon as an attempt is made to stop them." [Allen and Oswald, 1976]

Also in 1976 there was a report of neonatal withdrawal symptoms - important not least because drug withdrawal symptoms in a newborn baby could hardly be attributed to psychological dependence of any kind. The mother in this case had taken therapeutic doses of chlordiazepoxide thoughout her pregnancy, and her new-born twins had both had a withdrawal reaction. [26] This claimed to be the first report of its kind, although a tentative report along similar lines had in fact been published in 1969. [27]

Now, if there were only two reports of neonatal withdrawal in the 15 years the benzodiazepines had been used, why should one not conclude that this problem was extremely rare ? One answer is that, although it took 15 years before the first report of neonatal withdrawal from a benzodiazepine, it took much longer with the barbiturates. The first reports of neonatal withdrawal from barbiturates were published in 1972, nearly 70 years after the barbiturates first appeared [28] - but that did not mean that the barbiturates were really safer in this respect. It meant that doctors had not previously recognised withdrawal symptoms in babies - or had not reported them if they did.

The wider point is that the frequency and timing of published adverse drug reaction (ADR) reports may give an entirely misleading impression about the scale of the problem. This was the point missed by Dr John Marks - who, in 1978, produced detailed evidence which made the risks of benzodiazepine dependence seem negligible. At the time, his conclusions were widely accepted and, for several years, they underpinned the defence of the benzodiazepines in the UK and abroad.

Top marks for benzodiazepines

Marks was with Roche when chlordiazepoxide first appeared; he wrote the first review of the drug to appear in the UK. Later he became Managing Director, but then he left the company to become Director of Medical Studies and Tutor at Girton College, Cambridge. He was at Cambridge when he wrote his book, The Benzodiazepines: Use, Overuse, Misuse, Abuse. His book was prepared with much help from Roche, though Marks said he took full responsibility for any errors it contained.

With help from Roche, Marks had compiled what he believed to be a full list of 118 medical reports, published between 1961 and mid-1977, which gave "at least minimal information" about benzodiazepine dependence. He claimed that his evidence "overstated the incidence of published benzodiazepine dependence". He then analysed the 118 reports, making "every effort ... to be critical but unbiased", dividing them into three categories. He thought some articles gave acceptable evidence, while others were weak - and others he rejected outright.

A total of 18 articles were rejected from Mark's analysis, on the grounds "that inspection of the original publication has shown there is no evidence of dependence". These included the 1973 Mayo Clinic study; [29] also the 1975 letter from the hospital doctor in Boston [30] who said that he had seen "several patients" having withdrawal symptoms after routine treatment with benzodiazepines. Marks ignored the later in his analysis on the grounds that "the text quoted number of cases as 'several'."

Some reports Marks altogether missed; others he dismissed. One he rejected was the 1972 report by Dr Anthony Clift who (like Dr Frank Wells) had demonstrated that long-term consumption of hypnotics could be greatly reduced simply by encouraging patients to use them sparingly. Clift had also shown that patients were just as likely to get in trouble with nitrazepam (Mogadon) as with a barbiturate, (amylobarbitone). Dr Marks' conclusion was: "unfortunately the study must be regarded as invalid as there is no clear evidence presented of dependence".

Marks was also cool about two early studies [31] which had looked at the effects of abrupt withdrawal after four months on therapeutic doses of chlordiazepoxide. He reviewed these in two sentences, the operative one saying that the authors themselves had stressed "that it is far from clear whether these symptoms were those of withdrawal or a recurrence of the anxiety state". The authors had actually concluded that their results "support the occurrence of a minor abstinence syndrome of the barbiturate type".

Marks also considered part of the report by Maletzky & Klotter [1976]. He noted how different their findings were from just about everyone else's - suggesting that it was very hard to believe that there could be much addiction to diazepam, independently of addiction to alcohol and other drugs. Marks was unable to accept that the alleged victims of diazepam might include more than a small proportion of people who did not have a general problem with drugs.

"Against this background it is very difficult to evaluate the recent report by Maletzky & Klotter. Taken at its face value, this appears to show that a high proportion of patients taking diazepam presented some evidence of dependence. Unfortunately their data are not adequate to assess the incidence and their finding that those previously admitting alcohol or drug abuse showed no difference from the remainder casts doubt on their report."

Having analysed the published evidence on benzodiazepine dependence, Marks distinguished between two main kinds of case. Among the reports he had collected were 401 more or less convincing cases in which patients had also abused alcohol or other drugs. He had also found 57 cases, where alcohol was not involved, with "presumptive evidence of benzodiazepine dependence", mainly "within a therapeutic setting". On this basis, Marks concluded that the risk of dependence was extremely low, considering the amounts of benzodiazepines prescribed. He also questioned the extent to which the drug might be responsible.

"The concept of a dependence-producing 'capacity' or 'potential' which resides in a drug itself has been questioned by some authorities in respect of drugs other than narcotics. These authorities suggest it is more relevant to speak of 'dependence prone individuals' who abuse a variety of substances and can develop dependence on any or all of them."

However, if drugs did contribute to dependence, Marks pointed out that it was "widely agreed" that the risk with benzodiazepines was very much lower than with barbiturates. He then estimated the order of risk involved, by relating the numbers of reported cases of dependence to the total numbers of prescriptions for benzodiazepines issued over the years.

"The dependence risk with benzodiazepines is very low and is estimated to be approximately one case per 5 million patient months 'at risk' for all recorded cases and probably less than one case per 50 million months in therapeutic use."

This analysis involved basic errors of technique as well as serious errors of judgement. The main flaw was the assumption that the incidence of published cases necessarily gave any indication of the true incidence. It did not and could not be expected to: such estimates could be meaningful only if the ratio of reported-to-actual numbers of cases were known. Marks did not know this and apparently made no attempt to assess it. He should have realised that, if a number of individual doctors had reported several cases each, dependence could not possibly have been as rare as his precise calculations suggested. Even more so with hospital reports: if only a few hospitals reported a series of cases, it was very risky to assume there had been no cases at all in the overwhelming number of hospitals reporting nothing.

After making these precise (but essentially irrelevant and meaningless) calculations, Marks then suggested that the WHO Expert Committee's assessment of the dependence risk for benzodiazepines was obsolete. Having congratulated its authors [32] on their "masterly monograph", Marks tactfully suggested that a reclassification of risk from "moderate" to "low" would bring the WHO into line with "many experts in the field". A footnote identified the experts he had in mind: all had attended the Roche-sponsored 1976 roundtable on Valium: a discussion of current issues.

Marks went on to praise the WHO Expert Committee for its 1964 definition of the different types of dependence, and its various manifestations - and then proceeded to define benzodiazepines as exceptions to the general rule. Should the dependence risk with benzodiazepines be compared to the risk associated with barbiturates ? Marks view was that "it would probably be wiser to regard them as separate groups at the present time".

Marks' methodology was hardly questioned; his conclusions were very widely reported and well received. They proved most influential and were cited again and again.

Roche back in Washington

Towards the end of the 1970s in the US, publicity about benzodiazepine dependence increased - and public pressure eventually led to hearings before a Senate Sub-Committee on Use and Misuse of Benzodiazepines in 1979. These were not the first congressional hearings in which the benzodiazepines had featured, [33] but were the first to review and begin to tackle the question of dependence.

Senator Ted Kennedy's sub-committee recorded over 500 pages of evidence from patients, clinicians and research workers as well as from Hoffman La Roche and the Food & Drug Administration. Its report included many written submissions, also one or two confidential memoranda from Roche. One was a 1977 internal review in which Roche acknowledged that "abuse and misuse poses a continued confrontation" [34]. There was concern that sales of Valium in the US had dropped by 3 per cent during in 1977, although they were still worth nearly $1/4 billion a year.

Another internal document partly explains why Roche found it so hard to accept that benzodiazepines could produce dependence of the barbiturate type. Roche had apparently never researched the issue: an internal 1979 memorandum to the US company's chairman disclosed that Roche had neither conducted nor supported any studies on dependence and long-term effects of diazepam. This document also suggested that independent criticism of the company's products tended to be dismissed by Roche not only as unscientific; but also as something of an affront, an attack by "hostile" or "unfriendly" critics.

The company determined that its response should be to "continue to promote Valium on every call to objective physicians and institutions". Roche's overall aim was to identify from among these "objective" physicians those who would be prepared to promote the use of Valium on the company's behalf. At local level, this meant identifying psychiatrists who were high prescribers of Valium and heavily promoting the product to them. At regional and national level, the aim was to reverse declining sales' trends by "utilising a core group of key speakers". The defence of Valium and other benzodiazepines was orchestrated and cast by Roche to an extent which doctors could not have appreciated. The level of company involvement was outlined in a 1977 memorandum to Roche sales managers in the US Western region.

> "*Regional Strategy:* Increase Valium promotion in the institutions and utilise 'champions' and influentials to help handle the overuse confrontation. *Tactics:* Each division will establish a list of at least four Valium 'champions' by the end of February. These physicians will be utilized as speakers at staff meetings in the institutions and/or medical meetings. The list of physicians available for this purpose could be local influentials, i.e. senior residents in psychiatry or attending staff physicians with high levels of recognition. 'Experts' recognised statewide or nationally in the area of psychtropic drug use might also be considered."

Among the sales aids Roche used were reprints of articles published in learned journals. They included copies of reports by Hollister [1977] and Greenblatt & Shader [1978], both of which emphasised that diazepam and other benzodiazepines only rarely caused physical dependence - which they seemed to equate with "addiction". In their 1978 review, Greenblatt and Shader devoted one section to "Sorting out terminology", noting that "the terms tolerance, addiction, habituation and dependence are subject to much misunderstanding". They then defined their own terms, suggesting some definitions which had been largely abandoned by the WHO in 1964.

Greenblatt and Shader's detailed review made two main points. One was that "widespread concern about benzodiazepine addiction is based largely upon irresponsible journalism rather than sound scientific evidence". The other was that there was nothing much to be said about "habituation or psychological dependence" on benzodiazepines, because there was so little reliable evidence to go on. Nevertheless, they concluded that "in the vast majority of cases" there was nothing to indicate inappropriate, excessive or dangerous use. They believed that continued use of the benzodiazepines reflected the continued presence of anxiety or insomnia - warning that these symptoms might well be mistaken for a withdrawal reaction if treatment were suddenly stopped.

1 Greenblatt, 1976
2 Cohen, 1976
3 Blinick et al, 1976
4 Regent & Wahl, 1976
5 Regent & Wahl, 1976
6 Swanson et al, 1973
7 Retterstoll & Ropstadt, 1969
8 Floyd & Murphy, 1976
9 Fruensgaard, 1976
10 Greenblatt & Shader, 1978
11 Hollister, 1977 [b]
12 Erlichman, 1986
13 Hussey, 1974
14 Haskell, 1975
15 Covi et al, 1969, 1973
16 Committee on the Review of Medicines, 1980
17 Dennis, 1979
18 Anderson, 1980

19 Dunnell & Cartwright, 1972
20 Freed, 1976
21 Stevens, 1966
22 Greenfield, 1983; General Medical Counsel, 1987; Steering Group, 1990
23 Williams, 1961
24 WHO, 1970
25 General Practitioner, 1975
26 Athinarayanan et al, 1976
27 Bitnun, 1969
28 Desmond et al., 1972; Bleyer & Marshall, 1972; Schweigert, 1972
29 Swanson et al, 1973
30 Haskell, 1975
31 Covi et al, 1969, 1973
32 Isbell & Chruschiel, 1970
33 Smith M, 1985
34 US Senate subcommittee, 1979

Chapter 10

SHARPENED PERCEPTIONS OF RISK

"Mr Carter-Jones asked the Secretary of State for Social Services what study his Department has made of possible addiction to valium; if the Chief Medical Officer has advised doctors on treating such addiction and withdrawal symptoms; and if he will make a statement."

"Dr Vaughan: The Committee on the Review of Medicines (CRM), with an expert sub-committee including eminent psychiatrists, has made a comprehensive study of all aspects of the clinical use of benzodiazepines, including diazepam, the active ingredient of Valium. On the basis of present knowledge the CRM has concluded that addiction potential was generally low .... It is not the practice for the chief medical officer of the Department to advise doctors on clinical matters within their own responsibility. Publication of guidelines and consequent revision of data sheets will give doctors sound information on which to exercise their clinical judgement."
[Hansard, 5 March 1980, Col. 278w]

Problems for the elderly

Towards the end of the 1970s, the benzodiazepine market peaked and levelled off; between then and the mid-1980s, demand in the UK stayed at around 30 million NHS prescriptions a year. Over the same period, however, a profound change in prescribing habits led to great shifts in fortune. By the time the upheaval was over, Roche products had lost much ground; Wyeth's had done very well; and a third major company had entered the market. The underlying reason for this shift was concern about drug accumulation in the elderly: the essence of the problem was explained in a letter published in the *British Medical Journal* back in 1972.

THE NEXT STEP IS YOURS

Changing her prescription to short-acting Serenid-D
would reduce the risk of a fall.

Serenid-D *

Preferred for the elderly   oxazepam

Potentially hazardous sedation and impaired co-ordination resulting from accumulation, as seen with long-acting tranquillizers, tend not to occur.[1]

The letter came from the Department of Geriatric Medicine at Newcastle General Hospital, and described a condition which was thought to be was seriously affecting elderly people on nitrazepam (Mogadon). By this time, many patients had been changed from barbiturates to nitrazepam: "Nitrazepam is popular because of its rapid effect and is widely used in residential homes and elsewhere, where it is convenient or necessary for old people to be 'switched off' with the lights." [1]

The main symptoms of the condition were confusion, disorientation, and lack of coordination - all of which were liable to be misdiagnosed in elderly people as evidence of progressive brain disease. The letter illustrated the problem with the case of a 75-year-old woman referred to the hospital after a suspected stroke. She had been in an old people's home for six years, and had previously been "ambulant, continent and oriented" - but then there was a complete change. Her case history evoked the image of drooping heads on the bromide wards seen by Dr William Sargant, 40 years before.

> "Despite statements to the contrary made in advertising literature, nitrazepam (Mogadon) seems a particularly unsuitable hypnotic for old people. Members of this department have come to recognise a characteristic syndrome of disability caused by nitrazepam, of which the following case is typical:
>
> " ... She had become dysarthric [notably, slurred inarticulate speech], confused and disorientated and, if left undisturbed, would sit staring blankly into space. She tended to fall to the left and to stumble when attempting to walk. Specific questioning elicited the information that she looked better and seemed mentally more alert when in bed than when sitting out and that she had been taking one tablet (5mg) of nitrazepam nightly for at least a year. We advised stopping the nitrazepam and on review three days later she was said to be 'completely her own self' and had gone out on a charabanc trip. After four months she remains well." [Evans and Jarvis, 1972]

Drug accumulation is especially serious for elderly people: as the body ages, it becomes less efficient, so it becomes increasingly difficult to clear drugs like nitrazepam from the body. With repeated dosing, concentrations of the drug tend to build up and up, until toxic levels are reached. And because some toxic effects mimic states of senility and illness, they may be missed.

Such problems are greater with benzodiazepines which tend to stay in the body for longer, having longer half-lives. And so, from the late 1970s, there developed a strong correlation between the market share of a drug and its half-life. Most of Roche's benzodiazepines had long half-lives, and their sales began to decline. The worst hit were nitrazepam (Mogadon) in the UK and flurazepam (Dalmane) in the US.

Dalmane had become enormously popular in America since 1970 - and the reason for its later decline was also the reason for its popularity early on. Its great advantage was that it worked for longer than other sleeping pills - because it tended to accumulate, producing higher and higher levels of drug in the body. In 1974, Dr Kales and his sleep research team had found it different from the others: the effects of most hypnotics began to wear off after only a few days of continuous use, but flurazepam (Dalmane) went on working for at least a month.

America wakes up

By the late 1970s, the message was beginning to sink in. In August 1977, President Carter called for studies to review the safety and usefulness of hypnotic drugs, "especially the barbiturates" and an extensive review was begun by the Institute of Medicine (IoM) of the US National Academy of Sciences. The IoM report, published in January 1979, criticised the overwhelming lack of hard evidence, above all.

> "Of drugs marketed in the United States, only flurazepam has been shown to affect sleep for a long as 28 days of continuous use, and then only in 10 insomniac subjects. Most other hypnotics that have been studied in the sleep laboratory appear to lose their sleep-promoting properties within three to 14 days of continuous use. There have been no published reports of a hypnotic having been clinically evaluated by sleep laboratory methods for more than four weeks or with more than ten insomniac subjects. Nor have any hypnotics been fully assessed with respect to such daytime measures as patient mood, occupational performance, or psychomotor skills." [IoM, 1979]

When treating sleep problems...

When Dalmane is prescribed –

it promptly induces sleep[1] and gives the patient a good, full night's sleep.

When Dalmane is no longer prescribed –

problems associated with withdrawal are less likely with a hypnotic such as Dalmane than with short half-life benzodiazepines.[2,3]

DALMANE 15mg
flurazepam

because stopping is as important as starting

ROCHE

The IoM report was also scathing about the studies that had been done. Most had been sponsored by the drug industry; no studies had been done in the US to show the extent to which daytime impairment was caused by sleeping tablets taken the night before.

"Approximately 150 studies of hypnotic drug efficacy were reviewed in the course of preparing this report; all but a handful were sponsored by pharmaceutical companies. The results of most of these are extremely difficult to interpret. There has been a failure to set high standards of interpretability, replicability, and general validity in the published studies ... It is noteworthy that nearly all the investigations of residual adverse effects of hypnotics on daytime psychomotor performance tests have taken place overseas where support was provided by the respective foreign governments." [Ibid, p. 151]

The IoM found that "psychiatrists appear to have virtually abandoned the barbiturates in favour of flurazepam", and the result was that increasing numbers of chronic users of sleeping pills felt bad the following day. Some felt dull or a bit hungover - but others, and especially the elderly, sometimes became badly disoriented and confused. There was concern about the effects of these drugs on the mind. It was also feared that they contributed to accidents; for example, traffic accidents and broken bones after falls.

These hangover effects, according to the IoM, outweighed the advantages Roche claime for flurazepam - but the company continued to promote Dalmane as a more effective hypnotic and less toxic than barbiturates in overdose. In addition, Dr Kales' team had found minimal rebound after withdrawal of flurazepam (because the drug cleared the body slowly) and Roche later discreetly advertised that Dalmane caused less dependence because of this. See advertisement.

The IoM report did not focus attention on dependence as such. It discussed the non-medical use of hypnotics, but otherwise identified the problem mainly in terms of "nightly reliance on drugs for sleep". As Clift [1972] had also found, this was "equally likely to arise with either benzodiazepines or barbiturates". The IoM also concluded that these two were "probably equally effective in short-term use" and otherwise suggested that benzodiazepines were perhaps not as different from the barbiturates as generally believed. Their relative safety in overdose was an advantage - but there were still reasons for concern.

"The committee finds that insufficient evidence has been given to undesirable or hazardous effects of long-acting benzodiazepines that are not found with the barbiturates. These include the accumulation of long-acting metabolites, increased probability of adverse reactions with age, and an increased probability of adverse reactions in patients with diminished kidney function. Benzodiazepines also share a number of hazards with the barbiturates." [Ibid, p 12]

"... Although the benzodiazepines are regarded as much less potent respiratory depressants than the barbiturates, they are not entirely safe in this regard." [Ibid, p 27]

The IoM noted that continued use of hypnotics might actually worsen rather than improve the quality of sleep, [2] but left it at that: "It is still an unanswered question ... [whether] ... patients are being helped or whether they continue regular use because of physical or psychic dependence or both". However, the IoM did recommend tighter controls over drug testing, advertising and labelling; better information and warnings for patients; and greatly improved standards of prescribing. The report identified lack of professional education as an important reason for what was evidently a mess.

"Although hypnotics are widely prescribed, the committee finds that physicians receive little specific education or clinical training in the physiology of sleep and use of hypnotic medication. The committee urges that major professional education efforts be developed in this area, and that the efforts should not be sponsored solely by the pharmaceutical industry." [Ibid, p 13]

Britain sticks with benzodiazepines

Meanwhile, in Britain, the Committee on Review of Medicines (CRM) reported its own conclusions and recommendations on barbiturates. The CRM review was published in the *British Medical Journal* in 1979. By this time, the Committee believed that long-term use of barbiturates even at therapeutic doses could lead to both physical and psychological dependence: "barbiturates have a high addiction potential". It concluded that barbiturates were not lastingly effective and decided they should no longer be used to treat daytime anxiety at all. The CRM said barbiturates should be reserved for cases of "severe intractable insomnia" - meaning in practice that they should be used only by patients already severely dependent on them.

In the UK, therefore, the barbiturates were much more clearly distinguished from the benzodiazepines than in the US. By the end of the 1970s, the barbiturates had been dumped by the CRM; while the benzodiazepines had had a major boost from the ex-Roche man, Dr John Marks. Marks had emphatically distinguished between barbiturates and benzodiazepines, and had also advised that, in practice, doctors seemed to use the latter quite well. After reviewing what seemed to him to be the relevant evidence, Marks had concluded that the benzodiazepines were not excessively used. He suggested that further studies were needed, but ...

> "Prior to this we can only suggest, on the basis of the limited evidence, that psychotropic drugs appear to be used conservatively by doctors (ie underused) rather than overused, that their current consumption is not excessive relative to the level of emotional morbidity in the community." [Marks, 1978]

Not everyone shared this view, to judge from one or two asides in the medical literature of the 1970s. One of the speakers at the 1972 symposium had remarked, for example, that so many people were on tranquillisers in his area "that a partner suggested we might as well put chlordiazepoxide into the tap water"; [3] and in a 1975 paper another doctor likened tranquilliser prescribing to recommending a double whisky three times a day. [4] And by the time Marks' book was published in 1978, other experts were becoming more inclined to question the high levels of benzodiazepine consumption. One was Professor Malcolm Lader, a psychopharmacologist at the Institute of Psychiatry in London. In a commentary called Benzodiazepines - the opium of the masses ? Lader [1978] suggested there was a growing problem, because: "the indications for these drugs are being insidiously widened and the boundary between normality and illness increasingly blurred." [5] The same point was made by a senior FDA man at the US Senate hearings in 1979.

> "The whole history of their promotion has been through the years a series of attempts to suggest, sometime subtly and sometimes not, that these drugs are useful in treating diseases beyond anxiety and in coping with the everyday stresses of life, and we have a long and running com-

mentary between ourselves and the manufacturers in attempting to keep the advertising in line."

Another prominent UK critic was a psychiatrist, Dr Peter Tyrer. Back in 1974, Tyrer had created something of a stir with his report, The benzodiazepine bonanza; and four years later, he followed this up with a report on psychotropic drug prescribing in general practice. Tyrer used a different approach to Marks. Instead of trying to relate the amounts of benzodiazepines used to the estimated incidence of mental illness in the community, Tyrer tried to find out whether mood-altering drugs were being rationally prescribed. He reported how psychotropic drugs had been prescribed for the 287 patients referred to his clinic between 1974 and 1977.

Tyrer found that half these drugs had been incorrectly prescribed. One quarter of the patients had been taking benzodiazepines for over a year, often unnecessarily and sometimes "apparently ... regardless of whether regular treatment was indicated". In addition, one in every six patients on benzodiazepines was taking two or more of these drugs at the same time. Given the similarities between benzodiazepines, Tyrer thought this reflected: "a disturbing level of ignorance of pharmacological action", which made doctors all the more vulnerable to "seductive advertising". He suggested that "a basic grounding in the pharmacology of psychotropic drugs might help practitioners to avoid prescribing errors of this kind". [6]

There were, however, great variations in the way patients were treated by different doctors. In some practices, the policy was to issue repeat prescriptions only if patients were seen from time to time by a doctor - though the "routine consultation interval" ranged from one week to two years. Overall, patients could expect to be seen by a doctor on average about every 5 or 6 months - though a small percentage of patients were not seen "for many years, some not for over ten".[7]

A not-so systematic review

The Committee on Review of Medicines published its report, Systematic Review of the Benzodiazepines in the British Medical Journal in March 1980. It was a confused report and it seems doubtful that it was in fact the thorough investigation it claimed to be. One reason for doubt is that it cited only two pieces of evidence to support its conclusions. The first was little more than a press release about the US Institute of Medicine report on hypnotics - but not the report itself. The other was the book by Dr Marks - which by this time was being quoted and cited as the definitive statement on benzodiazepine dependence by just about everyone in the field.

The CRM fell straight in. Overlooking the possibility that the true incidence of dependence might be far higher than the incidence of reported cases, the Committee arrived at the same conclusion about the scale of the problem as Marks had done. By adding up the number of Yellow Cards received over the years (but overlooking that there were no more reports of dependence for barbiturates than benzodiazepines), the CRM independently arrived at the same absurd estimate of the problem.

"The number dependent on benzodiazepines in the UK from 1960 to 1977 has been estimated to be 28 persons. This is equivalent to a dependence rate of 5 - 10 cases per million patient months" [CRM, 1980]

With round figures to prove it - that benzodiazepine dependence was a once-in-a-professional-lifetime experience - the CRM then confusingly went on to describe something closer to the reality. It acknowledged that people sometimes did experience symptoms on withdrawal, even after short courses of treatment at therapeutic doses. It also recognised that withdrawal symptoms such as "anxiety, apprehension, tremor, insomnia, nausea and vomiting" might sometimes be misinterpreted as underlying illness - which in turn could have explained why there was so much repeat prescribing. However, the Committee then went on to say that it did not consider this evidence of "true dependence". The official view was that such symptoms were generally mild and transient and could readily be overcome by gradual withdrawal. In parliament, the minister said that these withdrawal symptoms "are not indicative of dependence". [8]

The CRM also "found no evidence which could justify the preferential use of any particular benzodiazepine in either anxiety or insomnia". This may have reflected concern specifically about the promotion of nitrazepam (Mogadon) as a hypnotic - when other benzodiazepines, promoted for anxiety, would have done just as well. However, the CRM statement needs some qualification. It is now better understood that there are factors which make some benzodiazepines more suitable for use as hypnotics than as sedatives, and vice versa. None of the benzodiazepines has a specific action on symptoms of anxiety or insomnia - but some are more selective as hypnotics (or anxiolytics) than others. These differences are mainly to do with the rate at which different benzodiazepines are cleared from the body - some faster than others. It is possible, for example, to select a benzodiazepine for use as a hypnotic, less likely to cause residual (hangover) effects during the day.

The CRM went on to warn of the potential dangers for elderly people of drug accumulation with long-acting benzodiazepines. It also agreed that there was "little convincing evidence" that benzodiazepines were effective in long-term use, endorsing the IoM view that most sleeping tablets worked for only 3 - 14 days in continuous use. The Committee also adopted the gold standard the FDA had been using for several years: there was no convincing evidence that benzodiazepines were effective for anxiety for longer than four months.

This conclusion seems to have been based on a 1973 study [9] which was probably never intended as more than a very rough guide. The study had suggested that, after four months, it seemed possible to distinguish true withdrawal effects from effects that might be attributed to recrudescence of an underlying illness. This study did not prove that benzodiazepines went on working for as long as four months; it showed only that clear evidence of dependence could be seen if benzodiazepines were used for longer.

From the Committee's point of view, the main purpose of the review had been to suggest changes that needed to be incorporated in benzodiazepine data sheets. The changes proposed by the CRM were modest (nothing like as tough as the labelling proposed for barbiturates) and broadly in line with Marks' thinking. Neverthless, it took the best part of five years for most data sheets to begin to change. The main reason was lack of cooperation by the companies: they had been angered by the CRM's review, as the medical director of the ABPI said in a letter to the British Medical Journal. Dr Eric Snell complained that the CRM had not consulted the industry before publishing its views, and said that its report lacked "scientific validity" as a result. Snell's letter hinted that the CRM's failure to consult was a foolish discourtesy which had led to errors, because only the industry understood the full picture.

> " ... the guidelines for data sheets were drawn up without the normal consultation to be expected and were finalised without full examination of the available evidence from manufacturers. Companies have an unri-

valled data source on their own products, accumulated
both nationally and internationally. Failure to take such
information fully into account can easily lead to imperfect decisions." [Snell, 1980]

On the other hand, the CRM review was criticised in the *Drug &*
Therapeutics Bulletin, for ducking the problem of what to do about the
many people who continued to be anxious on these drugs.

"The Committee has to some extent fudged the issue of
benzodiazepine dependence ... If the CRM believes that
benzodiazepines produce dependence, it should have
said so more clearly. More studies are urgently needed,
especially of withdrawal after long-term use." [*DTB*,
1980]

Warnings in data sheets and the new BNF

Most of the 1980/1981 data sheets for benzodiazepines made no reference to dependence risk. Wyeth's drugs were the only ones with
warnings - though what they said was rather reminiscent of what
Henry Maudsley had described 100 years before as "melodious words
which express no definite ideas but are pleasing discharges of vague
and incontinent emotion". From 1980/81 to 1986/87, Wyeth data
sheets said this:

"Prolonged or excessive use of benzodiazepines may
occasionally result in the development of some psychological dependence with withdrawal symptoms on sudden discontinuation. This is more likely in patients with
a history of alcoholism, drug abuse or in patients with
marked personality disorders ..."

Perhaps because it had to fight so hard with the industry to achieve
so little - perhaps also because so few doctors referred to data sheets
anyway - the DoH then decided to transfer an important responsibility to the medical and pharmacy professions. The aim was to communicate effectively to doctors sound, basic information about the many
drugs they prescribed - including some guidance about their risks.
The result was the launch in January 1981 of a radically new version
of the *British National Formulary (BNF)*, a concise, basic drug prescribing guide. The DoH agreed to pay for it to be sent free to all doctors
and pharmacists twice a year - enough to keep the data pretty fresh.

The new *BNF* was produced by a professional secretariat, working under a "Joint Formulary Committee" set up by the British Medical Association and the Pharmaceutical Society of Great Britain. Back in 1981, the doctors' representative on the committee was Dr Frank Wells: by then, he had left general practice in Ipswich to join the staff of the BMA. Also on the Committee was Dr John Griffin, representing the Department of Health. Later, both men joined the ABPI: Griffin became Director in 1984, and later appointed Wells as Medical Director. Both are still there.

On a close reading, the new *BNF* communicated most of the basic safety information that doctors needed to know about prescribing benzodiazepines. Indiscriminate and careless prescribing was acknowledged and censured. Short-term treatments were recommended, and only for patients with clearly disabling anxiety or insomnia. Warnings were given about rebound and withdrawal problems, and doctors were also specifically advised to tell patients about the symptoms they might get when treatment was stopped. It look years longer for this information to sink in.

The companies were not at all pleased by the arrival of the new *BNF*, and the Association of the British Pharmaceutical Industry issued a press release to say so. The ABPI's statement grumbled on: "views with some concern ... drastically revised format ... without any consultation ... lacks the comprehensiveness [of data sheets] ... not consistent with ... potentially misleading ... value judgements ... difficult to envisage the value and usefulness to doctors ...".

Just a few weeks before the publication of the *BNF* - in response to a critical Social Audit report [10] - the ABPI had emphasised that its own *Data Sheet Compendium* was the most useful source of prescribing information. Few doctors actually referred to data sheets; [11] nevertheless, the ABPI emphasised how very important they were.

> "In the UK, the best source of information which will enable a doctor to decide if and how a product is to be used is the ABPI compendium of data sheets which contain as a minimum all information on the product required by law (and frequently more). Indications, dosage forms and recommendations, warnings and contraindications and other information are all set out in full in data sheets and do provide an adequate basis for a prescribing decision".

Standards overseas

The Social Audit report which had prompted this statement had drawn attention to systematic differences in warnings that companies issued in different countries. The ABPI's statement dismissed the Social Audit report as ignorant, explaining that this happened for reasons beyond a drug company's control:

> "Response to medicines differ from country to country just as the incidence of disease varies. Since expert views on perceived benefits and risks vary it is not surprising that dosage recommendations and cautionary statements required by regulatory authorities also vary considerably from country to country." [12]

However, standards also depend on the behaviour of pharmaceutical companies and the effectiveness of drug regulation - as can be seen most clearly by looking at drug use in developing countries. Standards in third world countries have always tended to be relatively low, [13] and the evidence to this day suggests not only a failure to meet basic health needs, but also a lack of concern to improve.

> "Sir, - At a recent meeting in Pakistan, I was told that the urban poor, suffering from diseases associated with over-crowding and polluted water, spend much of their small incomes on useless or inappropriate medicines. Not all of these are 'quack medicines' provided by native healers. Some of the worst examples of quackery can be found in advertisements by ethical multinational pharmaceutical companies, taking advantage of the fact that drugs can be easily bought from pharmacists and that local drug-control legislation is weak or ineffective ..." [Birley, 1989]

The writer (then President of the Royal College of Psychiatrists) gave examples to illustrate his concern. He cited a claim by the Swiss company, Sandoz - "with Restoril (temazepam) patients do not experience drug dependence". The US firm, Parke Davis stated that "Verstan (prazepam) may provide an advantage in certain patients prone by history to drug misuse"; while Roche said that Lexotanil (bromazepam) "resolves anxiety and relieves the strain on the heart ..." Birley commented:

> "These are misleading statements. There are also claims for other drugs which are not part of the UK pharmacopoeia. If these claims are correct, then British doctors

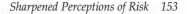

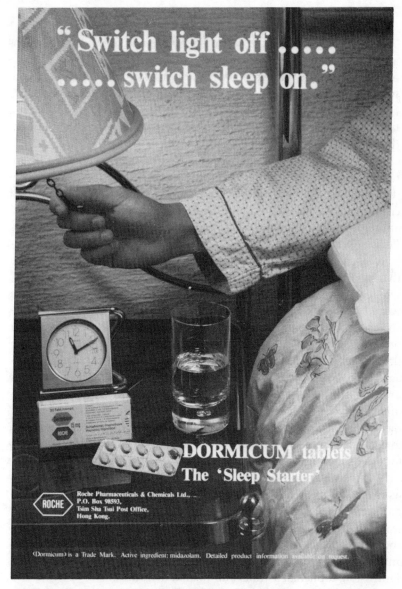

This 1986 advertisement from Hong Kong promotes midazolam - an ultra short-acting benzodiazepine available in the UK for use as a pre-anaesthetic. (See chapter 15.) This advertisement suggests that midazolam (Dormicum) puts patients out like a light, perhaps with the further implication of its place in bedtime routine. The advertisement suggests no risk of rebound, loss of effectiveness or dependence

and their patients are missing out on a therapeutic revolution." [Ibid]

Lack of control over the benzodiazepines and other drugs remains a serious problem in most if not all developing countries. Their governments typically have neither the resources nor the expertise to control companies and methods of drug distribution. In most developing countries, qualified pharmacists are still outnumbered by drug traders, and prescription-only drugs can usually be obtained just for the money, without any prescription at all.

One striking difference between here and there is in the use of combination products - drugs which combine two or more different ingredients in the same medication. An example is a Roche product which combines chlordiazepoxide (the ingredient of Librium) with an antidepressant - still available in the UK in 1991, although rated in the *British National Formulary* as "less suitable for prescribing".

Why are such combination products undesirable ? One reason is that an antidepressant might well be prescribed for months or years, whereas benzodiazepines should not be: by then, their effectiveness would be diminished and the risk of dependence high. Another reason is that different individuals tend to respond very differently to benzodiazepines - needing either higher or lower doses to get the desired response. If someone responds best to half or twice the average dose of diazepam, it does not mean they need half or twice as much of an antidepressant as well. The trouble with combining ingredients in fixed-ratio combinations is that the prescriber cannot adjust the dosage of each of the different drugs in the pill - so everyone tends to get an average sort of dose, which for some people will be too low, for others too high.

Most combination products are by their nature irrational, but the world is full of them. [14] In the late 1980s, for example, combination products including diazepam were sold in India for: pains, sprains, stiff joints, arthritis, lumbago, sciatica, colics, pancreatitis, duodenal and peptic ulcer, gastritis, nervous dyspepsia, irritable colon, allergy, muscle spasm, vomiting, hyperacidity, dysmenorrhoea, menorrhagia, depression, bronchial asthma and related disorders. [15]

Against this background, the WHO tried in 1982, and again in 1983, to persuade the UN Commission on Narcotic Drugs to schedule the benzodiazepines. Its aim was to get better record-keeping and to ensure that benzodiazepines were supplied only on prescription throughout the world. The scheduling would have made little difference to the control of benzodiazepines in the most developed countries - except perhaps in Belgium, where they were then considering allowing benzodiazepines to be sold without prescription.

However, WHO was thwarted at both attempts. The *Lancet* reported that this was "in the face of heavy lobbying by the pharmaceutical industry" - and that Wyeth apparently played a leading part:

> "The industry's strategy was to persuade governments that these drugs presented no significant public health problem, that they could be effectively controlled at national level, that international control was a waste of resources, that the requirements of the conventions would impose onerous administrative burdens on signatory states and that WHO's arguments in support of scheduling were not supported by solid data and were ill-founded. Wyeth Pharmaceuticals commissioned papers from the Health Management Institute (which has close links with the industry) directly attacking WHO and its expert review group on psychotropic substances. These papers and the manner of their distribution irritated some members of the Commission."
> [*Lancet*, 1984]

There was some irony in this, because three years later Wyeth was to defend Ativan by calling on the authority of the same expert committee. [16] Eventually, in 1984, the WHO committee did manage to get 33 different benzodiazepines scheduled, having argued that all benzodiazepines "be treated as similar compounds in terms of abuse liability". Wyeth took this to mean that Ativan was no different from the rest.

Nationality and Ativan dose

Differences of opinion might well have explained minor variations in the kinds of warnings doctors received. But could this also have explained marked discrepancies in the dosage recommendations made in different parts of the world ? Why was it, for example, that patients taking Ativan in the UK, South Africa and Australia, would get about twice the dose given to patients in North America, Argentina and the Philippines ?

At least until the late 1980s, Wyeth advised doctors in some countries that lorazepam 2-3mg/day was the appropriate daily dose "for the vast majority of patients" - whereas in the UK the company suggested up to 4mg/day, just for anxiety that was "mild". [17] In North America, Wyeth also emphasised the need for careful adjustment of dosage, and sold a 0.5mg tablet to help achieve this.

> Canada: "Dosage must be individualised and carefully titrated in order to avoid excessive sedation or mental or motor impairment ...The daily dosage should be carefully increased or decreased by 0.5mg depending on tolerance and response." [18]

> US: "For optimal results, dose, frequency of administration and duration of therapy should be individualised according to patient response. To facilitate this, 0.5mg, 1mg and 2mg tablets are available." [19]

In the UK, however, Ativan was sold only in high-strength tablets - 1mg and 2.5mg - and this made a decisive difference to the treatments given. It would have been much harder to make sensitive dosage adjustments using the 1mg pill - although Wyeth did not stress the need for this. In the UK data sheet, Wyeth told doctors that the correct dosage might be arrived at, in effect, by slightly overdosing some patients - and then waiting for tolerance to develop, until the initial side effects went away.

> "Daytime drowsiness may be seen initially and is to be anticipated in the initial treatment of anxiety. It will normally diminish rapidly and may be minimised in the early days of treatment by giving the larger proportion of the day's dose before retiring." [Ativan data sheets, 1974 - 1990/91]

The reasons for the different dose recommendations and tablet strengths in the UK and North America can be traced to the three main studies that Wyeth relied on to support its application for a product licence for Ativan in the US. All were done in America after the launch of Ativan in the UK; and all three were done to a common trial protocol (design). They were open (unblind) trials, comparing the effects of lorazepam and diazepam over 6 months; and their results were reported in papers by Drs Siassi et al, 1975; Antonelle & Katz, 1977; and Gross, 1977.

These were three very important trials. They clearly suggested, among other things, that the dosage of Ativan (lorazepam) recommended in the UK was around twice as high as it should have been.

In all three studies, patients were rated for anxiety using a standard measure, the Hamilton Scale. Patients with "mild" anxiety were altogether excluded - and patients with "moderate" anxiety outnumbered those with "severe" anxiety by about 2:1. Yet all of the 100-odd patients on lorazepam were started on 3mg/day - the dose that British doctors were told to prescribe for patients whose anxiety was "mild". All patients in the three US trials then had their starting dosage increased or decreased according to their response. However, none of the three investigators exceeded a maximum dosage of 6mg/day - the amount recommended for "moderate" anxiety in the UK.

The report from Dr Siassi gave no detailed information about the dosages patients actually received. But Antonelle was more specific: all but 2 of his 28 patients took 3mg/day lorazepam or less - and, as there were 9 severely anxious patients in his study, this meant that at least 7 severely anxious patients had responded well to lorazepam 3mg/day. In other words, most American patients suffering from "severe" anxiety responded well to the same dose of Ativan that British patients would have been given if their anxiety was "mild".

By contrast, Dr Gross had found it necessary to increase the dosage for 80% of his patients by the second month of the study, and he specified the usual dosage of lorazepam given as "4 to 5 mg/day". In spite of this, Gross reported - as did the other two investigators - "that there was no evidence of tolerance to efficacy over prolonged administration". They appeared to mean by this that there was no evidence of patients escalating the dose to counteract any loss of drug efficacy. The implication was that lorazepam went on working, and that there was therefore no risk of dependence.

The great range of results that can be obtained - even when investigators follow the same protocol - was also illustrated by the side effects reported in these trials. Dr Antonelle's patients - who received the lowest doses - reported the most side effects: a quarter of those on lorazepam (and 39% of those on diazepam) had one or more side effects, mainly sedation, lethargy and weakness. The other two investigators said none of their patients experienced significant side effects at all.

These three investigators were, however, unanimous in their assessment of dependence - whatever that meant. At the end of the 6-month trial, drug treatment was apparently stopped abruptly: no evidence of drug dependence was found, and all three made a point of saying so in the summaries of their reports. The ethical implications of abruptly withdrawing drugs from moderately and severely anxious patients were not discussed.

And there is a postscript. At the US Senate sub-committee hearings in 1979, Senator Kennedy asked the President of Roche Inc, Robert B Clark, how he would explain the internal memorandum addressed to him, which said that Roche had neither conducted nor sponsored studies of long-term efficacy or dependence with diazepam. Clark replied that, in fact, three particularly relevant studies had been done, in which diazepam had been abruptly withdrawn from patients after 6 months treatment, with no evidence of "psychological or physiological withdrawal symptoms". He was referring to the lorazepam v diazepam studies by Drs Siassi, Antonelle and Gross. The Roche President did not mention that these were open studies, conceived as evaluations of a competing drug, and that only 50-odd patients on diazepam had been involved.

1 Evans & Jarvis, 1972
2 Kales et al, 1974
3 Watts, 1972
4 Wilks, 1975
5 Lader, 1978
6 Tyrer, 1978
7 Dennis, 1979
8 Hansard, 5 March 1980, col 278w
9 Covi et al, 1973
10 Medawar, 1980
11 OHE, 1977
12 ABPI, 1980
13 Melrose, 1982; Chetley, 1990
14 Medawar, 1984 (b)
15 MIMS India, 1987
16 Cohen, 1987
17 Ativan data sheets, 1974 - 1988/1989
18 Canadian Pharmaceutical Association, 1981
19 Physician's Desk Reference, 1982

Chapter 11

READING THE WRITING ON THE WALL

"The frenzied activities of a sensation-hunting press influence regulatory agencies towards ensuring that they have an open and shut case before issuing a warning about hazards related to a product's use ... an early warning based on preliminary evidence, which could be exploited by the media and blown up into a full-scale panic, causing distress to maybe hundreds of thousands of patients using the drug, is undoubtedly contributing to the developing of an 'information lag'. Judgements of drug regulatory agenices must be the subject of balanced benefit-to-risk judgements and must not be influenced by the clamourings of media and politicians" [Griffin & D'Arcy, 1981]

More trouble with Ativan

Official prescription figures suggest that the systematic review of the benzodiazepines by the Committee on Review of Medicines [1980] had little overall impact on consumption. However, it did accelerate the general shift in prescribing away from long-acting benzodiazepines, and this meant that drugs like lorazepam (Ativan) and oxazepam (Serenid-D), became more often used. Temazepam was another, introduced as a hypnotic in 1977: there was a Wyeth brand, Normison; and Euhypnos, from the Italian company, Farmitalia Carlo Erba.

The switch to these shorter-acting compounds helped to disclose dependence problems with benzodiazepines, especially lorazepam. Withdrawal symptoms from these compounds tend to come on sooner, and the reaction is more intense and feels more severe. Nowadays, when doctors help patients to withdraw from lorazepam and drugs like it, they often first switch patients to a longer-acting drug, usually diazepam. It allows a more gradual reduction of dose.

The first reported case in the UK of a major withdrawal reaction from lorazepam was very nearly overlooked. In October 1979, Dr Peter Tyrer reported in the *Lancet* a case involving seizures following withdrawal from an antidepressant drug, mianserin. In passing, Tyrer mentioned that his patient had also stopped taking lorazepam at the same time - and this prompted a response from a hospital in Ontario. The writer said that he and his colleagues had seen four cases of convulsions following withdrawal from a benzodiazepine in the previous year - two involving lorazepam - and he wondered whether Tyrer and his colleagues might have picked on the wrong drug. Tyrer's patient had a withdrawal reaction three days after stopping a six-week course of lorazepam 7.5mg/day and, in view of the warnings in the Canadian data sheet, it seemed that lorazepam rather than the antidepressant could be to blame.

> "The Canadian product monograph on lorazepam recommends that 6mg/daily should not be exceeded and that the drug should not be given for more than 6 weeks. Thus the dose used in the last two cases reported here and in Tyrer's patient were quite high and the exposure was long enough to precipitate convulsions on abrupt withdrawal of lorazepam." [Einarson, 1980]

Tyrer replied that, when he and his colleagues reported their case, they had not been aware of any published reports of seizures following withdrawal from lorazepam. They had also taken into account Marks' view that major abstinence reactions from benzodiazepines were very rare - specifically recalling his estimate of one such case per 5-50 million patient months. However, Tyrer said he now accepted that lorazepam was probably implicated. This was partly because he had just come across another patient who had convulsions four days after stopping lorazepam (5-15mg/day for two years). Even so, Tyrer was reluctant to accept that lorazepam was mainly responsible for the withdrawal reaction in the first patient, because he had not taken the drug for long.

> "As the patient in our earlier report had a seizure three days after stopping lorazepam we feel that lorazepam withdrawal must have been a contributory cause of the seizure. This is unlikely to be the sole explanation because the patient had taken lorazepam for only six weeks and there is no indication that physical depen-

dence on lorazepam or other benzodiazepines can take
place over so short a time." [Tyrer, 1980]

This case underlines the importance of precedent in recognising
adverse drug reactions. Until the first convincing report appears, doctors tend to hold back - as if assuming that adverse drug reactions
don't happen unless they've happened before. This case also empha-
sises the need for adequate information and warnings. Dr De Buck,
for example, had in 1973 encountered one, if not two, cases of convulsions following withdrawal from lorazepam after only three weeks of
high dose treatment - and if his experience had been reflected in the
data sheet, Tyrer and other doctors might well have reached different
conclusions. But the Ativan data sheet did not mention this, nor
another case of lorazepam withdrawal reported from Denmark in
1976. [1]

This poverty of communication was such that an experienced psychiatrist and his team did not consider the possibility of a withdrawal
reaction to lorazepam, because their patient had used the drug as recommended in the data sheet. This was ironical because, only a year or
two year earlier, Tyrer had examined benzodiazepine prescribing in
general practice, and concluded that GPs were in need of "a basic
grounding in the pharmacology of psychotropic drugs". General
practitioners would have been even less likely than Tyrer to recognise
lorazepam withdrawal for what it was.

But Tyrer was not the only specialist who was uncertain about the
withdrawal effects of lorazepam. In March 1980, a US medical journal
responded to a reader's query, saying that "no reports of lorazepam
reactions have been published" [2] - and then a neurologist from Leeds
reported two cases of lorazepam withdrawal seizures, claiming they
were the first reports of their kind. [3] Meanwhile, two further cases
were published in the US literature - but this time the authors emphasised that these were not the first reported cases, because they had
finally discovered the 1973 report by De Buck. Pointing the finger in
the general direction of Wyeth, the authors noted that "this dangerous
side effect has been overlooked in the American literature". [4]

There then appeared a crop of similar reports about lorazepam
withdrawal. [5] Just as lack of published reports tends to discourage
reporting, so the publication of the first reports of an adverse drug
reaction tend to stimulate many more of the same. Two reports published in 1980 suggested, for the first time, that lorazepam might be

more likely than other benzodiazepines to cause serious reactions on withdrawal.

A report from New Zealand described eight cases of serious benzodiazepine withdrawal in hospital patients on therapeutic doses. [6] Four cases involved lorazepam, prompting the authors to ask whether shorter-acting benzodiazepines were more likely to cause dependence problems - just as shorter-acting barbiturates were. Similarly, lorazepam was implicated in 20 of 45 cases of major withdrawal reactions from benzodiazepines reported from the psychiatric clinic at Göttingen University. After a review of patient records, the authors concluded: "Among the benzodiazepines, lorazepam appears to have a particularly high addiction potential." [7]

In the meantime, the warning published in the Ativan data sheet remained unchanged: "prolonged or excessive use of benzodiazepines may occasionally result in the development of psychological dependence with withdrawal symptoms on sudden discontinuation". Around 30 million prescriptions for lorazepam were written in the UK before this data sheet warning was finally changed in 1988/1989.[8] Many patients had become aware of the problem long before then.

"My sister suffered from a gynaecological complaint for which, after considerable investigation had failed to produce a satisfactory physical explanation, the doctor (deciding the cause was psychosomatic) prescribed Ativan, three per day. The gynaecological complaint persisted and after nine months or so, my sister became aware that she was becoming increasingly 'muddled and forgetful' (her words). She attributed this, by a process of elimination, to the Ativan and decided to reduce the dose to one per day. Having successfully done this, she then attempted to cease taking them completely. As soon as she gave up taking them she suffered from 'ringing in the ears', 'giddiness' and generally 'felt terrible'.

"She returned to her GP, expressed concern about this, and asked for assistance, explaining that she thought she was suffering from withdrawal symptoms. The doctor denied that this was possible, and said that the symptoms experienced when she gave up the Ativan were 'a further indication of her nervous state'. My sister then pointed out that her gynaecological complaint had not improved, that she was hoping to become pregnant and that this was an additional reason for wishing to be drug free. The doctor merely told her to wait until she actually became pregnant and to continue taking Ativan.

"Two months later, she returned, pregnant, and by chance saw a different doctor. She asked him two questions, firstly, whether evidence existed concerning any possibly harmful effects of Ativan on the foetus and secondly, she again queried the possibility of withdrawal symptoms.

"She persuaded the doctor to go through the drug book and finally to phone the drug company. The doctor then informed her, that as Ativan was a relatively new drug, no research had been done into its effects on a foetus, but it was 'unlikely to have any adverse effects'. He further told her that it was now known that a small proportion of users did suffer from withdrawal symptoms of the kind she had experienced and he was very apologetic.

"My sister went home determined to cease taking Ativan; she retired to bed, and lived through what she describes as 'the worst week of my life'. She has taken no tranquillisers since, and has no recurrence of her withdrawal symptoms; her pregnancy was marred by the fact that she might possibly have harmed her baby, and it was a great relief to us all, when, last June, she gave birth to a healthy boy." [Hinton, 1980]

Market penetration and drug half-life

By the early 1980s, there were 17 different anxiolytic or hypnotic benzodiazepines on the market in the UK - generally with little to distinguish them apart from their half lives. The half-life of a drug defines how long, on average, it takes for half the amount of drug ingested to be cleared from the body; the mid-point measurement is used because drugs are not cleared at an even rate.

The half-life of a drug or metabolite (break-down product) is an average figure: individual response varies greatly, notably with age. As people get older, and their bodies become less efficient, drugs tend to stay in the body longer - but response can be unpredictable, nonetheless.

The average half-lives of the main benzodiazepines and their main active metabolites are shown in the Table opposite. This list includes several pro-drugs - drugs which have no effect themselves, which are broken down to an active drug in the body. Active drugs are in turn broken down into active and inactive metabolites. The main active metabolite of diazepam and many other benzodiazepines is desmethyldiazepam, which is in turn broken down into oxazepam. See Table.

The half-life of a benzodiazepine (and its metabolites) broadly indicates three main things. It suggests how long the effects of a single dose are likely to last. It also indicates whether or not a drug tends to accumulate in the body: any drug with a half-life of about 12 - 16 hours or more would tend to accumulate if taken regularly. Finally, the shorter the half-life, the sooner one can expect withdrawal effects to appear, and the more severe they may seem to be.

As the Table shows, the benzodiazepines introduced nearer to 1980 tended to have shorter half-lives and fewer, if any, metabolites. This reflected concern about drug accumulation, and naturally it handicapped later entrants to the market, such as ketazolam and prazepam, which were essentially similar to diazepam. On the other hand, the trend to prescribing shorter-acting benzodiazepines favoured the two drugs introduced by the US-based Upjohn Company - triazolam (Halcion), a hypnotic; and an anxiolytic, alprazolam (Xanax).

By about 1980, there was therefore intense pressure on manufacturers trying to introduce new longer-acting drugs - partly because of the changing prescribing trends, also because of the difficulties in differentiating their products from existing brands. In this, companies were both helped and handicapped by the results of clinical trials.

The manufacturers were helped because the methods used in clinical trials - then as now - were generally not sensitive enough to show how marginal the differences were between essentially similar drugs. On the other hand, manufacturers were handicapped because any comparison of like with like might come up with insignificant or inconclusive results. This can be seen from the studies on clobazam (Frisium) reviewed by Koeppen [1979]. In five trials, clobazam was found to cause more daytime drowsiness than diazepam; in seven trials, diazepam caused more drowsiness than clobazam; and no difference was found in the other two. The manufacturer's slogan was, nevertheless, uncompromising.

Benzodiazepines and their metabolites

Generic name (brand, manufacturer) and year of UK introduction	*Mean plasma half-life (and range) of drug and active metabolites (hrs)*
Chlordiazepoxide (Librium, Roche) 1960	17 (5 - 30) Metabolites (including desmethyldiazepam): 14, 40, 65
Diazepam (Valium, Roche) 1963	30 (20 - 90) Metabolites (including desmethyldiazepam) 10, 65
Nitrazepam (Mogadon, Roche) 1965	24 (18 - 34) Metabolites: inactive
Oxazepam (Serenid-D, Wyeth) 1966	10 (6 - 20) Metabolites: inactive
Medazepam (Nobrium, Roche) 1971	Pro-drug: 1.5 Metabolite (desmethyldiazepam) 65
Lorazepam (Ativan, Wyeth) 1972	15 (8 - 25) Metabolites: inactive
Clorazepate (Tranxene, Boehringer-Ingelheim) 1973	Pro-drug. Metabolite (desmethyldiazepam) 65
Flurazepam (Dalmane, Roche) 1974	Pro-drug: 1 Metabolites (including desmethyldiazepam) 65, 75
Temazepam (Normison, Wyeth; and Euhypnos, FCE) 1977	15 (8 - 38) Metabolites: inactive
Clobazam (Frisium, Hoechst) 1979	18 Metabolite: 42
Triazolam (Halcion, Upjohn) 1979	3 (2 - 5) Metabolite: 7
Ketazolam (Anxon, Beecham) 1980	Pro-drug: 1.5 Metabolites (including desmethyldiazepam) 30, 65
Lormetazepam (Loramet, Wyeth; and Noctamid, Schering) 1981	9 Metabolites: inactive
Prazepam (Centrax, Warner) 1982	Pro-drug. Metabolite (desmethyldiazepam) 65
Flunitrazepam (Rohypnol - Roche) 1982	20 (19 - 22) Metabolites: largely inactive
Bromazepam (Lexotan, Roche) 1982	12 (8 - 19) Metabolites: inactive
Alprazolam (Xanax, Upjohn) 1983	14 (11 - 19) Metabolites: inactive

The UK company, Beecham Products, also claimed that its product ketazolam (Anxon) caused less day-time sedation than diazepam. This claim was based on two trials which compared the effects of single doses of ketazolam taken at night with diazepam given three times during the day. [9] A comparison between the effects of diazepam given once at night, and ketazolam three times a day, might have produced the opposite result - and a strict comparison would probably have shown no difference at all.

Beecham made other claims for Anxon which illustrate the limitations of the kinds of studies and trials relied on. On the basis of unpublished data, the company suggested that ketazolam caused less physical dependence in animals than diazepam, after long-term, high-dose administration - which perhaps partly explains why no warning about dependence risk appeared in the Data Sheet Compendium until 1989/1990. Beecham also claimed a higher margin of safety for their product: the data sheet said that ketazolam was "particularly appropriate for those patients for whom a simple once-daily dosage and a low incidence of side effects are important considerations".

Fewer side effects would evidently be an advantage for any patient - but again this claim was mainly based on the unrealistic comparison between ketazolam (one dose at night) and diazepam (three times a day). Indeed, until the data sheet was changed in the late 1980s, Beecham claimed that "in comparative studies the overall incidence of side-effects was no greater than that observed with placebo." As ketazolam is a benzodiazepine through and through, this claim revealed rather more about the design, conduct and interpretation of trials than it did about the drug.

Demonstrations of dependence

In the meantime, Dr Peter Tyrer and his colleagues had set up a clinical trial to find out what actually did happen when long-term benzodiazepine users tried to quit. Their report, published in the *Lancet* in March 1981, it concluded that a fair proportion of long-term benzodiazepine users were to some extent dependent on their drug.

Tyrer began by identifying from patients referred to his hospital unit those who had taken therapeutic doses of either lorazepam or diazepam for at least 4 months - but no other drugs besides. They identified 86 patients eligible for the trial, but found that just over half decided not to take part. These "refusers" had taken lorazepam or diazepam at higher doses and for longer than the rest. See Table.

The trial involved switching half of the patients to placebo and the other half to propranolol - all under double-blind conditions. (Propranolol is normally used to reduce high blood pressure, and sometimes to control panic attacks. Tyrer found that propranolol did not affect the incidence of withdrawal effects, but could somewhat reduce the severity of symptoms.)

Within three days of the switch-over, seven of the eight patients on lorazepam dropped out of the trial. Both during the trial, and in the later follow-up, it was found that patients who had been on lower

---

Withdrawing from benzodiazepines

	Mean daily dose and duration of treatment
68 patients on diazepam	
36 refused to enter trial	15.75mg/day - 4.6 yrs
11 entered but dropped out	11.8mg/day - 4.5 yrs
21 completed the trial	9.5mg/day for 4.0 yrs
18 patients on lorazepam	
10 refused to enter trial	4.7mg/day - 2.6 yrs
7 entered but dropped out	4.5mg/day - 1.6 yrs
1 completed the trial	1.8mg/day - 0.9 yrs

doses, and for shorter periods of time, were less likely to drop out or to relapse later. The results also suggested that patients found it harder to come off lorazepam than diazepam.

Depending on the criteria used, between about a quarter and a half of patients in the study had withdrawal symptoms and were judged to have been "pharmacologically dependent" on the drugs they took. The most common symptoms were insomnia in 57% of patients and "extreme dysphoria" (mainly anxiety, tension and depression) in 25%. Of the 40 patients taking part, 18 reported two or more symptoms on withdrawal, including the following:

Epileptic seizures		1
Muscle twitching and muscle pain		7
Sensory changes	- touch	1
	- noise	6
	- vision	2
	- smell	1
Depersonalisation and derealisation		3
Impaired perception of movement		10
Difficulty in focusing		3
Retching or vomiting		4
Persistent headache and/or head throbbing		7

Around 1981, Professor Malcolm Lader and his colleagues, Drs Petursson and Hallstrom, also published several papers on withdrawal from long-term benzodiazepine treatment. [10] The essential difference from Tyrer's work was that Lader's patients were gradually withdrawn from their drugs. Nevertheless, all patients had distinct reactions, including several more symptoms to add to Tyrer's list: impaired memory and concentration; loss of appetite; weight-loss; depression, perspiration; photophobia (intolerance of light); and paresthesia (tingling, crawling or burning sensation in the skin).

In their 1981 review, Petursson and Lader concluded that, as 2% of the adult population were long-term users of benzodiazepines, many thousands of patients might be at risk of dependence. The 16 patients involved in their main study had not been representative of the whole population; they had all been referred because of their inability to stop taking benzodiazepines on their own. Nevertheless, these patients had been taking benzodiazepines at normal therapeutic doses for some years - as did over 750,000 other people in the UK at that time. By the early 1980s, some of them were beginning to protest.

Dependence by the sackload

In 1982, the voluntary agency, Release, published its report *Trouble with Tranquillisers*; it had been prompted by what were described as "horrific anecdotes by the sackload". [11] The evidence they gave was not strictly scientific, but it was still enough to suggest that Marks' definitive estimate of one case of dependence for every 4 million users each year might be far out.

Rather surprisingly, the British Medical Association dismissed the Release report, on the grounds that it contained nothing new. An under-secretary from the BMA, Dr. Frank Wells, was quoted as saying that the Release report "was three years too late. Doctors were now aware of problems with the benzodiazepines". [12] Wells added that he believed that withdrawal problems were nothing like as bad as they were with barbiturates - a view which reflected not least the results of his own 1973 study, which had assumed that benzodiazepines were not drugs of dependence.

But there was not in fact much evidence that doctors were aware of the risks and problems for their patients. Until the mid-1980s, doctors continued to prescribe about as many benzodiazepines as before - which meant they would have seen relatively few cases of withdrawal. And doctors who were more familar with withdrawal phenomena perhaps tended to understate patients' feelings in their reports. The following, for example, described what the investigators summarised as withdrawal which was "moderately uncomfortable but neither life-threatening or incapacitating".

> "He reported that he had continued to feel well until the third evening after starting on the new capsules. At that time he began to feel acutely anxious and shaky, developed diarrhea, was perspiring heavily and felt quite depressed. Over the next four days, he became increasingly uncomfortable ... He was observed to be agitated, diaphoretic [profusely sweating] and in obvious distress. His pulse was rapid and bounding." [Winokur & Rickels, 1981]

This particular patient knew why he was feeling awful and was also under close medical supervision. Other patients - less aware of what was happening, and unsupported during withdrawal - might have found the experience much more frightening. Thus, when people on benzodiazepines were asked directly about their experiences, they painted a picture far removed from mainstream medical opinion. This began to happen in the 1980s. For the first time, people in the UK began to explain how they felt, and the intensity of their response suggested that benzodiazepine dependence was neither benign nor rare.

An experiment run by the London Broadcasting Company (LBC), rather unexpectedly provided a fair illustration of what was then going on. Over a two-week period in May 1982, LBC organised a series of ten radio programmes, each about a different aspect of drug abuse. They also arranged for systematic analysis of the feedback: after each programme, listeners were encouraged to phone a trained counsellor at the radio station to discuss their concerns in confidence and off-the-air. The first programme - about solvent abuse - established a pattern which was sustained throughout the series. Whatever aspect of drug abuse was discussed in the programme, listeners mainly called about benzodiazepines.

> "Many people, most of them women, telephoned about their consumption of tranquillisers such as lorazepam (Ativan) and chlordiazepoxide (Librium) ... Articulate women with well modulated voices explained how they took their pills every morning and panicked if they could not find them. The counselling team realised slowly that addiction was the programme's central theme ... Most counsellors had not heard of Ativan, but it soon became a familiar name on this programme, and callers' concerns about it outweighed any other drug." [Webb, 1982]

The counsellors on the LBC telephones were mainly health education officers and staff from voluntary agencies concerned with drug addiction - and this response from listeners fundamentally challenged their beliefs about "the drug problem" too. The counsellors consistently found that most callers did not want to discuss what the producers had assumed to be the problem. However, by the time the third programme in the series was due, the counsellors were prepared. This was to be on prescription drugs, and inevitably attracted an even greater response than before.

> "By this time, the team had realised that tranquillisers were the main problem (76 per cent of the 113 calls

received so far), so it was expected that this programme would produce a large response. Sure enough, 290 calls were received when drugs on prescription were discussed. Of these, 268 wanted to discuss Valium and Ativan, and 140 of those enquiries concerned reducing the dosage." [Ibid]

By the end of the series, LBC had taken 899 calls about tranquillisers - six out of every ten calls received. It is therefore not surprising that there was a continuing focus on tranquillisers in media reports. Many of these were prepared with active support and encouragement from the National Association of Mental Health (MIND).

The prime mover at MIND, Ron Lacey, was behind two especially important initatives. One was a survey reported in *Woman's Own* in 1984 - to which over 7,000 people replied, "in frightening detail". Most had been taking tranquillisers for over four years; most had tried to quit; and most had failed. Lacey was also closely involved with the BBC-TV consumer show, *That's Life*.

In June 1983, *That's Life* reported the stories of "three people who felt they had become hooked on tranquillisers". Because of the enormous response, *That's Life* then did their own follow-up survey of over 2,000 viewers, and also commissioned a MORI opinion poll on tranquilliser use. The results of both surveys were reported in a later TV programme; and in a paperback, published by the BBC and MIND in 1985. [13] From this date - and no doubt partly because of the publicity - UK sales of benzodiazepines began to decline.

The MORI survey suggested that about 3.5 million adults in the UK had taken a benzodiazepine tranquilliser for over four months. The survey of viewers also revealed serious dependence problems, closely linked to quality of care and duration of drug use. There were 93 questions in the BBC/MIND questionnaire, dealing with patterns of drug use, dependence and experience of withdrawal. Most replies came from people who had been taking benzodiazepines for over five years, usually without effective medical supervision. Almost all had tried to quit, and nearly half had failed.

"A picture emerges from the survey of many hard-pressed doctors, confronted with a wide variety of physical and mental symptoms, with far too little time to be able to explore all the possible reasons for them. The survey revealed:

- Most patients saw their doctor for less than 10 minutes on that first visit when the drugs were prescribed.
- Half the patients were not even told they were [prescribed] tranquillisers.
- 9 out of 10 were not told they are only effective for a short time, nor warned about side effects.
- 9 out of 10 were given repeat prescriptions, enough to cover a period of longer than 4 months.
- 62 per cent have now been taking them longer than 5 years.
- 40 per cent, nearly a thousand people, have taken them longer than 10 years.
- 93 per cent of the people who took part in the survey have tried to give up tranquillisers.
- Only just over half - 57 per cent - succeeded." [Lacey and Woodward, 1985]

By the mid-1980s, dependence on benzodiazepine was therefore widely recognised as a reality, at least by many patients who used them. By this time, there were several self-help groups in the UK, also something of a campaign to publicise the risks. As well as Ron Lacey at MIND, there was Dr Vernon Coleman, a former GP turned writer. He concentrated on problems with Ativan, and increasingly emerged as a thorn in Wyeth's side.

Much the same had been happening in the US, but earlier and on a grander scale. Barbara Gordon's book, *I'm dancing as fast as I can* [1979] was filmed; it was about a television celebrity, whose withdrawal from Valium was described as a journey "to hell and back". Also at about this time, the Health Research Group, in Washington DC, was preparing its report, *Stopping Valium*. This was a more formal critique by Dr Sidney Wolfe and his team, dealing with the public and personal health hazards of benzodiazepine dependence. The emphasis was on how to avoid them, with practical advice about how to quit. Early in 1982, Hoffman La Roche Inc took the Health Research Group to court to try to stop publication, on the grounds that the words Valium in the title was an unwarranted infringement of copyright. Roche lost: Valium was a trade mark, but it was held to be a sort of hallmark as well.

1 Korsgaard, 1976
2 Imoto, 1980
3 Howe, 1980
4 de la Fuente et al., 1980
5 Barton, 1980; Stewart, 1980
6 Khan et al., 1980
7 Kemper et al., 1980
8 ABPI, Data Sheet Compendium, 1988/89

9 Fabre et al., 1978; Multicentre study, 1980
10 Lader; 1981; Hallstrom & Lader 1981, 1982; Petursson & Lader, 1981, 1982
11 Kirby, 1982
12 Kirby, 1982
13 Lacey and Woodward, 1985

Chapter 12

PENNIES BEGIN TO DROP

"Following a review of the world literature a few years ago, I concluded that the benzodiazepines ... had a negligible dependence risk as used in therapy (Marks, 1978). Recent published evidence suggests that a reappraisal of this conclusion is desirable." [Marks, 1983]

Too little too late

Early in 1983, Wyeth sent out a special Dear Doctor letter to all prescribers. Ostensibly a safety measure, it repeated the advice about gradual withdrawal after high-dose, long-term treatment with Ativan - to avoid what were still described as occasional "psychological" reactions. In an accompanying pamphlet, Wyeth advised that, on the basis on the past 20 years' experience, the dependence risk with benzodiazepines appeared to be one case per 50 million patient months. [1] In the meantime, Dr John Marks had abandoned this 1978 estimate: he had decided that there was a greater risk of dependence than he had originally thought, especially with shorter-acting benzodiazepines, notably lorazepam.

In 1983, Marks published a new review, The benzodiazepines - for good or evil. Five years had passed since he suggested that the risk of therapeutic dependence was negligible; he recognised that the situation had changed. He noted there had recently been a sharp rise in the number of reported cases of dependence, and said he was also influenced by "the incidence of clear evidence of a withdrawal reaction when normal therapeutic doses have suddenly been withdrawn". In guarded terms, he explained having previously offered a precise but definitively inaccurate view of dependence risk.

"I previously suggested on the basis of reported cases that dependence on benzodiazepines was a rare phenomenon. Reported cases cannot be regarded as a valid

representation of the true level of dependence, and I suggested that studies in which patients were deliberately
withdrawn from therapeutic doses of benzodiazepines
would be desirable. Several of these studies have now
been undertaken." [Marks, 1983]

By this time, most data sheets did include a note about dependence
risk. But the message reflected the official view of 1980, that the risk
was very low - and there was little evidence in data sheets of the other
modest warnings that the Committee on Review of Medicines had
proposed. In March 1984, a letter in the *British Medical Journal* complained that only one of the 17 benzodiazepine data sheets carried any
warning about lack of long-term efficacy. It pointed out that the CRM
had said in 1980 that an appropriate warning on this was needed in
data sheets "particularly in view of the high proportion of patients
receiving repeated prescriptions for extended periods of time". [2]

Next to this letter in the *BMJ* was a response from the ABPI medical
director, Dr Eric Snell. He pointed out, as he had said in 1980, that the
industry considered "it was misleading for 'guidelines for data sheets'
ever to have been issued ahead of the process of discussion and
appeal" - loftily adding, "fortunately this has not been repeated". [3]
His letter hinted that the reason for the delay in introducing data sheet
warnings was that manufacturers had decided to challenge the CRM
advice, using the elaborate and time-consuming appeals machinery in
the Medicines Act.

" ... manufacturers have the right of appeal against decision of the licensing authority and we deplored the publication of guidelines for data sheets before this right had
been exercised." [Snell, 1984]

Although the CRM was under no legal obligation to consult the
industry beforehand, the companies were legally entitled to stall - the
result being that the warnings which eventually did appear reflected
outmoded views. Indeed, until 1988, there were still three benzodiazepines whose data sheets had no warnings about dependence at all
- triazolam (Halcion, Upjohn), ketazolam (Anxon, Beecham) and
clobazam (Frisium, Hoechst). [4]

However, by 1985, the CRM's advice on efficacy had found its way
into most data sheets - though it was hardly a warning. It said: "Little
is known regarding the efficacy or safety of benzodiazepines in long-
term use". This was a scrupulous half-truth. It was entirely true, but it

also entirely obscured the evidence that efficacy wore off and dependence wore on, especially with hypnotics. This same empty little statement appeared in data sheets into the 1990s. It was placed in the Further Information section, at the end of the data sheet, where it was most likely to be overlooked. And because it was not a warning (but further information) manufacturers were not required to include it in the small print in their advertisements.

Perhaps partly because of the quality of data sheets - but in spite of the adverse publicity - a small but significant proportion of doctors apparently remained unaware of the risks involved. A survey of 58 GPs in Southampton - carried out between 1983 and 1985 - identified six doctors who either "believed that benzodiazepines were not drugs of dependence, or did not know if they were". [5] This evidence was thin, but if it were representative of the wider picture, it would suggest that around 3,000 doctors in the UK (with around 6 million patients between them) may have been less informed on this topic than an attentive viewer of *That's Life*.

The Limited List

Until the mid-1980s, GPs enjoyed virtually unfettered clinical freedom to prescribe. They were generally allowed to prescribe more or less what they pleased, leaving the NHS to pay the drugs bill. However, in November 1984, that principle was challenged for the first time when the DoH announced it was to introduce a Limited List of drugs. The Limited List excluded about 1,800 preparations which the Department said the NHS would no longer pay for - leaving around 15,000 (including all dosage forms) available for prescribing. Although the aim of the Limited List was to save money, it also encouraged rational prescribing, since nearly all of the excluded drugs were relatively unimportant medicines. Most had been designated in the *British National Formulary* as "less suitable for prescribing", since 1981.

The drugs excluded from the Limited List were mainly an assortment of essentially similar antacids, multi-ingredient cough medicines, minor pain killers and the like - but they also included most benzodiazepines. The goverment proposed to limit the number from 17 to three - leaving only diazepam, nitrazepam and temazepam available on the NHS. The reasons for excluding the rest were unprecedented. They specifically included trying to reduce the number of me-too drugs and controlling over-prescribing.

"The NHS spends £40m a year on benzodiazepine sedatives and tranquillisers. This group of drugs has expand-
ed rapidly in recent years and includes a large number of
expensive proprietory products with essentially similar
characteristics and with no significant advantage in normal clinical practice over the small number of generic
benzodiazepines. There is also a widespread feeling in
the medical profession that prescribing levels for the benzodiazepines are far higher than in clinically justified."
[Clarke, 1984]

There was a furious response to the government's proposals, from
many quarters. This was partly because it threatened the doctors' clinical freedom; partly because of the financial implications for companies - also because the Limited List proposals were represented as yet
another attack by the forces of Thatcher on the NHS. Opposition came
from individual companies, the Association of the British Pharmaceutical Industry (ABPI), the British Medical Association (BMA), from the
Labour opposition in parliament and elsewhere. The ABPI mounted a
£250,000 advertising campaign; the BMA refused to cooperate with
the DoH; and the Labour Party fell in with the industry.

Just a few months before the Limited List proposals were first
announced, Dr John Griffin left his senior position at the DoH to
become Director of the ABPI - in spite of the Health Minister's objection. [6] When the Limited List proposals were published, the ABPI
launched a series of full-page advertisements, accusing the goverment, among other things, of "threatening our entire health-care system"; of trying to "divide the rich from the poor and create a two-tier
health service;" and of requiring children, the elderly and the poor "to
have to put up with less appropriate medicines".

These arguments flatly contradicted Griffin's earlier views. Until
1984, he had been the government representative on the committee
which ran the *British National Formulary*. The *BNF* had criticised most
of the excluded medicines, and had also complained for years about
the over-prescribing of benzodiazepines. In addition, Griffin was on
record as believing that innovation in the drug industry was "directed
towards commercial returns, rather than therapeutic needs". In a 1981
paper, in which he and a DoH colleague reported an analysis of all
new drugs introduced during the 1970s, he had been scathing about
me-toos.

"The pattern of introduction on to the United Kingdom market over the last ten years fully justifies the criticisms levelled at the pharmaceutical industry by Franz Gross (1979) which were as follows: 'Drug research within the pharmaceutical industry is in a critical phase, since it lacks innovating impulses and in many companies beats tracks ... Instead of limiting the numbers of drugs that are qualitiatively and quantitatively quite similar to those already available, many drug companies are copying or slightly modifying successful therapeutic principles, with the result than an abundance of analagous drugs is offered, not rarely with exaggerated claims for efficacy ... We have a plethora of closely related penicillin and cephalosporin derivatives, of topical corticosteroids, of diuretics or of minor tranquillisers ... the temptation to look for a share of a big cake exceeds all too often rational and scientific reasoning. It should always be kept in mind that the main impulse for the development of a new drug is therapeutic need, and that, if a disease can already be effectively treated, a new medicine must offer advantages which are more than marginal'." [7]

Individual companies also lobbied hard against the Limited List proposals. Roche, for example, sent circulars to over 25,000 GPs, including a printed letter complete with SAE, for doctors to sign and send to their MPs. The Roche letter asked MPs for their views on the Limited List proposal - adding that their replies would be of interest to patients and might therefore be posted on surgery notice boards. One Conservative MP described this initiative as "the most disgraceful form of lobbying I have ever encountered". [8] Kenneth Clarke, the Minister of Health, was also outspoken about the opposition from both the BMA and the ABPI. Unusually, the DoH published his criticisms of both, and publicised them as press statements.

"I am, as I have said before, willing to see you at any time to discuss the real proposals we have made. I do not approve of any kind of campaigning that tries to cause needless alarm to patients to draw them into the lobbying. If you must advise your members to involve their patients, then at the very least the doctors should be given a clear and accurate description of the proposals. I

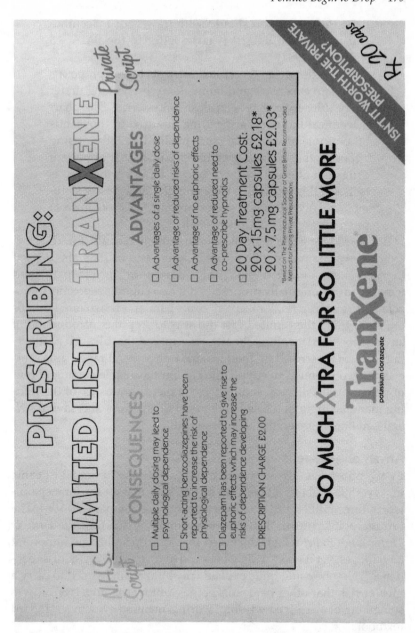

Clorazepate (Tranxene) was excluded from the Limited List. In this 1985 promotional piece, Boehringer Ingelheim tried to persuade prescribers there was less risk of dependence with its product

must insist that you should withdraw your inaccurate and misleading letter." [Clarke letter to the BMA, 13 December, 1984]

"The reaction from the vested interests to our proposals to contain expensive and unnecessary prescribing under the health service has been close to hysterical. The pharmaceutical industry is spending hundred of thousands of pounds on alarmist and misleading advertising opposing the scheme. They have claimed that important drugs not affected by the proposal will be banned. It is tactics of this sort which have brought the industry's promotional activities into such disrepute." [Clarke in DoH press release, 11 December 1984]

But considering the intensity of the campaign against it, the government was bound to give ground. By the end of 1985, the revised Limited List included not only diazepam, nitrazepam and temazepam, as originally proposed - but also chlordiazepoxide, loprazolam, lormetazepam, lorazepam, oxazepam and triazolam. Perhaps the main thing the Limited List did was to stop the introduction of any new benzodiazepines - because it required that all such products in future be prescribed by their generic rather than brand name. This encouraged chemists to supply the cheapest available version of out-of-patent drugs, thereby ending the complete dominance of the leading manufacturers in the sedative-hypnotic market - and saving several £ million more on the NHS drugs bill.

Ativan out of line

By the mid-1980s Ativan was in trouble. Until the Limited List came in, Wyeth had about 80 per cent of the NHS market for lorazepam - worth three million prescriptions a year to the company, in 1984. The turning point came in the following year, by which time the *Drug & Therapeutics Bulletin* had concluded that lorazepam had no important advantages, yet it was "widely believed to carry a great risk of dependence". No-one could quite explain why lorazepam seemed to carry a greater risk that other benzodiazepines, but by the mid-1980s it was something of a received wisdom, worth a mention even in a standard textbook.

"Unfortunately it [lorazepam] appears to have a peculiar capacity to induce dependence and withdrawal of the

drug can be particularly difficult, a substantial disavan-
tage." [Laurence & Bennett, 1987]

Ativan began to get a singularly bad name only after it had been on
the UK market for about ten years. It all started in about 1981, when
Tyrer's report first suggested that people seemed to find it harder to
come off lorazepam than diazepam. Then there were clinical reports
from specialists in benzodiazepine withdrawal which singled out
lorazepam. Some of these reports came from clinics where doctors
were trying to help people to come off lorazepam - by switching them
to diazepam first, to ease the symptoms of withdrawal.

Towards the end of the 1980s, the pressure on Ativan was great,
and Wyeth had to go to some lengths to defend itself. On one occasion, a senior Wyeth man was filmed in the US having a full-blooded
swing with his golf club at the feet of an intrepid and unusually
provocative investigative journalist, from BBC-TV. The Wyeth man
was on the golf course at the time; his game had been interrupted by
Roger Cook, plus film crew, insistently asking him what he proposed
to do about the many people in the UK concerned about Ativan.

Ativan repeatedly featured in the popular press and media, as well
as in medical journals - and questions were raised in Parliament,
again and again. By 1986, Dr Vernon Coleman was running a newsletter, *Life without Tranquillisers* - which focused attention on lorazepam
most of all. Coleman and others [9] also lobbied the CSM about the drug
- while the CSM gave the impression of not wanting to know.

"Your comments regarding lorazepam are noted but I am
afraid that the confidentiality requirements of the
Medicines Act 1968 prevent our discussion of possible
regulatory action or consideration by the Committee on
Safety of Medicines of named licenced products. If your
concern regarding lorazepam arises from your professional use of this product then you will know that it is
possible for you to report any adverse drug reactions
which you have experienced to the Committee on Safety
of Medicines by means of the Yellow Card scheme. I have
enclosed a copy of a Yellow Card report form which you
may wish to use in the circumstances which I have mentioned." [Mann, 1986]

In the meantime, Wyeth indignantly denied that Ativan was any
worse than other benzodiazepines - though the company also tried to

keep quite a low profile in saying so. Wyeth avoided interviews, but this was its full statement for another BBC-TV programme *(Brass Tacks)* about Ativan, transmitted in 1987. This was the occasion when the company called on the authority of the WHO expert committee whose work it had previously sought to discredit. [10]

"Lorazepam was licenced in 1974 by the Committee on Safety of Medicines. In April 1985 its continued prescription on the NHS was reviewed and approved by a panel of experts appointed by the DHSS. Lorazepam was included in a list of only three benzodiazepine tranquillisers available for NHS prescription and is now produced by several different manufacturers.

"Lorazepam has a proved record of efficacy for short-term treatment in anxiety. Many millions of patients, both in this country and worldwide have benefited.

"There is no evidence to suggest that more than a minority of patients are affected by benzodiazepine dependence. Furthermore there is no scientifically proven evidence to suggest that lorazepam creates more dependence than other benzodiazepines, only anecdotal impressions.

"The data collected to date provide no basis for differentiation among benzodiazepines.' Reference WHO Code MNH 81.37[33] - 1981. In 1984, WHO, in making recommendations to the United Nations Commission on Narcotic Drugs recognised the therapeutic usefulness of benzodiazepines and recommended that all available benzodiazepines be treated as similar compounds in terms of abuse liability.

"Over the years this Company has recommended that treatment with these products should be given for short periods only. This is reflected in the literature produced by the Company for the medical profession and Product Data Sheets have been updated in collaboration with the DHSS.

"The benzodiazepine group of drugs, of which lorazepam is a member, replaced barbiturates as the standard treatment for anxiety when the latter group of drugs proved to be dangerous in overdosage and also

subject to abuse. The benzodiazepines have been shown
to be a safer alternative." [Cohen, 1987]

By then, the Committee on Safety of Medicines seems to have been actively wondering what to do. Early in 1987, the Committee was sent a short unpublished paper on *Problems with Lorazepam*, by Dr Heather Ashton, from the clinical pharmacology unit at Newcastle University. Her report was partly based on clinical experience with over 500 dependent patients - 30 per cent on lorazepam. She had concluded that the recommended dose of lorazepam was too high.

Ashton recommended 3-4mg/day as an appropriate dosage of lorazepam for moderate to severe anxiety - the amount the data sheet still suggested for anxiety that was mild. She also told the CSM she thought tablet strengths should be reduced and that lorazepam should be phased out over a period of, say, five years. In the meantime, she suggested that the 2.5mg tablet should be abandoned and that new tablets of 0.5mg and 0.25mg be introduced. She also thought that a 0.125mg tablet would be useful for patients undergoing a difficult lorazepam withdrawal.

About a year later, the CSM [1988] published its first ever statement on benzodiazepines. It did not specifically mention lorazepam. It said only that "No epidemiological evidence is available to suggest that one benzodiazepine is more responsible for the development of dependency or withdrawal symptoms than another." This seemed to be another scrupulous half-truth: though there was no reliable evidence from scientific surveys, there was other evidence to go on. For example, there were the three US studies from the mid-1970s, by Drs Gross, Antonelle and Siassi. They had all found that lorazepam 3-4mg/day was an appropriate dose for moderate to severe anxiety - and the FDA had been persuaded this was so.

And then in 1988, a legal action began in the UK on behalf of several hundred people claiming compensation for dependence on Ativan. By 1992, over 12,000 claimants had joined this action; and diazepam and several other benzodiazepines were involved. But the numbers of Ativan claims originally exceeded all the others put together, and this put all the more pressure on both Wyeth and the CSM.

In public, the CSM and the Department of Health persisted in denying that there was any special problem with lorazepam. However, in 1989, Wyeth got a UK product licence for a half-strength (0.5mg) tablet, and the Ativan data sheet advice on dosage was radically changed. There was miminal publicity, considering the significance of the change. No special effort was made to communicate or explain the new policy to prescribers: it was essentially a small-print change in the data sheet.

In the new data sheet, the dose for insomnia was halved - and lorazepam was no longer indicated for mild anxiety at all, let alone at a dose of 1-4mg/day. From 1989/90, Ativan was indicated only for severe and moderate anxiety - also at a dose of 1-4mg/day - and that is how things now stand. [11]

1 Scrip, 1983
2 Murray & O'Leary, 1984
3 Snell, 1984
4 Medawar, 1988
5 Cantopher et al, 1988
6 Deitch, 1984

7 Griffin and Diggle, 1981
8 Daily Mail 07-12-84
9 Ross 1986; Ashton, 1987 (b)
10 Lancet, 1984
11 Data sheet 1991/92

Chapter 13

REBOUND AND CONFUSION

"Undoubtedly irresistible compassion is behind most benzodi-azepine dependence. The feeling that some help must be given, however imperfect, is deeply ingrained and hard to resist." [Benson, 1988]

Xanax

Alprazolam (Xanax, Upjohn) was the last of the anxiolytic benzodiazepines, introduced into the UK in 1983. Given the established competition, perhaps Xanax would never have been launched if it had not been able to claim some feature to distinguish it from other products. But the DoH (the Licensing Authority) had allowed Upjohn to promote Xanax for "anxiety associated with depression" on the strength of two suggestive, but far from conclusive trials.

"Alprazolam is unremarkable an an anxiolytic but its activity in anxiety associated with depression, if confirmed, could prove useful. However, it is premature to recommend alprazolam for this purpose because its dependence liability has yet to be assessed." [*Drug & Ther Bull*, 1983]

A year or so after the launch of Xanax, the government published its proposals for the Limited List. This was a major blow for Upjohn, and the company responded by looking for a loophole. As the government's proposals applied only to benzodiazepines prescribed for anxiety or insomnia, Upjohn tried to press the advantage of its approved indication for alprazolam for "anxiety associated with depression". Early in 1985, Upjohn sent out a Dear Doctor letter which suggested that "as depression can frequently complicate anxiety", their product remained "an important option in patient therapy". [1] However, the Department did not think it that important, since alprazolam was still excluded from the final version of the Limited List. It has therefore been little prescribed in the UK, though it became a best seller in the US.

One reason for excluding Xanax from the Limited List was its cost - 27 times more than the cost of generic (unbranded) diazepam. Another casualty of the Limited List was Roche's latest benzodiazepine, bromazepam (Lexotan) - which cost twice as much as Xanax, and over 50 time more than diazepam. These are at the high end of kind of the price differentials that the present patent system allows.

However, the decision to exclude Xanax from the Limited List probably also reflected concern about its dependence liability. This was an important consideration, partly because the recommended dosage of alprazolam for "anxiety associated with depression" was around four times higher than the dosage recommended for plain anxiety. This implied that the severity, if not the incidence, of withdrawal symptoms, would have been correspondingly greater.

The first published study on alprazolam dependence inexplicably concluded that the risk was low. The investigators put 40 patients on alprazolam and 29 on lorazepam, and after six months switched them to placebo. They found that nearly half of all patients reported withdrawal effects, including about one-third who dropped out. However, just over half of the patients "made no comment or complaint, indicating they were not even aware of being given placebo" - and on this basis, the authors concluded that these drugs caused "minimal withdrawal effects". [2]

However, alprazolam proved a potent drug of dependence from early on. This was partly because of the drug it was, but may also have resulted from the timing of the launch. By 1983, shorter-acting benzodiazepines like Xanax were increasingly in the firing line, because of their apparently greater dependence risk. Doctors were on the look-out for trouble, and from then on there were more and more of reports of withdrawal reactions from alprazolam, some quite severe.

Published reports about alprazolam suggested several problems. It seemed that withdrawal from therapeutic doses of alprazolam was sometimes accompanied paranoid and other psychotic reactions; [3] and it was also suggested there were some between-dose rebound effects, ie symptoms of withdrawal felt before the next dose was due. [4] There were also reports that the manufacturer's recommendations for

gradual withdrawal were unsuitable for some patients - and that even more gradual withdrawal, perhaps under cover of a long-acting benzodiazepine, might be required. [5]

In 1987, Upjohn modified its recommendations for gradual withdrawal, suggesting the dosage was reduced at half the rate suggested before. This new advice was spelt out in some detail in the US label, but not in the data sheet in the UK. [6]

Halcion in Holland
The US-based Upjohn Company had first entered the benzodiazepine market in the late 1970s with triazolam - a hypnotic, called Halcion.

The launch of Halcion was well-timed: by the end of the 1970s, there was much concern about hangover effects with longer-acting benzodiazepines, but triazolam had a very short half-life, so there was no problem with drug accumulation. However, soon after its introduction into Holland, there was a major public scare and in mid 1979 Halcion's licence in Holland was withdrawn.

The trouble started with an alarming paper in the Dutch medical press, which was immediately taken up in the lay press. A psychiatrist, Dr Cees van der Kroef, reported that triazolam was liable to cause acute psychotic reactions, notably paranoid and confused thinking. As they were still unfolding, the events were described and analysed in a classic essay by Dr Graham Dukes. It began by contemplating triazolam as a molecule.

> "Sooner or later, something like this was bound to happen; for twenty years chemists have been manipulating the basic chlordiazepoxide molecule in an attempt to increase potency, improve specificity, or merely evade patents; the benzodiazepine concept has proved surprisingly resistant to all this, and such efforts have generally resulted at most in a slight quantitative shift in the spectrum of biological activity; yet at a given moment one is certain to exceed the limits within which a structure-activity relationship holds good, and end up with a benzodiazepine of sorts which induces agranulocytosis, phocomelia - or psychosis. Whether triazolam represents such a novum is at this point in time not clear, nor does it in the present context matter; the point to be made is merely that one cannot extrapolate for ever and with impunity from the Librium example." [Dukes, 1980]

When Dukes said that something like this was bound to happen, he was referring not so much to the alleged effects of triazolam - but to the uproar following publication of the van der Kroef report . As Dukes put it, "Conclusions intended for modest nine-point type (' ... a highly toxic hypnotic, which can rapidly induce major psychiatric disorders ...') were magnified into headlines". The trouble started after van der Kroef reported that four of his eleven patients treated with triazolam (up to 1mg/day) had experienced serious psychiatric problems. These were exemplified by the case of a 53-year-old woman lawyer "suffering from psychogenic depression and insomnia":

"The insomnia improved at once, but psychically she rapidly went downhill. Progressively she became paranoid. Several times she asked me what the new hypnotic contained - LSD perhaps? - for she felt that she was bordering on a psychosis. She felt shut off from the world; it was as if she no longer belonged in society. Her friends asked her what was happpening to her, so strangely was she behaving. She became increasingly restless and felt that she had to be continually on the go. She developed hyperaesthesia; she could no longer tolerate the odour of her own body and became hypersensitive to sounds. When she was on the street it seemed to her that cyclists and cars exhibited a rolling motion. After two months I too began to suspect, particularly in the light of experience with an earlier patient, that all this might be a consequence of her taking triazolam. The drug was withdrawn and replaced by nitrazepam. Within a day she felt herself again. The people around her noticed the difference and recognized her old self again. The paranoid traits, the hypermotility urge and the hyperaesthesia disappeared in the course of two days..." [7]

Once in headlines and on the air, this report prompted hundreds more reports from Dutch doctors, and protesting letters to the Department of Health, mainly from people who believed the drug had harmed them. The atmosphere in Holland was such that, within a month, the authorities had the drug withdrawn, suspending its licence initially for six months.

Dukes was at this time Vice Chairman of the Netherlands Committee for the Evaluation of Medicines - in which capacity he felt that the climate in Holland made any dispassionate assessment of the drug impossible. This was not only because of the noise from the media or the weight of the mail. Dukes also thought that many doctors were confusing reality with appearance, partly because of the uncertainties surrounding psychiatric diagnosis, also because of the powerful effects of suggestion. The Dutch authorities had responded to the outcry by asking doctors to report any similar cases they suspected - but Dukes believed that the atmosphere was so charged that, "for every well documented case report that the question elicits there may be five, ten or twenty which have been founded on suggestion alone".

Dukes actually wrote his essay towards the end of 1979, at a time when "the jury was out": Halcion was then nearing the end its six-month suspension, and drug regulatory authorities all over the world were then trying to decide whether they should follow the Dutch example, and take Halcion off the market. And this timing underlined the central point of the essay. At the time, Dukes had his doubts both ways: triazolam might or might not prove as dangerous as it appeared. What seemed most relevant to him was that any decision was likely to be a bad one, and no answer likely to be right.

"The verdict, whatever it may be, is bound to be followed by the same process of over-simplification which has characterized the story from the start. If the accused is discharged, many will be induced to conclude that the accusation was hollow from the beginning; the benzodiazepine circus will go on as if nothing has changed. If triazolam is condemned, we shall be far too eager to forget the extent to which a nucleus of truth was concealed among false evidence, poor science and amorphous thinking."

The jury stayed out for over a decade. A verdict finally came in August 1990, when the Dutch authorities allowed the reinstatement of Halcion, but for use at a lower dose. The decision, as Upjohn saw it, brought Holland into line with world medical opinion. [8] The consensus throughout the 1980s was that triazolam was effective and acceptably safe - at least at lower doses than 1mg/day. However, this was not the last word on the subject: worrying evidence about the effects of triazolam accumulated rather than went away.

Triazolam problems unresolved

Concern about the effects of triazolam (Halcion) on behaviour never really went away. By 1985, the number of adverse drug reaction reports of memory loss, confusion, bizarre or abnormal behaviour, agitation and hallucinations sent to the US Food & Drug Administration exceeded by 8-30 times the numbers of reports about temazepam and flurazepam, the other main benzodiazepine hypnotics. [9] But although these reports were highly suggestive, they did not prove to the FDA's satisfaction that triazolam was more hazardous than these other two. Minor changes were made to the US label in 1989 but, apart from this, nothing much was done. In spite of increasing evidence of

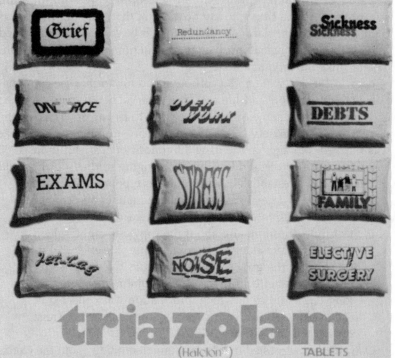

When short-term problems cause insomnia

Grief

Redundancy

Sickness

DIVORCE

WORRY

DEBTS

EXAMS

STRESS

FAMILY

Jet-Lag

NOISE

ELECTIVE SURGERY

triazolam
(Halcion®)   TABLETS

lets patients sleep on them

the risks - notably from Oswald et al in the UK and from Kales et al in the US - Halcion had become the best selling benzodiazepine hypnotic in the US, and in the world.

Doubts about triazolam continued to grow, in spite of the Dutch authorities' decision in 1990 to reinstate the drug. A year before they did so, Professor Ian Oswald (from the sleep research unit in Edinburgh) wrote to the *Lancet*, to say he thought that "van der Kroef was right", and that triazolam "should no longer be sold". Oswald argued that agitation, amnesia and psychotic reactions constituted a syndrome, linked to rebound anxiety.

Back in 1982, Oswald and a colleague had found that the combination of the very short half-life and long interval between doses taken each night, caused some triazolam patients to feel anxious during the day. [10] Rebound anxiety was also evident on stopping the drug - as was marked tolerance to the drug's hypnotic effects. But in his 1989 letter, Oswald also accused Upjohn of arranging studies which would necessarily fail to establish how serious this rebound anxiety was.

> "Quality of data always rests on the manner and care of collection. Upjohn's studies consistently used a breakfast-time questionnaire about the previous night's sleep with a final question: 'Did you have any side effects?' Little wonder the grogginess emerged as the supposedly only adverse effect of triazolam. Upjohn sponsored no long-term studies in which information was collected in the evening about feelings, or events such as quarrels, during the day." [Oswald 1989]

Oswald also suggested that lack of understanding about the effects of triazolam on personality resulted from Upjohn's failure to investigate the drug in anything other than short-term use. "Upjohn-funded research has concentrated on dosing for 1-7 nights", he said - not enough to investigate the problem of rebound anxiety. Oswald said that there were only three reliable studies on this. Two were from his own unit at Edinburgh - and one of these specifically confirmed what van der Kroef had reported, ten years before.

> "All three found that regular nightly triazolam causes daytime anxiety. In Edinburgh, 21 subjects took triazolam 0.5mg and their daytime anxiety rose to become significantly greater than placebo baseline, but only by the third week. At the university department of geriatric

medicine in Cardiff, 22 patients took triazolam 0.125mg and, by 3 weeks, daytime restlessness became signifi- cantly enhanced, associated with anxiety and irritability. Subsequently in Edinburgh, 40 patients took triazolam 0.5mg, 40 took placebo and 40 took lormetazepam 2mg, and again by 3 weeks the triazolam takers had become anxious compared with placebo or lormetazepam-takers. van der Kroef's observations about derealisation, panics, development of paranoid ideas, loss of weight and per- sonality changes were also confirmed." [Oswald, 1989]

The CSM quietly re-investigated triazolam in 1989 - but nothing came of it, apparently because they had not received enough Yellow Cards to justify action. Thus, lack of ADR reports (inertia) helps to define policies on drug safety. No data sheet changes were made. Instead, the CSM asked Upjohn to carry out another post-marketing surveillance study - whose results would not be due until 1994.

Then, in April 1991, a new report from Dr Kales' sleep research team in Pennsylvania established that triazolam 0.5mg consistently produced next-day memory impairment - apparently far more so than either temazepam or placebo.[11] Similar effects had also been reported from time to time at the doses recommended in Britain (0.25mg and 0.125mg). However, at these lower doses, the hypnotic effect of triazo- lam is weak - less than that of standard doses of temazepam.[12] Partly on these grounds, Dr Kales and others joined Oswald in suggesting that triazolam should be withdrawn.

In August 1991, the temperature rose again, as Upjohn made a large ($6m?) out of court settlement in the US of a claim that Halcion had led a patient to murder her mother. This was one of three separate cases in which a US criminal court had dismissed or reduced murder charges, on the grounds the defendants had been under the influence of triazolam. [13] Upjohn began from this time to face increasing num- bers of civil actions both in the US and UK.

The re-investigation of Halcion in the US forced Upjohn to disclose, for the first time, crucial data about psychiatric ADRs from a 1972 trial on prisoners (protocol 321). In September 1991 Upjohn sent these data to the UK and other authorities, apologising for a "transcription error". Very soon, the CSM asked Upjohn to withdraw the drug, reportedly writing: "If the information had been presented completely and correctly, it is highly unlikely that the committee would have been able to recommend the grant of product licences".

But Upjohn refused to withdraw Halcion, and in October 1991 the UK authorities suspended its licence. Upjohn said it was astonished and gave notice of appeal. At the time of writing, Halcion is off the market in the UK, but not elsewhere. World sales before the crash were $250m per year. The jury is out again.

Halcion data sheet warnings

Triazolam was one of the first drugs in the UK to be involved in a formal post-marketing surveillance (PMS) scheme - a procedure more routine nowadays. As a condition of the product licence, the Department of Health asked Upjohn to organise a study to monitor the effects of triazolam in everyday use. The study was apparently requested before the uproar in Holland - and its reassuring conclusions helped the UK authorities and Upjohn to ride the storm. The study involved 600 GPs and 3,000 patients - one-third of them on triazolam for over a month. Upjohn reported that, "Side effects were low and similar to those found in controlled clinical studies with other benzodiazepines." [14]

From the outset, triazolam was recommended in the UK at a much lower dose (0.125 - 0.25 mg/day) than in Holland and elsewhere - and this would also explain why there was less trouble with Halcion in the UK. In other parts of the world, Halcion was originally supplied in a 0.5mg tablet as well as at lower dosages - but by the late 1980s, many countries had withdrawn this high-strength version from sale, also reducing the recommended dose.

In this respect, the UK licensing authorities seem to have been more prudent than many of their counterparts abroad. On the other hand, it is worth contrasting UK policies on warnings with those in the US - because here the British authorities seemed to lag far behind. Consider, first, the warning about rebound effects and drug tolerance in the UK data sheet (1990-1991).

> "Tapering the dose of Halcion may decrease the incidence of recurrent insomnia on drug discontinuation. Patients who have taken benzodiazepines for a long time may require a longer period during which doses are reduced ...
> "The preponderance of data from sleep laboratory studies indicates that there would be no significant tolerance

development, drug accumulation or withdrawal effects
after cessation of treatment."

Compared with the US warning, the UK data sheet reflected almost a studied lack of urgency and concern. The word "may" diluted any warning, and the word "rebound" did not appear at all. In addition, the suggestion that little tolerance developed might easily have been misunderstood. Tolerance leading to rapid, gross escalation of dosage may be rare, but tolerance to the hypnotic effects of triazolam develops quickly - as the US label (data sheet) said.

"After two weeks of consecutive nightly administration,
the drug's effects on total wake time is decreased, and
the values recorded in the last third of the night approach
baseline levels. On the first and/or second night after
discontinuance (first or second post-drug night), total
time asleep, percentage of time spent sleeping, and
rapidity of falling asleep were significantly less than on
baseline [pre-drug] nights. This effect is often called
'rebound insomnia' ..." [*Physicians' Desk Reference*, 1990]

Equally, the UK data sheet (1990/91) suggested there were no significant withdrawal symptoms when triazolam was stopped - except that it didn't actually say this. It said that no significant withdrawal effects had been seen in short-term sleep laboratory studies - ie after about a week or so of normal dose treatment. Upjohn itself had established that around half of all general practice patients took Halcion for over two weeks [15] - but gave no information about the effects of withdrawal for them. Until ten years after the UK launch of Halcion, the data sheet said nothing about dependence at all.

The essential difference between warnings in the US and UK seems to be that UK data sheets tend to acknowledge side effects only when there is pretty clear evidence of actual harm. By contrast, the US authorities have tended to act earlier, on evidence of risk. Thus, US warnings about dependence on benzodiazepines have been stronger, and have appeared sooner, than in the UK.

The difference between these two approaches (risk v harm) can be seen by comparing information given to doctors about possible side effects of drugs. The lists below use triazolam as an example, to show how the content of side effect warnings has differed in the US and UK.

Possible side effects/adverse reactions warned of both in the
UK and US (1990): drowsiness, dizziness, confusion,

headache, light-headedness; taste alterations; CNS depression; depression with suicidal tendencies; antero-grade amnesia [loss of memory of recent events]; abnor-mal psychological reactions; paradoxical aggressive outbursts; excitement [UK] or agitation [US]; falling; transient insomnia after stopping drugs; hallucinations; somnabulism [sleepwalking]; pruritus [itching]; skin rash; blurred vision; hiccups; palpitations; epigastric discomfort [stomach upset]; diarrhoea; burning eyes.

Possible side effects/adverse reactions warned of only in US (1990): increased wakefulness towards the end of the night; increased daytime anxiety; euphoria; tachycardia [increased heart rate]; tiredness; fatigue; dry mouth; dreaming/nightmares; insomnia; paresthesia (tingling, burning feeling in skin); tinnitus (ringing in ears); dysesthesia (impaired senses, especially touch); weakness; congestion; slurred speech; jaundice; changes in libido; menstrual irregularity; incontinence and urinary retention

The same difference can be seen in warnings for many other drugs. It reflects the different enforcement philosophies of the UK and US authorities, and the resources that go with them. In mid 1991, 350 professional and other staff worked on medicines control in the UK, [16] compared with over 8,000 in the US Food and Drug Administration - expanding to perhaps 17,000 staff by 1997. [17]

This would partly explain why drug warnings in the US have tended to spell things out and to emphasise risks much more - typically in more straightforward language than used in data sheets in the UK. The main difference seems to be that the US authorities scrutinise every word of the label, while the UK authorities have tended to leave it to the manufacturers to explain things in their own way.

The differences between UK and US warnings therefore go deeper than is suggested just by lists of possible side-effects. This can be seen, for example, by comparing the warnings given on triazolam (Halcion) in pregnancy, depending on which side of the Atlantic the prescriber was on.

UK data sheet, 1990/91: "Safety for use during pregnancy has not yet been established".

US Physicians' Desk Reference, 1990: "Benzodiazepines

may cause fetal damage when administered during pregnancy ... Halcion is contraindicated in pregnant women ... Teratogenic effects: Pregnancy Category X" [this is an FDA rating: '...there is absolutely no reason to risk using the drug in pregnancy ... studies or reports ... have shown fetal risk which clearly outweighs any possible benefit to patient']. " ... the child born of a mother who is on benzodiazepines may be at some risk for withdrawal symptoms from the drug, during the post-natal period".

Under the present system of UK medicines control, the Committee on Safety of Medicines is legally protected from any requirement to explain and justify why it permitted triazolam to be used on such terms - or indeed why the drug was ever withdrawn. We understand the decision to withdraw the Product Licence was influenced by, among other things, fear of involvement in litigation, and by knowledge of the imminent transmission (14 October 1991) of Tom Mangold's hard-hitting *Panorama* programme on Halcion, on BBC TV.

1 Upjohn, 1985

2 Cohn & Noble, 1983

3 Levy, 1984; Noyes, 1985; Vital-Herne et al., 1985; Browne, 1986; Bleich et al., 1987

4 Raschid et al., 1987 [pre-publication manuscript]

5 Levy, 1984; Brier et al., 1984; Noyes, 1985; Zipursky et al., 1985 Noyes et al, 1986; Raschid et al., 1987; Bleich et al., 1987

6 Physician's Desk Reference, 1988; ABPI Data Sheet Compendium, 1990/91

7 (Translation by) Dukes, 1980

8 Upjohn, 1990

9 Wolfe SM (Ed), 1990

10 Morgan and Oswald, 1982

11 Bixler, Kales et al, 1991

12 Kales & Kales, 1986; Seidel, Cohen et al, 1986; O'Donnell & Balchin, 1988; Kales, Manfredi et al, 1991

13 Wolfe SM (Ed), 1990

14 Macleod, 1981

15 Macleod, 1981

16 Medicines Control Agency, 1991

17 SCRIP, 1991

Chapter 14

ISSUES FOR THE 1990s

"The recent 'benzohysteria' has clouded medical opinion to such a degree that some patients are denied effective and appropriate anxiolytic therapy or, worse, are forced into acute withdrawal states by having their benzodiazepines abruptly discontinued. Many patients believe they may have a valid claim for compensation as a result of taking benzodiazepines and many will be disappointed. On the other hand, if the popular press and more recently the legal profession had not taken up arms against the overprescription of tranquillisers, the issue of benzodiazepine dependence would still remain a medical curio only for the pages of medical journals. The media and lawyers have undoubtedly altered prescribing practices, mostly for the better." [Hallstrom, 1991]

Limitations of long-term use

Until recently, drug dependence was defined by doctors. They generally saw it in terms of non-therapeutic use, involving small numbers of people who conspicuously presented a threat to themselves or others. The nub of the problem was self-intoxication, rather than compulsive use. It led to unacceptable behaviour, illness and sometimes death. However, from about the 1980s, dependence became recognised more as an iatrogenic problem, a disease caused by medicine itself.

From about that time, consumers began to define what dependence meant to them, and the definition was extended to embrace other areas of concern. One related to the patient's feelings of loss of identity and self-esteem from being fettered to a drug - also some anger about being exposed to the risk of dependence, but not adequately warned. Secondly, withdrawal from drugs after normal treatment became defined as a greater problem than before - and recognised as often a very difficult and painful experience, with effects (notably depression) that sometimes continued for long after the drug had finally left the body. [1] In addition, people began to think more about the possible adverse effects of prolonged exposure to a drug, which dependence implied.

The consequences of long-term benzodiazepine use - apart from possible reinforcement of dependence - are still poorly understood. As data sheets still say, "Little is known regarding the efficacy or safety of benzodiazepines in long-term use". The information collected about side effects - notably under the Yellow Card scheme - mainly concerned acute and relatively clear-cut symptoms, mostly associated with short-term use. However, once patients began to describe what they felt, increasing attention was focused on the possible hazards of prolonged use - especially on mood, behaviour and mind.

The CSM's 1988 statement about benzodiazepine dependence and withdrawal confronted this problem basically by advising doctors against long-term use. It advised that benzodiazepines be used only for short courses of treatment (2 - 4 weeks) and only when anxiety or insomnia were disabling or severe. The CSM also declared that: "The use of benzodiazepines to treat short-term 'mild' anxiety is inappropriate and unsuitable." Nothing was said about giving advice to patients, in spite of the obvious need to do so. [2]

The CSM's recommendations were quickly incorporated into data sheets, without the appeals and long delays there had been before. One reason for this was was that the Committee's statement tallied closely with the recommendations of a small working party on benzodiazepine dependence set up by the Royal College of Psychiatrists in 1987. The working party included Dr Tyrer and Professor Lader, as well as a staff member of the CSM, Dr Graham Burton (who joined Upjohn UK, as Medical Director, in 1991).

The CSM said nothing new about the possible long-term effects of benzodiazepines on personality, although it made one recommendation which dimly reflected such concern: "In cases of loss or bereavement, psychological adjustment may be inhibited by benzodiazepines". The Royal College of Psychiatrists (RCP) made the same recommendation and, unlike the CSM, explained why. The RCP concluded that the harm benzodiazepines could do was directly related to their tendency to cause loss of memory. The RCP suggested this could cause problems in any acute crisis, but the implications of memory loss for other coping mechanisms were not discussed.

> "Amnesia is frequently a real side-effect of benzodi-
> azepines and not just a figment of the individual's imag-
> ination or a coincident symptom of emotional disorder ...
> It is often inadvisable to prescribe benzodiazepines to a
> patient in an acute crisis as the amnesic property of these
> compounds may not allow patients to make an optimum
> response to the situation which they are facing. In cases
> of loss or bereavement, the psychological adjustment to
> this trauma may be severely inhibited by benzodi-
> azepines and any tendency to denial could be rein-
> forced." [Priest, 1988]

The history of sedative-hypnotic drugs to date has been marked by belated recognition of drug-induced psychiatric disorders - chronically mistaken as evidence of illness or a character disorder, rather than something to do with the drug. These drugs have have repeatedly proved to be very subtle in their deleterious effects, though it could hardly be said that the bad news ever came right out of the blue. Reports of acute adverse reactions may, for example, also signal low-level, long-term effects.

Early isolated reports of explosive withdrawal from benzodiazepines later turned out to be related to widespread but "sub-clinical" drug dependence, and the same may apply to other psychiatric effects. It took over 20 years to establish the relationship between this particular iceberg and its tip; how much more will be known 20 years from now ? It is tempting, for example, to speculate that the relatively clear-cut cases of depression reported as acute reactions to benzodiazepines may be some portent of many other less obvious cases, unnoticed or unreported elsewhere. But in the meantime, it is hard to be sure.

> "Although depression is frequently attributed to [benzo-
> diazepines] the evidence is not wholly convincing since
> the patients were usually taking other additional drugs
> and/or were suffering from cerebrovascular or convul-
> sive disorders. Furthermore the relief of anxiety may
> 'unmask' coexisting depressive features." [D'Arcy &
> Griffin, 1986]

A variety of impairments of mind, memory and mood have been linked to chronic benzodiazepine use; experienced observers have described these effects in terms of the blunting of emotional life, and "emotional anaesthesia". [3] But again, the available evidence tends to be suggestive rather than scientifically conclusive. The same uncertainty applies to another focus of concern, indirectly suggested by a senior member of the CSM, in a paper published back in 1975. It was by Professor David Grahame-Smith, a neuroscientist with a special interest in adverse drug reaction monitoring by the CSM.

Grahame-Smith questioned whether even the fleeting use of some psychotropic drugs might cause far-reaching changes in behaviour. His point was that drugs could make a lasting impression on the mind, just as significant life events can - and that with both, the effects may continue long after the stimulus has gone.

> "In other words, on the first exposure to the drug changes have occurred in the brain which remain after the drug has been stopped which alter subsequent responses to various stimuli. Just as experience alters our future behaviour so do drugs. Many people appear to think that the individual remains more or less unchanged after using drugs, say pot, or the successfully weaned heroin addict, but I think that animal experiments and the writings of many previous drug users show that profound alterations in the brain can occur which change the individual for life and cannot be eradicated..." [Grahame-Smith, 1975]

Grahame-Smith illustrated his concern by referring to heroin and cannabis - perhaps choosing these examples of notable drugs of abuse to emphasise his point. Yet it would be hard to exempt benzodiazepines from such an assessment on pharmacological grounds. Cannabis, for example, does not cause recognised withdrawal symptoms, and benzodiazepines have been reported to cause more cognitive impairment than opiates. [4] However, in the same paper, Grahame-Smith defined dependence on benzodiazepines as a different sort of problem, seemingly more to do with coping, attitude and willpower.

> "There is little evidence that physical addiction to benzodiazepines is important though undoubtedly in maladjusted individuals psychological dependence may occur, but by and large with the benzodiazepines this is not a great problem." [Grahame-Smith, 1975]

Understanding of the long-term effects of drugs on behaviour (including the effects on offspring resulting from foetal exposure [5]) were still very limited by the early 1990s. There is almost certainly scope for radical revision of present-day views - including widely held beliefs about the role of personality in creating and sustaining dependence. There also remains to this day something of an unhealthy tendency to distinguish between us and them - in spite of the fact that substance abuse by doctors is estimated at about 30-times as common as among the general population. [6] It is not known how many doctors abuse benzodiazepines, but nor does it much matter what drugs are used.

> "One of the common notions about drugs, especially alcohol, but also other psychoactive drugs is that there is a 'we' and a 'they'. This notion implies that there are those who use the drug in some safe way: 'we' have a distribution from high to low, but still a safe use. Then there are those people - the undesirable types - who mis-use the drug, and 'they' go from low to high also. We believe that somehow there are two populations. The fact is that if you take a large enough sample, you find that the curve is smooth, that you move from abstinence to the highest level of consumption in a smooth distribu-tion." [LeBlanc, 1975]

A dependence-prone personality?

By the mid-1980s, authoritative estimates suggested that between 200,000 and 500,000 people (varying according to the criteria used) [7] were dependent on benzodiazepines - and higher estimates have been made since. [8] It is still unclear why some people get dependent, others not, after the same exposure to drugs.

There is little evidence that physiological factors consistently make a difference - though one factor was noticed in the study of abrupt withdrawal by Tyrer and associates in 1981. They found that patients who experienced withdrawal symptoms also tended to clear benzodi-azepines from their bodies relatively fast. For reasons apparently to do with physiology rather than personality, some people in effect withdrew the drug from their own bodies faster than others - and were more likely to have marked withdrawal symptoms as a result. However, this effect was not discernible when benzodiazepines were withdrawn gradually, as Tyrer reported in 1983.

Indeed, Tyrer's 1983 study emphatically concluded that personality factors were *more* significant than pharmacological and other factors in predicting the prevalence of withdrawal symptoms. The investigators decided this after making standardised personality assessments of the patients in the study, and then comparing those who had withdrawal symptoms with those who did not. They suggested that patients with a "passive dependent" personality type were especially prone to withdrawal symptoms - whereas patients with the opposite personality type were not.

As the Table shows, Tyrer and his colleagues in fact found that most cases of dependence involved "normal" people - and that normal people were just as likely to experience withdrawal symptoms as not. But the investigators also suspected that exceptionally timorous and meek people were more likely to become dependent; while obsessionally independent (anankastic) people were not - the implication being that pharmacological dependence and physical withdrawal symptoms might be subdued by some sort of psychological resource.

Differences between patients with and without withdrawal symptoms [after Tyrer et al, 1983]

	Patients with withdrawal symptoms	Patients without withdrawal symptoms
Mean duration of treatment(months)	45.5	35.9
Personality type:		
- sociopathic	1	0
- passive-dependent	3	1
- anankastic	1	3
- normal	11	16

This main finding was based on a tiny sample, not enough to draw any firm conclusions. However, Tyrer also compared a whole range of personality traits (including in this analysis patients who were "normal") - with liability to withdrawal symptoms. He then found that patients with five traits (resourcelessness, lability, impulsiveness, sensitivity and irresponsibility) were more likely to have withdrawal symptoms than others. On the other hand, none of the following characteristics seemed to make any significant difference: pessimism, worthlessness, optimism, anxiousness, suspiciousness, introspection, shyness, aloofness, irritability, aggression, callousness, childishness, dependence, submissiveness, conscientiousness, rigidity, eccentricity, hypochondriasis.

Much later, in 1991, Tyrer and a colleague reported the results of another study on the effects of personality on withdrawal.[9] This time they found that patients with passive-dependent disorders were more likely to complete withdrawal from benzodiazepines than patients rated anankastic.

These rather confusing and contradictary results hardly supported the conclusion that personality type was more significant than pharmacological and physiological factors as a predictor of dependence. Since the role of these other factors is still only poorly defined, such a conclusion must be tentative at most.

But even if liability to dependence were related to personality factors, what difference would it make in practice ? It would be far beyond the capacity of most doctors to do the kind of screening of patients that Tyrer used. A very sensitive diagnosis (using relatively crude diagnostic criteria) would be needed to be able to reliably predict which patients might become dependent on benzodiazepines, which not. And even the most sensitive screening would probably miss more cases than it would identify. It would seem far more useful to moderate prescribing and to advise and encourage patients to cut down consumption. It was demonstrated around 25 years ago that this could reduce drug dependence to a fraction of the level it might otherwise reach. [10]

Other benzodiazepines?

The question of whether the dependence risk with some benzodiazepines is greater than with others arises partly because, in the looming legal action for compensation, most claims concern lorazepam (Ativan) - and most of the rest, diazepam (Valium). Some benzodiazepines were not involved at all.

This may seem all the more surprising because, for example, temazepam (eg Normison, Euhypnos) has been the most widely used benzodiazepine in the UK since the mid-1980s, and oxazepam (eg Serenid D) had been used as an anxiolytic for 25 years - without either ever emerging as a major problem drug. Does this necessarily mean that these and other benzodiazepines would, at comparable doses, carry a lower dependence risk than the drugs most involved in legal proceedings ?

Not at all. There would certainly be some connection between the amount of critical publicity for each drug and the number of claims pursued - but less publicity does not mean a cleaner bill of health. Too many confounding factors are involved - including the fact that many patients might not realise that the drugs prescribed for them were also benzodiazepines, like Ativan and Valium, and so would not make claims.

Another important factor would be how much a particular drug was used by different categories of patients (eg the elderly), and what the drug was used for. Clinical reports of dependence on benzodiazepines prescribed for anxiety appear to be much more common than reports about dependence on hypnotics - but this does not necessarily mean any difference in risk. It could mean (we fear it does) that there was much less concern about dependence in the elderly, for whom hypnotics are most often prescribed.

There should be concern about any high levels of prescribing - especially of hypnotics, intended only for short-term use. Temazepam, for example, is now formally indicated in data sheets for treatment of up to 4 weeks, and only when insomnia is disabling or causing extreme distress - yet enough of this one drug is still prescribed to provide one in every six adults in the UK with a one-month course of treatment each year. This signals a continuing, major dependence problem; it also seems to support anecdotal evidence that withdrawal from temazepam is particularly hard. [11] Whether or not this is so, it does suggest that dependence on temazepam closely compares with the rest.

While there are some differences of degree between benzodiazepines, there are many more similarities of type. All carry a significant risk of dependence if prescribed for more than a few weeks, and they can all precipitate the same syndrome on withdrawal. Severe withdrawal symptoms from any of these drugs may be dangerous, and may feel almost unbearable at their most intense - especially when they come on suddenly and sharply, as they tend to with shorter-acting drugs.

Differences between benzodiazepines are much less important than how they are prescribed and taken. The determination of doctors and patients to reduce risks is clearly more important in reducing dependence than is the choice of drug - so there is still a long way to go. By the beginning of the 1990s, doctors were prescribing benzodiazepines much more sparingly than before, and a few had altogther rejected their use. [12] But general levels of prescribing are still very high, and dependence almost has to be the main reason for it. See Table.

Alternatives to benzodiazepines

The risk of dependence makes benzodiazepines potentially hazardous - but they are potentially very useful drugs too. They have done much good in their time, and clearly still have an important role in medicine. Drug treatment may be preferable to any available alternative in the short-term - for example, to break a vicious cycle of severe insomnia or anxiety, to give a patient breathing space and time.

There are alternatives to benzodiazepines and other drug treatments. The obvious one is alcohol, but it is also liable to get out of hand and often does. Benzodiazepines and similar drugs are sometimes prescribed to try to reduce this risk - and they are in some ways safer than the opiates, bromides and barbiturates that were used before. Still, it is worth bearing in mind the paradox that "safer" drugs tend to be more dangerously prescribed. Newer drugs, almost always seeming safer than they really are, will always tend to be prescribed as if they could not do harm - too much to ask of any potent drug.

The better alternatives to benzodiazepines, as always, involve prevention - through more automony, better tolerance of each other, more mutual dependence, better understanding, more sharing, less inequality, better ways of doing things, better ways of life. There are potentially great opportunities for all of these things, but formidable practical problems too. Another paradox is that it can be harder to see how much prevention is needed, if people chronically depend on drugs to help them forget about the sometimes grimmer realities of life.

Para-medical and medical alternatives to drugs include a wide range of non-drug treatments, notably counselling and analytic, behavioural and other psychotherapies. Such treatments aim to help patients better understand and cope with the underlying reasons for distress. They are more expensive than drugs and their availability is limited by cost - although the cost of short-term counselling might compare quite favourably with the cost of long-term dependence,

Number of NHS prescriptions for benzodiazepines 1978-1989 in Great Britain (millions)

	'78	'79	'80	'81	'82	'83	'84	'85	'86	'87	'88	'89
Temazepam	0.3	0.7	1.3	2.1	3.1	3.6	4.2	6.3	7.2	7.8	7.7	7.1
Nitrazepam	10.2	10.1	9.0	8.4	7.9	7.0	6.4	6.0	5.5	5.2	4.6	4.2
Diazepam	11.1	10.5	8.8	8.0	7.1	6.2	5.4	5.4	5.2	5.1	4.5	4.1
Triazolam	-	0.2	0.5	1.0	1.1	1.1	1.3	1.6	2.0	2.2	2.2	2.1
Lorazepam	1.8	2.1	2.4	2.9	3.5	3.5	3.2	3.1	3.1	2.9	2.1	1.7
Chlordiazepoxide	2.9	2.6	2.2	2.0	1.8	1.6	1.3	1.2	1.1	1.0	0.9	0.8
Oxazepam	0.7	0.7	0.7	0.8	0.8	0.7	0.6	0.7	0.8	0.8	0.6	0.5
Lormetazepam	-	-	-	0.0*	0.2	0.4	0.5	0.1	0.2	0.2	0.2	0.2
Loprazolam	-	-	-	-		0.0	0.1	0.0	0.1	0.1	0.2	0.2
Clonazepam	0.0	0.0	0.0	0.1	0.1	0.1	0.1	0.1	0.1	0.1	0.1	0.1
Clobazam	-	0.1	0.3	0.4	0.5	0.5	0.5	0.1	0.0	0.0	0.1	0.1
Alprazolam	-	-	-	-	-	0.2	0.3	0.1**	-	-	-	-
Flurazepam	2.1	2.3	2.3	2.2	2.2	2.0	2.0	0.5	-	-	-	-
Clorazepate	1.0	1.0	1.2	1.1	1.2	1.2	1.3	0.3	-	-	-	-
Flunitrazepam	-	-	-	-	0.0	0.1	0.2	0.1	-	-	-	-
Bromazepam	-	-	-	-	0.0	0.1	0.2	0.0	-	-	-	-
Ketazolam	-	-	0.0	0.1	0.2	0.2	0.2	0.0	-	-	-	-
Medazepam	0.3	0.3	0.2	0.2	0.2	0.2	0.1	0.0	-	-	-	-
Prazepam	-	-	-	-	0.0	0.0	0.0	0.0	-	-	-	-
Total	30.6	30.9	29.1	29.5	29.7	28.7	28.0	25.7	25.3	25.5	23.2	22.1

* 0.0 = fewer than 50,000 prescriptions

** Limited list became effective, April 1985

[Source: Hansard, 31 March 1988, cols 657-8w; 27 February 1990, 121-2w; 4 December 1990, 75-6w]

including the cost of the doctor's time. All of these therapies can work, sometimes extremely well - but they, of course, carry risks too.

And what of the drug alternatives to benzodiazepines ? The only survivor from Chapter 2 is chloral hydrate - a panacea in its day, and available as a standby ever since. In symbolic terms, the continuing use of chloral indicates that progress can be made without newer products, by using older ones more safely. If properly used, chloral seems reasonably efficacious and safe, about as good as the rest.

Still, Henry Maudsley was surely right when he suggested that drugs do not promote natural sleep - and it seems ironic that chloral should now be the only hypnotic available in the UK to claim that "a near natural sleep is induced and the REM/NON-REM ratio is not altered" (data sheets, 1981 - 1991). They are more circumspect about these things in the US; the US label said nothing about natural sleep, acknowledging that "chloral hydrate's effects on Rapid Eye Movement (REM) sleep is uncertain".

Another older non-benzodiazepine drug treatment for anxiety to survive into the 1990s was chlormezanone (Trancopal), sold by the Sterling-Winthrop group since 1961, but never really much used. Until about 1987, the data sheet stated simply that "the dependence potential of chlormezanone is not known". Since then, it has carried a statement reminiscent of the 1978 warnings about benzodiazepines from Dr John Marks.

> "As with sedative drugs, dependence may possibly occur when chlormezanone is given in high dosage or for prolonged periods, especially in patients with a history of alcoholism or drug dependence, or in patients with marked personality disorders. The possibility of withdrawal reactions to abrupt termination of chlormezanone after long-term treatment has not been studied. Gradual withdrawal may be appropriate."
> [Data sheet 1990/91]

Successors to benzodiazepines ?

By 1990, probably the major drug alternative to benzodiazepines for anxiety was buspirone, introduced by Bristol-Myers as BuSpar in both the UK and the US. Buspirone was launched in the late 1980s, and in both countries the promotion drew fire. Under pressure from the Health Research Group, [13] the FDA required Bristol-Myers to with-

BuSpar

buspirone

Anxiety therapy pure and simple

Starting dose: 1 x 5mg tablet t.d.s.
Maintenance dose: 15-30mg daily.
Patients should be treated for at
least four weeks.

draw a prominent advertisement featuring an air traffic controller -
"He needs anxiolytic therapy, but alertness is part of his job". In the
UK - where Professor Malcolm Lader was conspicuous in the launch -
criticism from Social Audit focused on promotion of the drug to the
editors of womens' magazines; and on poor information in the data
sheet.

   BuSpar was launched on the crest of a tidal wave of anxiety about
benzodiazepine dependence. In the brochures used to promote it, the
drugged patient was symbolised by a white swan, reflecting somewhat narcissistically on its own image in calm blue water. The caption

was "Anxiety therapy pure and simple" - as if it really could be. The main and most prominent claims - each referenced to a single and arguably inadequate source [14] - were as follows:

"As effective as the benzodiazepines in relieving anxiety"; "No evidence of dependence or abuse potential"; "Psychomotor performance unimpaired"; "Sedation similar to placebo"

At least the US Label made it clear that the effectiveness of buspirone "for more than three or four weeks has not been demonstrated in clinical trials". The data sheet said nothing about this; on the contrary, UK prescribers were told that "patients should be be treated for at least four weeks". It was also emphasised that, in some patients, the drug could take up to two weeks to work.

The BuSpar data sheet did not mention either 13 adverse experiences reported "frequently" in the US, nor 50 other "infrequently" reported events. The data sheet claimed that Buspar was "generally well tolerated", whereas the label said that about 10 per cent of patients in trials had stopped treatment because of an adverse effect. The most commonly reported was dizziness - although the UK data sheet said nothing about warning patients not to drive. Other side effects which could impair psychomotor performance included headache, nervousness, lightheadedness, excitement, palpitations, drowsiness, confusion, blurred vision, numbness, incoordination and tremor.

At the same time, BuSpar advertisements claimed there was "no evidence of dependence or abuse potential" - a reference to a report which emphasised that this was a preliminary view and that "further clinical experience will be necessary to confirm this". [15] Is there really "no evidence" of risk ? Is it merely superstitious to consider how often this has been emphasised in the past and repeatedly proved wrong ?

The main new contender as an alternative hypnotic was a drug called zopiclone (Zimovane); it too was promoted as a safer bet than benzodiazepines. Zimovane was licensed to Rhone-Poulenc in late 1989. It cost 20 times more than temazepam, the main competing drug, and at least the data sheet suggested it might be worth it. The operative words in the adverse reactions section were: "Mild ... mild ... minor .... very rarely ... occasionally ... more rarely ... rare and generally of minor significance".

Two years before it got its licence, Professor Malcolm Lader tested

A NEW CLASS OF HYPNOTIC
The First Cyclopyrrolone

Sleep serene ... awake refreshed

Zimovane ▼
zopiclone
No evidence of dependence
in clinical use

RHÔNE-POULENC

Further information is available on request from Rhone-Poulenc Pharmaceuticals, a division of Rhone-Poulenc Ltd, Dagenham, Essex RM10 7XS

the drug on ten volunteers. He found it effective over four weeks, and reported that rebound effects on withdrawal were so slight that it did not seem necessary to gradually reduce the dosage on withdrawal. [16] He also contrasted the effects of zopiclone and temazepam on mood: "Zopiclone was associated with feelings of being troubled, tense, antagonistic and bored whereas temazepam produced drowsiness, clumsiness, dreaminess and sadness".

Before Zimovane was licensed, three more clinical reports were published [17] which concluded there were no rebound effects when the drug was withdrawn - and the company reached the same conclusion in a review of 25 studies assessing rebound and withdrawal. [18] A company overview of all studies and trials, published at the time of the UK launch, claimed effectiveness with minimal effect on sleep patterns; no residual impairment of cognitive functions; and no rebound or withdrawal symptoms.

The data sheet faithfully reflected this, giving the manufacturers licence to advertise at the launch that there was "no evidence of dependence in clinical use". Instead of a swan (which would have looked silly in bed) the advertisements featured a teddy bear.

The *Lancet* (1990) reacted to this launch with an editorial - Zopiclone: another carriage on the tranquilliser train. This argued that rebound insomnia had been demonstrated in volunteers, and that Rhone-Poulenc had failed to test for it properly in patients. The editorial concluded that some of the claims made about the drug's dependence potential were "inaccurate to the point of being irresponsible".

And, towards the end of 1990, the CSM published a note in *Current Problems* about the 122 adverse reaction reports it had received in the first few months after the launch:

"A fifth of these reactions have been neuro-psychiatric reactions, a proportion similar to that found with other hypnotics. Many of these reactions were potentially serious and involved hallucinations (3 auditory and 2 visual), amnesia (4) and behavioural disturbances (10 including 3 cases of aggression). Most reactions started immediately or shortly after the first dose and improved rapidly on stopping the drug. Three patients had difficulty in stopping treatment (2 because of withdrawal symptoms and 1 due to repeated rebound insomnia). These reports underline the risk of dependency on long term use of zopiclone."

BuSpar and Zimovane, in different ways, illustrate continuing deficiencies in drug evaluation and promotion, and in the drug licensing process. These are discussed in more detail in the concluding chapter - with reference to drugs other than sedative-hypnotics. As a prelude to chapter, we ask if this style of new drug promotion for a new drug can possibly be justified - when studies and trials can fall so far short of establishing the truth, and when standards of reporting are so poor.

Perhaps the answer lies in compromise - recognising both the extra risk with new drugs, and the manufacturer's need to promote new products for all they are worth. One compromise might be to have a government health warning for all new drugs - a prominent box warning in all promotional materials, to convey the (privately expressed) views of the present Chairman of the Committee on Safety of Medicines:

"With a known chemical entity we have some idea of what ballpark we are in ... [but] ... by the time a drug is licenced we really know very little in the case of a new chemical entity about its possible risks." [Asscher, 1988]

Professor Asscher made these remarks to a mainly industry audience; they were not intended for public consumption. They seemed to make nonsense of the licence given, and the liberties taken, to emphasise publicly that major problems do not exist.

Matters of perspective

This case-history about benzodiazepines and related drugs leaves one outstanding question to be discussed. To what extent should this case history be interpreted as an isolated and self-contained problem, mainly something to do with the past - or be seen as more characteristic of the system of medicine as a whole ?

This story described only a very small part of what medicine is - and it concentrated on a single problem, albeit of long standing. The story ignored many other parts of medicine and had very little to say about its many achievements, some of which are indeed great. How do the parts of medicine described in this book relate to the whole, and are the bits described representative of the fabric of medicine and an integral part of its structure ?

If the whole of medicine were imagined as a great castle, this story might be seen as a short survey and guide of some baser bits of the building, including the dungeons. The survey does not begin to describe or value the whole building - but may seem relevant to the whole because it describes something of its foundations, including some obvious sources of damp, mould and rot. The story also reveals something about the human activity in the building and the spirit of the place.

Yet in some respects, this case history may seem unique. Dependence is different from other side effects, because it prompts people to continue with the drug, rather than stop it. Also, the benzodiazepines and similar drugs are exceptional because some of their side effects mimic the very symptoms for which they are most prescribed. Another distinctive factor in this case is the scale of prescribing over the years, and the tendency to treat everyday problems and all ills: "Whatever the diagnosis: Librium", as the advertisements used to say. The problem of dependence that was eventually revealed was on a commensurate scale.

In other respects, there seems to be nothing unique about this case-history. Typically, it does take years of use to establish how drugs work and what effects they have - and years longer for even quite basic information to pass between cultures, organisations, groups and individuals until finally it sinks in. The extent of the misunderstandings and the gaps in information that are liable to arise have been exemplified in this case-history by reference to variations in dosage and the risk of long-term adverse effects. Still, after 30 years of extensive use, "little is known" about the long-term effects of benzodiazepines - not even if they go on working in the long term (which we very much doubt).

There were three benzodiazepines - lorazepam, triazolam and midazolam (discussed later) - all used at some time during the 1980s at a dosage around twice as high in some countries as others. Where such discrepancies did exist, always the lower dosage was later found to be more appropriate - and the same has proved true with other drugs. [19] If it takes numerous trials and perhaps many years of clinical use to discern a marked difference in response, when the identical drug is used at a dose of either x or 2x, clearly the sensitivity of drug testing and analysis is not high - and should not be too much relied on.

There are equally profound gaps in understanding with many other kinds of drugs and treatments - but it is not the uncertainty in itself which does the harm. The real harm is done when this relatively high level of ignorance is not reflected in drug control policies, and in marketing and clinical practice. What is known about drugs today does by far surpass what was known even only a few years ago - but for exactly this reason, one has to assume that the amount known this year may seem quite inadequate next. By definition, one will never know enough without some reckoning of how much is not known - a reality often ignored. [20]

We hope this case-history will be accepted partly as a study of the quality of drug information, and methods and styles of communication - quite as much as a study of any particular class of drugs. We believe that the examples given illustrate standards which apply quite generally to methods of data collection and styles of reasoning, argument and analysis. These standards, and the rules which apply to generating and presenting data, are not peculiar to this case history: they reflect aspects of standard practice in the system of medicine as a whole. Of particular concern are the extent of unconscious bias; the degree of scientific illiteracy; and the overwhelming weight of over-optimistic and uncritical product assessments.

The roles of the main actors - the companies, government, doctors and consumers - are discussed more in the next chapter, with particular emphasis on the relationship between government and consumers. But just to judge from this case history, all of the actors seemed to play their parts true to form.

Patients tended to be patronised, treated like dependants, and many behaved accordingly: passive, trusting and consuming ever more. Others did protest and, at first, faced enormous resistance. Their experiences were for many years overlooked, and their views scorned - but eventually there was enough unison for common sense to begin to prevail. Collectively, consumers were largely disregarded, their opinions barely canvassed - though they had all the raw data the whole time. Consumers do not yet enjoy more than basic, even primitive, rights within the system of medicine - the rights to safety, to be informed, to choose and to be heard.

Most doctors continued to prescribe benzodiazepines on some scale, apparently taking very much for granted that this helped patients and that all was well. Many doctors didn't know nearly enough, but tended to behave as if they did - unduly encouraged and reassured by publicity and soft data it would have been much safer to ignore. Over the years, the profession as a whole demonstrated a startling capacity for prejudice and denial, and a corresponding problem when it came to learning from mistakes. But there were also fine exceptions to the rule - doctors who took good care; who thought about what was going on and asked the right questions; and who spoke out about policies and practice that seemed to make no sense. They are not yet an endangered species, but there are not nearly enough of them - and they need much more support.

The pharmaceutical companies sought to dominate professional and public opinion, by generating more and more evidence of benefit while tending to overlook the risks. The companies might claim that they strike some balance between good sales and good sense, yet seemed at times almost intoxicated with their own cause, unable to distinguish readily between honest criticism of its products and persecution of themselves. [21] Drug risks will always be unacceptably high so long as the industry tends to pour money into demonstrating product benefits, while pouring cold water on allegations of risk - calling on quite different standards of investigation and proof in each case.

Can the industry have it both ways ? Can it be allowed such influence over the law and practice of medicine, given its compulsion to stimulate and supply demand ? What is the point of making more and more magic bullets, if companies then block the view and spoil the doctors' aim ? Is the industry fit to lead - as in many ways it clearly does - when it professes to observe high ethical and scientific standards but, in practice, is so driven to sell ? The following view could be right, wrong, or something in between - but it is the view of an experienced observer and a prominent apologist for the industry, (also the leading critic of its critics).

> "The essence of the problem is the fact that what the industry wants so badly these days - to 'be valued for its contributions to society' - is not what the game is normally about. The pharmaceutical business - like every other business in the US - is about making money, and it is towards the goal of making the most possible money that industry executives normally devote their energies day in and day out." [Schwartz, 1991]

That spirit seems to have been catching on in the UK, [22] and is probably closer to the reality than government seems to understand. Thus, most members of the CSM also act as consultants to pharmaceutical companies, doing research for them or giving advice. The official view is that, provided such interests are declared, no conflict arises - and that such arrangements are inevitable and useful too. But it is hard for us to believe that this loss of independence does not profoundly affect the spirit of national drug policy and control.

This case-history suggests that Department of Health policy in medicine control is founded on three main principles - beyond earning revenue and reducing costs. One is to keep consumers and their representatives at bay; another is reliance on self-regulation by both the medical profession and the industry. Above all, the Department seeks to keep its head down - hoping, sometimes against all the odds, to avoid controversy and make problems go away.

Give or take the odd hiccup, both the industry and the medical profession have found it possible to work quite well with government on these terms. Consumers, on the other hand, might feel that government has demonstrated, at best, a desperate lack of imagination. Official policies seem ill-defined and to some extent ill-conceived - and in practice often appear faint, weary and weak. Government has largely isolated itself from consumers, operating pretty much independently of parliamentary scrutiny and control. It operates in secrecy to an extent which precludes any strictly scientific, independent assessment of the standards it sets, or the risks it takes.

More to the point, government seeks to justify keeping this distance from those it claims to serve, on the grounds that it is engaged in some strictly scientific endeavour - the implication being that lay views, because uninformed, would tend to corrupt the process. This case-history suggests that government action and inaction are determined in the main by political and economic, rather than strictly scientific considerations.

In the last analysis, this is not just a case-history of sedative-hypnotic drugs, but a case-study of power and dependence - also in spiritual, social, economic and political dimensions. We emphasise this in the concluding chapter - using different drugs as examples, to discuss in rounder terms what "the safety of medicines" seems to mean today.

1 Ashton, 1984; Olajide and Lader, 1984; Council of Europe, 1990

2 Clift, 1972; Wells, 1973

3 Ashton, 1984

4 Hendler et al, 1980

5 Fishman et al, 1983; Jacobsen et al, 1990

6 Pilowski & O'Sullivan, 1989; Rucinski & Cybulska, 1985

7 Drug & Ther Bull, 1985; Ashton, 1987 (b)

8 BMJ, 1991

9 Murphy & Tyrer, 1991

10 Clift, 1972; Wells, 1973

11 Drug & Ther Bull, 1985

12 Cohen, 1987

13 Salive and Wolfe, 1987

14 Medawar, 1988

15 Medawar, 1988

16 Lader, 1987

17 Anderson, 1987; Brun, 1988; Wheatley, 1988

18 Bianchi & Musch, 1990

19 Collier, 1989

20 Medawar, June 1988

21 Medawar, 1989

22 Tucker, 1984

Chapter 15

DEPENDENCE OR POWER?

"One of the real problems is that we do not have, in the UK, a 'drug policy'. What we have are small isolated pieces of legislation which have all been introduced as a result of specific problems. Thus the Medicines Act and the CSM were established to regulate the pharmaceutical industry. With the passage of time the CSM has gradually taken on some role in public and professional education but these activities are fraught with a range of legal and practical impediments." [CSM member, 1991]

Responsibility for safety

In the beginning, doctors generally assumed that the drugs they used were safe enough. If drug treatments went wrong, this was readily interpreted as an abnormal or idiosyncratic response - and when drug treatments proved altogether too much, doctors used to report they had "lost" their patient, as if the loss was mainly theirs. Until quite recently, it was rather taken for granted that good intent in medicine meant good effect. The drug could be interpreted as penance, indulgence or gift; whichever it was, the patient's recovery depended largely on confidence that the pill was good and would work.

Around mid-century, the pharmaceutical industry began to provide drugs which really could, and increasingly did make a decisive difference to the practice of medicine and human health. Something like euphoria then set in and it led to to excessive supply, promotion, prescribing and consumption. That trend has been punctuated by the thalidomide disaster and a succession of other nasty shocks - all reminders that very basic lessons about drug safety have still to be learned.

It took until the 1960s, for example, to appreciate the now seemingly obvious point that the foetus would be especially sensitive to drug effects. Equally, it was not widely recognised until the 1980s (after bitter experience with Opren) that elderly people face special risks as well. There is clearly much more to learn, notably about why identical drugs can elicit very different responses from different groups of people. As more potent and specific drugs are introduced, and as their effects become better known, notions of "average" and "normal" treatment and response will seem much more elusive than now.

The state of the art can be illustrated by reference to patients' genetic and ethnic differences, which can profoundly affect how they react to drugs. [1] Such factors are known to make a difference, but there is no systematic enquiry into what that difference really amounts to. Yellow Cards, for example, do not ask doctors to record the patient's race - unscientific, whatever else.

There will inevitably be drug disasters in future; some will underline how subtle the unwanted effects of drugs can be - and with others it will seem the problem was right under our noses all the time. Certainly, much progress has been made in reducing risks: towards the end of the 20th century, the need for some pre-screening and post-marketing surveillance is well recognised. Yet medicine is still at the stage when quite gross risks may not be noticed for years.

Perhaps the most important reason for this is that the authorities and experts still tend to think in terms of "the safety of medicines", rather than the safety of the people for whom they are prescribed. The powers that be continue to think and act as if safety can be achieved by looking ever more closely at the drug, but never too closely at themselves or at the system of medicines' control. They have yet to accept that the safety of medicines is very largely defined by the discharge of corporate responsibilities, and by the determination to protect human and civil rights.

The consumer movement has gathered this and has rapidly gained in influence since the 1980s - both in the UK and abroad - and if it is given to finding fault with the system, that seems understandable enough. The style of medicines' control in many respects gives cause for concern, but there is still precious little scope for dialogue between consumers and the authorities, let alone a spirit of partnership or trust. [2] If the courts are now becoming a more central focus for consumers, it is partly because they have no other way of expressing themselves. The authorities have put themselves beyond reach, and there is still no effective forum for consumer affairs in medicine.

Parliament has taken little concerted initiative in such matters, but clearly must. It needs urgently to establish the real impact of drug injury in the community, including its cost - and then to consider what and how much to invest in prevention. The time has also come for Parliament to reconsider the usefulness of the 1968 Medicines Act: it is the product of an age when patients, in pharmacological terms, were still treated somewhat like guinea pigs - and consumers regarded as sheep. The culture of secrecy which the Act enshrines increasingly alienates consumers and contributes to mutual mistrust. It is no longer possible to keep consumers out of the action, and seems increasingly provocative to try.

The need for effective parliamentary scrutiny has become all the greater with the creation of the single European market: initiatives on drug safety will increasingly come from the Community, and reflect EC standards more than domestic ones. A whole new legislative and administrative structure is to be built on a foundation which has only one cornerstone - the principle of free trade. An amendment is under discussion, but the Treaty of Rome still has no clauses relating to health - and many issues at the heart of health policy are now affected by the process of harmonisation. [3] There is a risk of deterioration of safety standards, not only because drugs are very different from other consumer products - but also because the drive to harmonisation will inevitably involve some compromise between stronger and weaker national systems of drug control. [4] The British system, whatever its limitations, is generally regarded as one of the strongest in the EC.

The EC member states have now agreed in principle to set up an agency to evaluate new drugs for marketing approval. It will take time to realise but, by mid-1991, individual member states were already bidding to host this new centre of power - though many basic issues relating to public accountability and the role of consumers had barely been explored. Nevertheless, there are opportunities for progress in some areas. For example, there is now a draft EC proposal to encourage the authorities to outline their reasons for licensing individual new drugs - and if this were implemented if could help to erode the secrecy on which the UK licensing system is now based.

In response to another EC directive, drug manufacturers are to provide patients, from 1992, with shortened and much simplified versions of the drug warnings they now supply for doctors. The quality of these new patient information leaflets remains to be seen, but the indications are that they represent but a small step towards informed consent to treatment. Understandably, the ABPI emphasised that information in the new leaflets should be comprehensible, pitched at the average British patient, with a reading age of nine. However, for ostensibly the same reasons, the industry also decided to limit what the leaflets would say (as well as how they say it), and to make them as brief as the regulations allow. This policy may well leave British consumers much less informed than their counterparts elsewhere. Parliament has played little or no part in this process, while the DoH has acted essentially as a passive bystander. It appears there will be no systematic scrutiny by the Department of leaflet warnings [5] - certainly none to compare with the approval process for data sheets, limited in value as this has proved to be. [6]

The wider point is that the pharmaceutical industry is taking more and more responsibility for the safety of medicines - now even to the extent of directly advising patients about the benefits of drug treatment and the risks they may run. This underlines the importance of effective self-regulation, as well as good laws. Whether the industry is yet capable of assuming responsibilities beyond those it already has seems at least debatable - and must be debated, out in the open, because of the importance of the issues involved.

The reality is that all countries need multinational pharmaceutical companies to supply safe and effective medicines. Whatever their capacity for regulation, and their approach to drug control, all countries have to rely on pharmaceutical companies to maintain reasonable standards themselves. Let it not distract from the main thread of the argument - continued in the main text - but the following example gives little evidence of a system dedicated to promoting trust.

Midazolam was the last of the Roche benzodiazepines: marketed in the UK from 1983, as Hypnovel. Because of its very short half-life and rapid onset of action, Hypnovel was promoted as an injectable pre-anaesthetic - eg to induce amnesia and twilight sleep in patients undergoing uncomfortable diagnostic examinations.

Three years before the UK launch of Hypnovel, Roche was apparently aware of potential safety problems with the drug - but did not act. The evidence comes from company documents, obtained in mid 1991 by the Public Citizen Health Research Group in the US. [7] One 1980 memorandum, from Roche US to the company headquarters in Basle, acknowledged there was some risk of respiratory arrest - especially when intravenous midazolam was used "for minor medical and dental procedures, in situations in which there usually is neither resuscitation equipment available nor personnel trained in the use of these measures". The memorandum said that such problems could best be avoided by supplying the drug in a more dilute form.

However, allegedly for marketing reasons, Roche introduced into the UK a concentrated version of midazolam (10mg/2ml), and soon after it began to learn of serious problems. A report prepared by Roche UK in late 1983 mentioned a market research survey of 12 doctors who had stopped using the drug; five had stopped because of serious side effects including respiratory depression, cardio-vascular instability, excessive sedation - and because of difficulties in giving the right dose. The Roche UK memo noted "Perhaps our thoughts of introducing a new dilution could overcome these problems".

On the surface, nothing much seemed to happen until five years after Roche apparently first recognised the potential dangers involved. Then, in February 1985, the CSM published a note saying it had received reports of seven cases of respiratory depression, including two patients who died. Elderly patients and people with chronic breathing difficulties were most at risk. These patients especially needed lower and precisely titrated doses - and the CSM announced that Roche had responded to their needs by introducing a diluted version of Hypnovel (10mg/5ml as opposed to 10mg/2ml).

Then in April 1986, Roche began marketing midazolam in the US. The drug had a different brand name, Versed, but was also sold as an injectable preparation for pre-anaesthesia. However, the dosage approved in the US was the same as the original UK dosage, and soon the difference showed.

"Inexplicably, the FDA approved a dose of Versed that was one and a half to two times higher than the doses used in Britain. As a result, doctors unwittingly gave their patients toxic doses of this anaesthetic which result in death from depression of breathing and heart function ... Versed had by January 1988 already killed 66 people from cardiac and respiratory depression." [Wolfe (Ed), 1988]

The less concentrated version was then introduced in the US, following criticism which focused mainly on the role of the FDA. But on the strength of the evidence it obtained in 1991, the Health Research Group petitioned the FDA to prosecute both the company and the employees concerned. Specifically, HRG alleged that Roche had failed to report to the FDA - just at the time it was considering the licence application - the details of foreign cases involving serious and fatal adverse effects. Yet again, the jury is out - but in secret session, in the UK.

Benefits and risks

Our case-history on sedative-hypnotic drugs has outlined the origins and the working of a system for making, selling and consuming products - and for understanding, examining and choosing medicinal drugs. These drugs range from very important to trivial and from highly to barely effective - and they carry greater and smaller risks. In the case-history we sought to show that it is not so much the toxicity of the drugs used, as the performance of this system, which defines how safe people are when they take prescribed medicines, and how safe they are entitled to be.

The UK authorities do not accept this approach. They maintain that the risks of drug treatment are very low, and the benefits great, and often the public is chided for failing to understand this: "there is a misconception on the part of much of the public that medicines ought not to produce any toxic or adverse effects"; [8] "there is no question that the public are obsessed with risk and benefit gets relatively little attention"; [9] and "the mirage of a truly safe drug has dominated public expectations". [10] The authorities stress that people need to understand that nothing is risk free, and that "a public that demands progress must be prepared for some risks". [11]

The established literature on risk and benefit tends to be highly economical with the reality; many papers disguise this by adding tables and figures which at a glance seem convincing - but which on close inspection seem no more relevant than Dr Marks' calculations of dependence risk. The data produced compares favourably the risk of an adverse drug reaction with other generally accepted and more remote risks, even being struck by lightning. Perhaps underlining the need for greater fortitude, the Chairman of the CSM has contrasted the risk of a fatal adverse drug reaction (ADR) to the risks for pilots in World War II, who faced an even chance of dying in any one year. [12] Professor Asscher put the risk of a fatal ADR at 1 in 100,000 - but because he specified no units (eg per drug exposure, per year or lifetime) the figure has no real meaning.

The experts and the authorities generally agree that benefits far outweigh risks, though they argue about the exact figures. But the more precise their calculations are, the more meaningless they seems to be - because the numbers used to express risk are based on data which are either missing or highly imprecise. One estimate, for example, has proposed that someone who took no drugs would gain 37 minutes of life, by reducing drug risks to zero - but would lose 15 years, by missing out on the benefits drugs bring. [13] Yet another estimate is critical of this approach - correcting the figures to one week of life saved and a loss of about 5 years. [14] The following statement is bolder than most, but it captures the spirit of the establishment view quite well:

> "In summary it would appear that treatment risks associated with prescription medicines are small (1 in a million on average) compared with many other risks that individuals accept. A glance at travel risks will confirm that the average patient is more likely to be killed in a traffic accident if she drives to the doctor's surgery than by the medicine that the doctor might prescribe. Yet this is no argument for complacency in risk assessment." [OHE, 1986]

On this sort of basis, the Director of the Office of Health Economics, George Teeling-Smith, has estimated that it might cost £55 million to save one life by setting up large-scale clinical trials, to try to define risks more precisely. [15] Such estimates suggest that investments in drug safety would hardly be worth it - but they muddy the water by emphasising only fatal cases rather than all drug injury; by basing estimates of damage on the reported incidence of (notoriously underreported) ADRs; and by overlooking that there are better and cheaper ways of preventing drug injury than by simply increasing the numbers of patients in clinical trials. The sum mentioned by Teeling-Smith would, for example, fund a major national programme of professional education - or more than quadruple the total annual budget of the new Medicines Control Agency, which in 1989 took over responsibility for all drug licensing and inspection.

The question of how much people actually do need and benefit from drug treatment seems every bit as thorny as the question of risk - though it is beyond the scope of this book to do more than mention some caveats about benefit which are often overlooked. One is that drugs, in the long term, and in a variety of ways, may perpetuate or worsen the conditions they are meant to treat. Classic examples are the many aspirin-like drugs, used mainly to treat osteoarthritis in the elderly. Because they effectively relieve the pain caused by natural wear and tear on the joints, they allow patients to overburden the joints still more - though they tend to reduce demand for surgical joint replacement.

The availability of efficacious drugs does not necessarily lead to enlightened social policy. For example, the introduction in the 1950s of more effective treatments for "schizophrenia" (as a result of which "psychopharmacology became, overnight, a bright new discipline in medicine") led directly to policies which were intended to place mentally ill people back into the community - but which left many isolated and destitute instead. [16] The drugs themselves are in no way to blame but, on both sides of the Atlantic, there is cruel evidence of the failure of this policy in prisons and on the streets.

Great as they sometimes are, drug benefits tend to be much exaggerated - with estimates based on limited and idealised data, and typically aggregated to the point where they become meaningless and unhelpful. Of what possible relevance could it be, in making any pertinent assessment of drug benefits and risks, to think in terms of minutes of life gained gained versus years lost?

In the real world, drugs are frequently over-used, poorly prescribed and wrongly taken by patients. They may also stand in the way of better alternatives and interfere with constructive adaptation to ill-health. It is certainly conceivable that the average medical intervention still does more harm than good [17] - even if it is now clear that at least the potential exists for much more good than harm.

In short, drug benefits tend to be assessed no more thoroughly than drug risks. Professional optimism runs deep and sometimes wild; accordingly, patients are expected to be grateful for treatment, and to trust it will be safe. A much quoted opinion is that, "if you don't want to try the risk of the drug, try the risk of disease". [18] This may seem engagingly blunt, but it could equally be seen as a form of emotional blackmail, or even as evidence of the arrogance of power. Either way, it seems absurd to suggest on the basis of the available data that there is a simple choice for the patient between benefit (with drugs) or risk (without them). The reality tends to be much more complicated, as the following example shows.

Many doctors have prescribed phenobarbitone for seizures in children - but would not know that it can cause a condition known as Dupuytren's contracture. As there are many other causes of this complaint, it was that much harder to pin it on the drug, and the suspicions first raised about phenobarbitone in the 1920s [19] did not harden until the 1970s [20] - and were not absolutely confirmed until the late 1980s. [21] Whatever the cause (not usually drugs) Dupuytren's contracture involves progressive deformation of one or more fingers: abnormal (non-malignant) growth of connective tissue causes the affected fingers to curl up close towards the palm.

Mrs N was first prescribed phenobarbitone as a three year old, after a febrile convulsion. That was in the early 1960s, when most children would routinely be treated in this way - though increasingly they are not. Occasional fits in children are not unusual, nor necessarily serious - and there are other reasons for avoiding drug treatment as well. These include "the frequency with which epilepsy is misdiagnosed, the length of time that children are ordinarily left on the drugs after their final seizure, the frequency of toxic blood levels in randomly sampled children, the freneticism with which difficult cases are medicated, and the oft-associated learning disorders..."[22]

Mrs N first noticed some deformation of her finger as a teenager, still on phenobarbitone. She was examined by her GP, but he advised her to sit on it, to try to straighten it out. Her condition deteriorated and two years later she had an operation - but after another three years, still on phenobarbitone, it was much worse. Mrs N was told at that time by a specialist that she needed urgent treatment - and, after a "regrettable" delay of 18 months, she was finally admitted for surgery. Her finger had to be amputated.

For the best part of 30 years, neither she nor her doctors had appreciated that there was any connection between taking phenobarbitone and Dupuytren's contracture. Recognition of this association came too late in the day - for the use of the drug is now declining. It is rare to find any warning in reference books; nor have warnings ever appeared in data sheets. In fact there are no longer any data sheets, because no branded versions of phenobarbitone (tablets) have been actively promoted to doctors since 1988.

Phenobarbitone has for years been the mainstay of drug treatment for young children with febrile seizures - in spite of the known risk of drug dependence and fears of adverse effects on intellectual performance. However, the extent of cognitive impairment has only recently been established. A recent report suggests this is a serious disadvantage, which may long outlast the period of drug administration - and which is not offset by any benefit of seizure prevention.

"In a well controlled study, 217 children under 3 years old, who had had at least one seizure and were at heightened risk of further seizures, were randomly assigned to phenobarbital or placebo. After two years, the mean IQ was 8.4 points lower in the treated group than in the placebo group - and six months later, after tapering off and finally ending drug treatment, the mean IQ was still 5.2 points lower. The proportion of children remaining free of seizures did not differ significantly between the groups. " [Farwell et al, 1990]

The pressures on the system
The UK system of drug control is dedicated to the view that drugs are safe enough, and committed to a belief in great benefit over tiny risk.

It follows that public discussion about the safety of medicines tends to be interpreted by the authorities as potentially dangerous - the rationale being that, if people get worried about risks, they may not take the drugs they need. As the benefits so far outweigh the risks, the argument goes, people should take all medicines they are prescribed, for their own good. This paternalism is one reason for the secrecy in the system; it also explains the official disdain for action groups, the media and press. These include "the so called 'investigative journalists' who flit from story to story leaving a trail of human misery far exceeding any damage that could conceivably have been caused by the products whose reputation they have destroyed" [23]

One central feature of this system is the belief that the safety of medicines is best achieved by making safer drugs - rather than by making drugs safer - and these two objectives often conflict. Making safer drugs is obviously worthwhile, but it is also a much slower, more expensive and less certain road to progress. If the objective is to reduce levels of drug injury now and in the foreseeable future, it must make more sense to try to encourage safer drug use. The extent of avoidable drug injury is not known, but it seems far too high. Few would put a figure on it, though Dr John Griffin (ex-DoH, now ABPI) has tried:

> "All my evidence seems to point to the fact that probably about 20% of adverse reactions that are due to drugs are due to drug interactions. About 20% are due to a 'bad' drug, and the other 60% are due to inappropriate prescribing." [*Scrip*, 1984]

The way in which new drugs are promoted, as if unseen risks could not exist, is a reminder of an important impetus in the system: the perception of drugs as products, and the operation of a market to match. It is a market open to all drugs which can meet basic standards of safety and efficacy, in which all products tend to be promoted as best. The Medicines Act positively requires that a product licence be granted, provided only that a drug is demonstrably more effective than placebo and apparently no less safe than other drugs indicated for the same conditions.

The result is far too many drugs - more than prescribers or patients need, and more than it is possible to use well or even sensible to try to.[24] The Chairman of the CSM himself has acknowledged there could be twice as many products as needed - but so long as the Medicines

Act prohibits comparative efficacy assessments, nothing much can be done about it. [25] In theory, the NHS could decline to purchase drugs that were not needed or wanted - but in practice the idea behind the Limited List proved too bold to pursue. Opposition from the industry (sales), the medical profession (clinical freedom) and in parliament (party allegiance) made this initiative fade away.

Regardless of their different abilities and experience as prescribers, GPs in the NHS are still permitted to prescribe many drugs that hospital specialists would never use. The formularies (drug lists) used in well-organised teaching hospitals often include no more than a quarter of the drugs available to GPs - evidence of the gulf that still exists between clinical freedom and effective prescribing. [26] The present state of play is illustrated by the continued use in general practice of over 200 products which, in the British National Formularly (1991), are formally rated "less suitable for prescribing". Many GPs still prescribe them, so the NHS still pays for them - or is it the other way round ?

There does not at present seem to be much prospect of change from within the system, not least because the DoH acts as the industry's sponsoring department. This means it is the duty of the DoH to promote the trade interests of the pharmaceutical industry, and especially to encourage its export performance. In the early 1980s, the Minister of Health, Kenneth Clarke, tried to transfer this sponsoring role to the Department of Trade - against opposition from his own Department, the Treasury and the pharmaceutical industry. He failed. [27]

The economic importance of the industry's contribution to the UK's balance of trade is considered to be so great that the DoH maintains its dual role to this day. To promote better prescribing, the DoH tries to restrain the industry - but to earn more from abroad (especially from new drugs), the DoH promotes its expansion. There has been no parliamentary scrutiny to examine the conflict between these two objectives and the nature of the compromises involved. A non-partisan (all party) enquiry into sponsorship could help to sort things out.

The main therapeutic justification for having so many products is to invest in better drugs for the future. Another argument, derived from the doctrine of clinical freedom, is to maximise choice - the implication being that you and your doctor can benefit from this great range of products, because just the right drug may be available for you. In practice, no doctor could choose sensibly from among the thousands of products available. Most GPs use only around 100 different drugs - though they have so many different, often irrational, preferences that they can, paradoxically, sustain a true sellers' market, between them.

The sheer number of essentially similar drugs has led to incessant, intense promotional activity - not only an impediment to the rational selection of drugs, but also a stimulus to excessive prescribing. Doctors tend to deny that promotional activities adversely affect their judgement - and that is part of the nub of the problem: doctors tend not to recognise the promotional element in much of what they learn, hear and see. The most corrupting and distracting aspects of drug promotion tend to be the least obvious.

> "So long as commercial promotion is identifiable as such, one can set it quietly aside and proceed with one's studies: but when promotion interferes with the flow of honest observation and opinion or masquerades as scientific evidence (and there is still many an editor and many a physician who will sell his soul for a mess of pottage) it can only impede and protract the analysis." [Dukes, 1977]

When pharmaceutical companies develop products which may bring in tens or hundreds of millions of pounds a year, they invest accordingly to promote them and expect a fast and high return. A company's fortunes, and even its survival, may well depend on the success of just a few products. So the companies tend to monitor their main brands very closely, seeking to control as much as possible of what is printed, said and thought about them.

Major companies run highly sophisticated intelligence departments; they routinely analyse individual doctors' prescribing habits, and systematically collect detailed information about the views of "opinion-formers" and leaders of the profession. In the process, companies help doctors with the right opinions to become more prominent, isolating independent critics at the same time. Drug companies can give formidable opposition - or they may be of great assistance to doctors in their professional work; send them to interesting and enjoyable meetings; enable them to speak and publish; and otherwise reward them well. Promoting doctors has become an integral part of promoting drugs.

Companies constantly feed professional opinion and then rigorously sift it and check it out, in order to reinforce their messages and target their products more effectively. The objective is both to encourage and to reassure and, as part of this process, the companies design, sponsor and write up countless studies and reports on their products. Inevitably, they play a major part in setting standards as they do so, and those standards still seem frighteningly low.

> "If one's first impression of the world's clinical literature is that of its fearsome immensity, one's second is likely to be that of its appallingly poor average quality. The two are obviously interconnected; the drug literature is overburdened by a vast volume of superfluous and even dangerous rubbish. The standards of medical journals ranges from the sublime (of which there are very few) to the disgraceful. No physician, confronted with this literature as a whole from week to week, can be very proud of what his profession is on average producing." [Ibid]

This systematic blurring of the truth is probably the most worrying aspect of drug promotion, because it is so pervasive. But in this competitive environment, there is also naturally a degree of outright malpractice - on occasions extending to bribery and corruption, oppressive treatment of conscientious employees and others, and the suppression and falsification of data. [28] Evidence of the extent of it is lacking, but one private industry estimate (quoted by the former editor of the *BMJ*) has suggested that perhaps 5% of clinical trials cannot be trusted because of misconduct of one form or another. [29]

But, in general, the present system suits the providers quite well. There is a high degree of unity and inter-dependence between them - notably because of the investment each has in perpetuating the view that the benefits of medicines are overwhelming, and that drugs are safe enough. Consumers have traditionally been kept at a distance from this tight alliance of government, industry and the mainstream medical profession - though increasingly since the 1980s, they have begun to challenge it, and to protest.

Still, the providers and receivers seem to be barely talking the same language and often not talking about the same thing. The providers tend to talk about catastrophic risk and say how low the figures are - while the receivers complain about all manner of drug injury, emphasising how much it hurts other people or themselves. This failure to communicate seems to be growing, because each side extrapolates from its own data to an extent that the other considers inexcusable. The providers believe that the public grossly exaggerates risk on the basis of a few published stories - while the public sees enough evidence of harm perhaps to feel quite alarmed when the authorities reflexively respond to news of drug problems by somehow communicating: don't worry, no drug is completely safe, and everything is under control.

Seen from the perspective of someone close to the human burden of drug injury, this attitude might seem dangerously complacent and quite deluded too. This can be appreciated by contrasting the formal report of a near fatal disaster with something closer to the feelings and experience of those most involved.

Our example concerns a much loved first child called Henrietta who, when she was three months old, suddenly became dangerously ill. Henrietta began to convulse and her breathing started to fail - all the more desperate for her parents because they lived deep in the country in Cornwall, with the nearest hospital 20 miles away. Imagine the drive to hospital - Henrietta's father trying to resuscitate her, her mother at the wheel with her hand on the horn - and then consider this cooler account of what went on.

"In 1987, I was contacted by the parents of a 3-month-old baby who had nearly died after treatment of an anal fissure with a [local anaesthetic] ointment containing 5% lignocaine (Xyloproct, Astra Pharmaceuticals Ltd). After several days of treatment, the infant convulsed and suffered respiratory collapse. She recovered after treatment in hospital. This child's parents wished to warn other doctors and parents of what appears to be a rare but potentially dangerous outcome, especially in infants and children. On their behalf I approached the CSM and the Association of the British Pharmaceutical Industry (ABPI) - in particular to complain about the data sheet for this product, which states that 'There are no known contraindications or side effects'. My complaint was that there were indeed known contraindications and side effects - and that, even if there were not, this was an unacceptable statement to make about any active drug.

"The Secretary of the ABPI's Code of Practice Committee pointed out that the content of data sheets (which are legally considered to be advertisements) are not covered by the industry's code of marketing practice. He also saw no objection in principle to the wording complained of.

"By contrast, the CSM agreed that the statement 'there are no known contraindications or side effects' was 'not generally acceptable'. The Committee also said these words had in fact been deleted from the Xyloproct data sheet in a review of the product made in 1985. However, 'through an oversight', Astra had omitted to change the data sheet so that the old and 'wrong' version will continue to appear in the ABPI's Data Sheet Compendium until 1989-90. The CSM said that 'The Department will be writing to the company about this'."

"The revised but unpublished data sheet for Xyloproct in fact still mentions nothing of the potential dangers of topical lignocaine, especially in neonates and infants, except for the unsurprising warning against the use in cases of 'known sensitivity' to this or that related local anaesthetics, suggesting also that this product 'is intended for use for limited periods'. The data sheet fails to say either why or for how long this might be [Medawar, 1988].

Present-day controls

The Medicines Control Agency (MCA) was set up in 1989, to take over the work of the old licensing division of the DoH. This change resulted from a review of the control of medicines - prompted mainly by industry complaints about delays in the licensing process which were eroding the patent life on new drugs. The review led to a streamlining of the approval process, but no other major change: it was concluded that the Medicines Act had worked well and that Britain had an enviable record in this field, "thanks not least to excellent professional judgement on benefit and risk". [30]

The MCA, still in the process of transition to full Executive Agency status, is run essentially as a business - mainly funded by the large fees that companies pay for licence applications. The new agency appears to be much more efficient than its predecessor, though at a price. The MCA even charges a £250 fee for admission to its annual meeting (ensuring overwhelming attendance by company representatives) and then has the gall to suggest that this might be an occasion to call it to account. Democracy has come to this ?

"The Agency wishes to hear and take account of the views of those to whom it provides services. Both morning and afternoon sessions will allow time for questions and views on any issues relating to the control of medicines in the UK." [Medicines Control Agency, 1991]

Together, the MCA and the CSM continue to work in almost complete secrecy - making it impossible to assess overall performance, or even to appreciate the significance of the bits of data that are released from time to time. Without detailed information, how would one decide, for example, whether to be concerned or reassured that about 60% of licence applications are turned down for lack of evidence of safety and efficacy ? [31] This could on the one hand suggest that the authorities have their critical faculties intact; on the other hand, it might seem worrying that many companies try to introduce so many new compounds on the basis of inadequate data.

In practice, there is no clear and sharp dividing line between acceptable and unacceptable evidence of drug efficacy and safety - any more than there are clear distinctions to be made between acceptable and unacceptable levels of drug risk. Much of the decision-making is about issues that can go one way or another; comparisons between different licensing authorities can reveal quite different ways of thinking, as the following example shows.

Fluoxetine (Prozac, Lilly) was first licensed in Belgium in 1986. It was launched the US in 1988 (and much hyped in the lay press) and introduced into the UK the following year. In the US it is indicated "for the treatment of depression", and in the UK for "the treatment of the symptoms of depressive illness, especially where sedation is not required" - the implication being that the drug might allow the UK user to lead a more normal life. However, the range of known psychiatric side effects suggests a drug which produces a markedly different response in different individuals. The response seems to range from feelings of drowsiness and fatigue in some patients, to nervousness, anxiety and insomnia in others

- with about 5% of all patients in pre-marketing clinical trials experiencing psychiatric side effects severe enough to stop taking the drug.

However, in 1991, the authorities in Norway and Sweden both turned down Lilly's application for a licence for fluoxetine. They outlined their reasons for this in a manner which, in the UK, might have attracted a criminal prosecution and a prison sentence of up to two years.

"The objections were that questions on the dosage for the treatment of depression had not been answered satisfactorily ... a published study had shown good antidepressant effects with doses as low as 5mg daily in nine patients, while the manufacturer recommended 20mg rising to 60-80mg. Since the product was only available in 20mg capsules there was no opportunity for adjusting the dose for individual needs." [Scrip, 1991]. [32]

Equally, the issues may be so fine that there can be basic disagreements between members of the same authority. But again, because of the shroud of secrecy, one cannot know how often this happens: as a rule, a drug is either licensed or not, with restrictions on use spelled out in data sheets. However, a recent leak [33] did reveal how close the voting can sometimes go.

Xamoterol (Corwin, ICI) was first licensed for the treatment of chronic heart failure in March 1988, and was promoted as "breathing new life into heart failure therapy". The data sheet listed no absolute contra-indications for use, and claimed "Corwin is well tolerated and adverse experiences are uncommon". Investment analysts voted it "the most outstanding new product of the year".

In the meantime, ICI had set up a study to monitor the effects of xamoterol on patients with severe symptoms of chronic heart failure - apparently seeking a further, specific indication for use. But this study was stopped in May 1989, when it was found that severely-affected patients were 2.5 times more likely to die than similar patients on placebo. The CSM was informed; ICI sent out a Dear Doctor letter in August 1989; and the data sheet was amended to warn against use in severe cases of chronic heart failure.

The question was, and still is: how safe was it to indicate a drug for use in mild and moderate forms of a disease - but to contraindicate its use in severe cases ? How
safe is safe, when degrees of severity of illness are poorly
defined, and when there is always the possibility of a
worsening of the disease ? Early in 1990, the CSM voted
on the issue: some members argued that xamoterol was
not safe enough and should be withdrawn, but the
majority favoured more warnings. Thus, in May 1990,
the CSM published a note on xamoterol in one of its
series of leaflets, Current Problems, and the data sheet
was amended once again.

It seems unlikely that this is an isolated example and probably
there are other drugs on the market which some members of the CSM
think should be withdrawn. However, the wider point is that Corwin
kept its licence because the majority on the CSM seem to subscribe to
the view that a drug's benefits and risks should be calculated on an
'ideal use' basis - assuming that prescribing standards will comply
strictly with data sheet terms. Such a policy has no proper scientific
basis, and must increase the risk of drug injury.

The limitations of these policies are underlined both by deficiencies
in data sheets, and by the natural reluctance of many doctors to study
them. A private survey in the UK (1990) suggested that a quarter of
doctors may never refer to the ABPI's *Data Sheet Compendium*, while
only about a third rate it very useful. By contrast, published surveys
indicate that the average doctor in the US consults the *Physicians Desk
Reference* ten times a week or more. [34] Patients also consult it: 14 million households in the US own a copy of the PDR, and twice that
number consult it. [35]

A further weakness of the CSM's 'ideal use' policy is the lack of any
systematic monitoring of prescribing standards - so there is no good
way of knowing how well warnings get through. The result is a high
degree of reliance on the Yellow Card system, plus the risks of delay.
But as our next example shows, even high and sustained levels of
ADR reporting do not necessarily lead to effective data sheet warnings, nor to appropriate restrictions on drug use.

Fenbufen (Lederfen, Lederle) has probably attracted
more Yellow Cards than any other drug - 80% of reports
being about adverse reactions affecting the skin. Fen-

Why should gastroenterologists recommend Lederfen in arthritis?

fenbufen

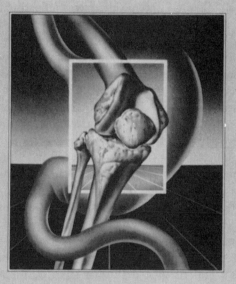

Because Lederfen has efficacy uncompromised by serious gastrointestinal side effects

bufen is one of many aspirin-like drugs used to treat osteo-arthritis and related painful conditions; it has a tidy stake in what is the most lucrative sector of the whole drugs market.

Fenbufen was introduced in 1980: the data sheet said it was well tolerated, though there was a fleeting reference to infrequent skin rashes and other minor reactions. In the meantime, the Yellow Cards kept coming - until the 1985 data sheet quietly introduced a radical new concept in prescribing: "Lederfen treatment should be discontinued immediately on appearance of a rash."

But still the Yellow Cards kept coming - which in itself was most unusual because, as the CSM later acknowledged: "Adverse reaction reporting rates for a drug tend to be highest in the first two years following marketing and then decline". [36] But the CSM had received more reports about fenbufen than any other drug on the market both in 1986 and 1987. This was not disclosed until September 1988, when there was a note in a Current Problems leaflet saying that a total of 6,000 Yellow Cards had been received, and that "some reactions have been serious". This prompted another spate of Yellow Cards, prompting a further note in Current Problems, in January 1989.

In the meantime, the data sheet was changed a bit, but it hardly reflected the very unusual profile of this drug - nor that the long-term drop-out rate due to ADRs might range from 12 to 22%. [37] It is also significant that the data sheet (1990/1991) indicated no reason for choosing fenbufen over many alternative drugs - which in turn raises a basic question about the interpretation of law. If a drug is mainly distinguished from many other painkillers by the number of Yellow Cards it spawns, on what basis does it hold a licence at all, let alone as a first-line drug ? This question seems all the more relevant, since fenbufen is not sold in the US, where the manufacturers are based - and because, in the UK, Lederle continues to promote fenbufen by claiming pretty categorically that it has no serious effects on the gut.

The wider question is how much the authorities should rely on Yellow Card reports and post-marketing studies - rather than on scrutinising licence applications and by commissioning and following up relevant reports. This was also a key question in the Corwin case: why hadn't the drug been tested on patients with severe heart failure before the licence was given ? This question goes to the heart of the present drug licensing and control system - and its considerable reliance on post-marketing data. This policy seems to be linked to more liberal licensing standards for more innovative drugs - though the risks of these new drugs are least understood. [38]

The official view is that scrutiny of a drug licence application can do no more than detect gross risks; and that actual risks can be determined only after a drug has been licensed and used by many patients, perhaps for many years. Albeit using a meaningless statistic (no units), the CSM has explained to doctors: "Perhaps only one patient in 1,000 will experience a severe adverse reaction from their medication. Such incidents are so rare that the pharmaceutical industry's clinical trials cannot be expected to detect them." [39]

But the problem is not only that some adverse reactions are rare. Many ADRs involve illness which also arise from other causes - and the greater the background incidence of such an illness (ie normal prevalence in the community), the less likely it is to be identified as a drug side effect. Thus, psychiatric symptoms (eg mental confusion, depression, anxiety) may be especially hard to detect - although even unusual but obvious physical signals (eg Dupuytren's contracture) may also be overlooked. Post-marketing surveillance is therefore an important part of drug safety - but is it not relied on too much, in relation to the kind of scrutiny given to a licence application? Consider, for example, the case of nomifensine (Merital, Hoechst).

> Merital was an antidepressant drug first licensed in the UK in 1977, and withdrawn worldwide in 1986. The CSM has cited this case as "a prime example of how the yellow card reporting system can provide important information even when a drug has been widely used for several years without causing undue suspicion". [40]
>
> "On the contrary, there had been suspicions about nomifensine since 1979. By then, Hoechst was sufficiently worried by reports of immune haemolytic anaemia among nomifensine users to launch a European surveil-

lance programme to study the immunological complications. In mid-1982, Hoechst collaborated with Swiss scientists to investigate circulating drug-specific antibodies in nomifensine-treated patients. The results, published in December 1983, showed specific antibodies to nomifensine in all [41] patients who had side effects to the drug, and also in 10 who had received the drug with no side effects. These findings suggested that nomifensine was highly immunogenic, apparently more so than any other drug then on the market.

"Much of this information came to light in a US Senate inquiry held in May 1986, that examined the circumstances in which the US Food and Drug Administration (FDA) had licensed nomifensine. This inquiry revealed that the FDA had refused to license the drug in 1979 and again in 1981, largely because of lack of evidence of efficacy. By 1984, the FDA was proposing to grant marketing approval but, because of some worrying reports of drug-associated fevers in nomifensine patients, to restrict the drug to second-line use. In a well-established antidepressant market, such a restriction would have made nomifensine commercially unviable and, not surprisingly, Hoechst objected strongly.

"Finally, the FDA approved nomifensine, along with a batch of other drugs, on Dec 31, 1984 - apparently in part to top up its annual approval figures. Meanwhile in May 1984, Hoechst had withdrawn its application to the Swedish Board of Drugs for approval for nomifensine after the Board had concluded that the drug was less efficacious than existing antidepressants and carried an unacceptably high risk of drug-induced immune reactions." [*Lancet*, 1988]

The demise of this drug in the UK began late in the day - in July 1985, when the CSM published a note about 33 Yellow Cards on nomifensine, including three fatal reports. It was probably this and other publicity which prompted a surge of reports which finally led to the drug's (voluntary) withdrawal. By then, the CSM had about 600 Yellow Cards (all suspected ADRs) but, apart from the continuing emphasis on this as a success story, not much more is known. There never have been public enquiries into such matters in the UK - so questions about such things as efficacy standards, literature awareness, company reporting requirements, contact with other regulatory agencies, and reliance on the Yellow Card scheme remain unanswered to this day. [42]

By contrast, the US Senate committee's report examined the FDA's performance in detail. As a result, the Agency was censured, and Hoechst was accused of withholding from the FDA important information, including notification of many serious and fatal ADRs. [42] After nearly five years of legal wrangling, the company agreed to pay a $202,000 fine, on two counts of unintentionally failing to report to the US authorities the details of side effects experienced by two patients who took the drug in Europe. [43]

This degree of reliance on spontaneous reports of ADRs also seems worrying because the Yellow Card scheme has gained very little acceptance by most doctors: the CSM's own figures suggest that over 80% never report ADRs at all. [44] Nor do most Post Marketing Surveillance studies appear to be of much use. An analysis of over 60 company-sponsored PMS initiatives suggests that "such schemes show no evidence of being able to detect new ADRs, nor do they offer any prospect of being able to advance the methodology". [45] This was the conclusion of Dr Myles Stevens of the International Drug Surveillance Department of Glaxo Group Research Ltd.

"Some of the factors which may have been responsible for these PMS schemes not detecting ADRs include; inadequate numbers, short duration of monitoring; collection of ADRs rather than adverse events; delay in onset of the ADR; delay in recognition of the ADR. There is no published evidence indicating that company-sponsored PMS schemes have revealed previously unknown ADRs." [Stevens, 1988]

Studies and trials conducted along these lines are a commonplace. They could simply be regarded as evidence of omission, reflecting badly on both the sponsors and on the sponsoring department - for the DoH accepts evidence of this quality in support of licence applications. However, one might also interpret this as evidence of a more or less unconscious grand design to demonstrate the safety of medicines by failing to seriously examine the risks.

Warnings and question marks

Data sheets still tend to reflect these failings. Most of them seem second or third rate, and some are pitiful. It does not seem surprising that most doctors look to other sources of prescribing information, as they will probably continue to do until the quality of data sheets improves.

The data sheet ought to be a definitive statement about how a drug should be used and what effects it may have. It should provide relevant, factual information, readily usable both as a learning tool and as a reference for doctors. It ought to contain indispensable information, all of which doctors should be expected (if not required) to understand before prescribing any drug. A data sheet ought to be uniquely reliable, fairly reflecting both what is known and not understood about the drug, and it should reflect the place of the drug in therapeutics as well.

A data sheet should convey the knowledge of the manufacturer, the collective experience of doctors, the wisdom of regulators and the care due to patients. Its purpose is to communicate essential and important information; to set standards for safe and effective prescribing; and to define limits for promoting a drug's use. Most data sheets fall far short of these standards; they also suffer from the weakness inherent in the law in failing to provide the comparative prescribing information that doctors really need.

The very design of data sheets gives them away. They are physically unappealing, clearly never conceived as tools that doctors need to use to protect patients. There is minimal signposting to crucial bits of information. There is nothing to see when new information has been added - nothing to distinguish what is more from what is less well known. Data sheets tend to be impenetrable and confused, mainly because they have been developed as legal instruments as well as therapeutic guidelines. As a medical text, the data sheet provides some information about the product - but because it is also a legal document, doctors may have to look very hard indeed to understand what a drug is really all about.

Part of what the drug is about is being a product, and data sheets quietly reflect this too. Products have to survive - so data sheets express confidence in them, above all keeping awkward questions out of sight and mind. There are no question marks in data sheets, though medicine is full of them. Data sheets avoid reflecting difficulties and uncertainties, because they are torn between different commitments. They are marketing instruments, as well as therapeutic and legal tools.

Caught between these uneasy objectives, data sheets have evolved as symbols of the triumph of obfuscation over clarity. What is becoming clearer and clearer in medicine is how much is not known, and how much more there is to learn - and data sheets do a wonderful job of concealing this. They disguise uncertainty by being sometimes pompous and often verbose; but also through understatement, abbreviation and omission. Soft data relating to benefits tend to be presented in a more robust and ebullient style - while discussion of risk is sometimes so brief as to seem almost airy. In some of the language and style, there are echoes of estate agency (each drug having the most desirable properties and unique advantages etc) - and also of undertakers (deferential verging on unctuous, but very remote). Data sheets, in their own way, reflect the basic instinct in medicine to hide uncertainty and to disguise bad news.

Data sheets do seem to be slowly getting better, but information retrieval is often still a nightmare. In particular, the parts of data sheets that discuss risks have evolved essentially as statements in code - perhaps meaningful for the authorities and companies concerned, but not for most doctors. Data sheets seem to have emerged as part of a contract between industry and government, rather than as clear instructions for use - the model for the US label. All too often, it seems as if statements in data sheets are 'not incompatible' with the evidence of safety and efficacy reviewed by the licensing authorities - just as advertisements are required by law to be "not incompatible" with the terms of data sheets. Misunderstandings can therefore arise at every point.

Under present law, it is not clear who should do what about this. Standards for data sheets have been developed piecemeal: their overall function has been only vaguely defined, and it is still far from clear who is really responsible for what they say. The terms of the Medicines Act leave the companies thinking that the government is responsible - while government has largely devolved responsibility to the companies themselves. The buck never stops.

Data sheets in their own way reflect the nature of the secrecy that underpins medicines control in the UK. They keep secrets by gently obscuring things, by leaving stones unturned, and letting doubts slip through the cracks. Data sheets tend to be studiedly cautious in discussing risk, to an extent which seems unsafe.

The culture of secrecy

Secrecy involves more than the systematic withholding of information: it is also a mentality and part of a culture. It is second nature wherever the first is power: endemic in government, and rampant in the system of medicines control. The secrecy in this system obscures, divides and rules. For the providers it helps in the struggle for independence and power - but like a side effect, it also creates and sustains the dependence of consumers.

As if to symbolise the dedication of this system to secrecy, the DoH publishes news about product licences granted, suspended or revoked in the columns of the most obscure and inaccessible organ, the *London Gazette*. The names of the drugs involved are to be found among long lists of bankruptcies and planning notices, and of the names of people in the postal and military services awarded Imperial Service Medals and the like.

The underlying reason for all this is that s.118 of the Medicines Act prohibits intelligent public discussion about the thinking behind licensing decisions. In the US and other countries - and perhaps before long in the EC - the authorities outline their reasons for granting a product licence in a document called the Summary Basis of Approval. In the UK, the authorities do not explain themselves, and prefer not to. This is especially true when more sensitive issues are involved - as anything to do with drug safety always is. Secrecy means not explaining things, and sometimes refusing to even to discuss them:

> "In the UK 105 medicinal products have had their licences withdrawn (suspended or revoked) since January 1st 1979, according to a parliamentary reply by Health Minister Tony Newton. A list of these products is to be placed in the House of Commons Library. In addition, for a variety of reasons, 15,645 product licences have been surrendered by companies, or have lapsed since that date. Mr Newton told Jack Ashley MP that a list of products where safety was identified by the licence

holder as a reason for product withdrawal could be produced 'only at disproportionate cost'." [SCRIP, 1988]

Such answers duck and fudge the issues. In this case, the issue is what the licensing authorities know about the safety of different medicines, not what the licence holder says - but either way, the official answer is that the facts are not worth finding out. This answer also obscures the point that, when the authorities become aware of safety problems, they will not usually revoke the product licence - instead, they invite the licence holder to withdraw voluntarily, to reduce pressure for any public explanation. However, this policy seems now to be changing: but secrecy seems to have increased.

Until mid-1988, product licences were suspended or revoked by the authorities at an average rate of about ten a year. Over the next three years, no drug lost its licence (until Upjohn refused to withdraw Halcion, in October 1991). This statistically significant change of policy coincided with the setting up of the Medicines Control Agency - but may also have been due to the increase in drug-injury litigation, and notably the high-profile class actions over the benzodiazepines, Opren (benoxaprofen) and Factor VIII (for haemophilia) contaminated with HIV.

For whatever reasons, the authorities appear to have become even more cautious about what they say and do. This is reflected not only in licensing decisions and in the terms of data sheets, but sometimes also in statements straight from the horse's mouth. As warnings, some CSM statements may seem almost incomprehensible, unless read entirely between the lines - as this next example shows.

Fenoterol (Berotec, Boehringer-Ingelheim) is an asthma drug, supplied in a metered-dose aerosol which delivers a precise dose per puff. It is a bronchodilator: it causes widening of air passages by relaxing bronchial muscle.

From about the mid-1980s, reports mainly from New Zealand (where this drug was much used) implicated fenoterol in sudden deaths from asthma. The evidence was not conclusive but it led the *Drug & Therapeutics Bulletin* [1990] to advise that "while doubts about fenoterol remain unresolved, it seems wise to avoid using it". A similar drug, salbutamol, was suggested as an alternative, as it did not seem to be implicated in any problem there might be.

Nearly a year later, the CSM announced in a *Current Problems* leaflet that a new half-strength formulation of Berotec had been introduced, and that the recommended usual dose of fenoterol had been halved. But there was no explanation, and no suggestion of any connection between dose and adverse effects. The only thing the CSM said was: "There is considerable evidence that fenoterol ... is an effective bronchodilator at doses lower than have been recommended previously. In consequence, the dosage recommendations have been revised". [46]

A new maximimum dose was recommended (800mcg/day) which was at the low end of the original recommended dosage range (600-1200mcg/day) - which the data sheet had previously described as "usually sufficient" for adults. Many patients had for years been taking an apparently excessive dosage, but the implications of this were never discussed.

The secrecy we are complaining of tends to protect the product more than the conscientious prescriber or his/her patients. It aids and abets misrepresentation and misunderstanding, and lack of proper accountability. It seems as dangerous as it is pervasive: minimal and insufficient information is available about the process of product assessment and evaluation; policy-making relating to risk and benefit; and about the interpretation and enforcement of law. And this secrecy goes much further than it needs.

"Much of what you (and I) seek would require repeal of section 118 of the Medicines Act which is the section concerned with secrecy. A small part of individual [licence] applications might be regarded as commercially confidential but the major proportion could, with little loss to anyone, be made publicly available. Similarly, I see no objection to Committee's papers being publicly available ... [CSM member, 1991]

We may at least conclude that the safety of (people who take) medicines remains in essence something of a mystery and an illusion. It might seem unfair to describe it as a sham, but it certainly seems shaming that so much evidence of drug risks is hidden - with much of it secreted to an extent which would be quite unacceptable (and illegal) in countries with freedom of information laws. All we can safely say is, that sooner or later, things will change here too - but not until enough of us insist.

1 Drug & Ther Bull, 1974; Nebert, 1981; Brit Med J, 1981; Goedde, 1986; Jacqz et al, 1986
2 WHO, 1983
3 Lancet, 1991
4 Hodgkin 1991
5 Robertson, 1988
6 Medawar, 1988
7 Public Citizen, 1991
8 McMahon, 1983
9 Burley, 1986
10 Lancet, 1981
11 Asscher, 1986
12 Asscher, 1985
13 SCRIP, 1987a
14 SCRIP, 1987b
15 Scrip, 1982
16 Thomas, 1983
17 Illich, 1976
18 Asscher, 1985
19 Maillard & Renard, 1925
20 Critchley et al., 1976; Laidlaw & Richens, 1982
21 Mattson et al, 1989
22 Werry, 1988
23 Inman, 1985
24 Ridley, 1986
25 Asscher, 1985
26 Hampton, 1983
27 Medawar, 1984
28 Medawar, 1989
29 Lock, 1988
30 Evans & Cunliffe, 1988
31 Rawlins & Jeffrys, 1991
32 Also: SCRIP, October 1990
33 Erlichman, 1990
34 Medical Economics Co, 1988
35 CBS, 1984
36 Committee on Safety of Medicines, 1988
37 Dukes (Ed), 1988
38 Rawlins & Jeffrys, 1991
39 SCRIP 1985,
40 Committee on Safety of Medicines, 1986
41 Rassaby 1988
42 US Senate, 1986
43 SCRIP 1991
44 Griffin, 1984; SCRIP, April 1985
45 SCRIP, 1987
46 Committee on Safety of Medicines, 1991

WHERE DO WE GO FROM HERE?

Reporting gut reactions

Is this a true and fair account, or not ? Is there really much wrong and enough concern about it ? Are there in fact much better, safer ways of doing things and could they ever really work ? To try to get round answers to these questions, we are are inviting readers (strictly in their personal capacities) to respond on one of the four tear-out Grey Cards (gut reaction report forms) that follow. If you feel like sending us a Grey Card (by FREEPOST) we would be very grateful; it would take just a few minutes of your time.

On one side of the Grey Card, we ask for a quick response (agree or not) to any of the following propositions.

1 There is not as much wrong with pharmaceutical medicine as this book suggests.

2 The safety of medicines depends on greater openness, scrutiny and public accountability.

3 The medicines control system deserves public trust.

4 The pharmaceutical industry can be relied on to put its own house in order.

5 The quality of drug prescribing is not nearly good enough.

6 Where standards of prescribing are too low, this is not the fault of the pharmaceutical companies.

7 Review and reform of medicines law is essential.

8 Much could be done to reduce levels of iatrogenic disease.

As well as seeking a response on these points, we want to encourage spontaneous reporting along the lines of the Yellow Card scheme. Just as Yellow Cards may help to spot adverse drug reactions, so Grey Cards might help to identify unsafe policies or practices.

On the other side of the Grey Card, there is space for any comments - an opportunity to identify any issue relating to the safety of medicine that particularly concerns you. It could be something to do with this book, or something else you think should be looked into or more widely aired. However you want to use the Grey Card, we would be very pleased to hear from you. All replies will be treated in strict confidence.

Social Audit will analyse Grey Cards, and report back what they say. We will profile all messages in such a way as to protect identities, and to secure improvements rather than focus blame. Our aim will be to identify and classify concerns, and to learn more about the extent and patterns of behaviour which seem to promote ill-health.

This will not be easy because (as you have read) ill-health may result from acts of omission as well as commission, and even when there is plainly good intent. Some conduct may be clearly unacceptable (eg data falsification, bribery), but often the issues are less clear cut (eg what is the probable risk to health of a particular method of promotion, or the message in an advertisement?) Issues which arouse concern may result from untypical and abnormal behaviour - or they may be linked to familiar and established practices (eg failure to communicate or give space; oppression of conscience).

We think such a confidential reporting scheme might help to air concerns. Just as patients may come under great pressure if they criticise their treatment - so can individuals within the providing sector who are critical of the organisations, professions and teams with which they associate. Such pressures - and the often dire consequences for isolated individuals who draw attention even to serious malpractice or major problems [1] [2] [3] - suggest the need for a cooperative and confidential reporting scheme. The value of a full-scale scheme might well lie in its protective and deterrent effects, as well by operating as an information exchange.

Social Audit will run this Grey Card scheme until the end of 1992 - and will seek to extend it thereafter if there is sufficient interest and support. If you give us your name and address (in strict confidence) we will send you in due course a free report of the analysis of Grey Cards received.

1 Adams, 1984
2 Beardshaw, 1981
3 Winfield, 1990

GREY CARDS

Please use both sides of this **GREY CARD** to report reactions to this book, and/or air any concern (see pages 248 and 249). **Send it to Social Audit Ltd, FREEPOST, PO Box 111, London NW1 0YW**

Please tick the appropriate box to indicate how much you agree or disagree with each of the following propositions

	Strongly agree	Agree	Neither agree nor disagree	Disagree	Strongly disagree
1 There is not as much wrong with pharmaceutical companies as this book suggests	☐	☐	☐	☐	☐
2 The safety of medicines depends on greater openness, scrutiny and public accountability	☐	☐	☐	☐	☐
3 The medicines control system deserves public trust	☐	☐	☐	☐	☐
4 The pharmaceutical industry can be relied upon to put its own house in order	☐	☐	☐	☐	☐
5 The quality of drug prescribing is not nearly good enough	☐	☐	☐	☐	☐
6 Where standards of prescribing are too low, this is not the fault of the pharmaceutical companies	☐	☐	☐	☐	☐
7 Review and reform of medicines law seems essential	☐	☐	☐	☐	☐
8 Much could be done to reduce levels of iatrogenic disease	☐	☐	☐	☐	☐

To help us analyse Grey Card reports, please give some information about yourself. It will be treated IN THE STRICTEST CONFIDENCE

Name..

Address..

....

Tel no (may we?)...............................

If you have professional experience in any of these areas, please indicate how many years'

Clinical practice ....

Medical research ....

Pharmaceutical industry ....

Health care administration ....

Government (re health care) ....

Consumer protection and law ....

Other ....

Please briefly indicate your speciality (eg GP, retail pharmacist) and/or the capacity (eg patient) in which you write

....

....

Please use this space for further comment or to outline any particular issue of concern

Please use both sides of this **GREY CARD** to report reactions to this book, and/or air any concern (see pages 248 and 249). **Send it to Social Audit Ltd, FREEPOST, PO Box 111, London NW1 0YW**

Please tick the appropriate box to indicate how much you agree or disagree with each of the following propositions

	Strongly agree	Agree	Neither agree nor disagree	Disagree	Strongly disagree
1 There is not as much wrong with pharmaceutical companies as this book suggests	☐	☐	☐	☐	☐
2 The safety of medicines depends on greater openness, scrutiny and public accountability	☐	☐	☐	☐	☐
3 The medicines control system deserves public trust	☐	☐	☐	☐	☐
4 The pharmaceutical industry can be relied upon to put its own house in order	☐	☐	☐	☐	☐
5 The quality of drug prescribing is not nearly good enough	☐	☐	☐	☐	☐
6 Where standards of prescribing are too low, this is not the fault of the pharmaceutical companies	☐	☐	☐	☐	☐
7 Review and reform of medicines law seems essential	☐	☐	☐	☐	☐
8 Much could be done to reduce levels of iatrogenic disease	☐	☐	☐	☐	☐

To help us analyse Grey Card reports, please give some information about yourself. It will be treated IN THE STRICTEST CONFIDENCE

Name..........

Address..........

....

Tel no (may we?)..........

If you have professional experience in any of these areas, please indicate how many years'

Clinical practice ....
Medical research ....
Pharmaceutical industry ....
Health care administration ....
Government (re health care) ....
Consumer protection and law ....
Other.......... ....

Please briefly indicate your speciality (eg GP, retail pharmacist) and/or the capacity (eg patient) in which you write

....

....

Please use this space for further comment or to outline any particular issue of concern

Please use both sides of this **GREY CARD** to report reactions to this book, and/or air any concern (see pages 248 and 249). **Send it to Social Audit Ltd, FREEPOST, PO Box 111, London NW1 0YW**

Please tick the appropriate box to indicate how much you agree or disagree with each of the following propositions

	Strongly agree	Agree	Neither agree nor disagree	Disagree	Strongly disagree
1 There is not as much wrong with pharmaceutical companies as this book suggests	☐	☐	☐	☐	☐
2 The safety of medicines depends on greater openness, scrutiny and public accountability	☐	☐	☐	☐	☐
3 The medicines control system deserves public trust	☐	☐	☐	☐	☐
4 The pharmaceutical industry can be relied upon to put its own house in order	☐	☐	☐	☐	☐
5 The quality of drug prescribing is not nearly good enough	☐	☐	☐	☐	☐
6 Where standards of prescribing are too low, this is not the fault of the pharmaceutical companies	☐	☐	☐	☐	☐
7 Review and reform of medicines law seems essential	☐	☐	☐	☐	☐
8 Much could be done to reduce levels of iatrogenic disease	☐	☐	☐	☐	☐

To help us analyse Grey Card reports, please give some information about yourself. It will be treated IN THE STRICTEST CONFIDENCE

Name..............................

Address..............................

....

....

Tel no (may we?)..........................

If you have professional experience in any of these areas, please indicate how many years'

Clinical practice ....

Medical research ....

Pharmaceutical industry ....

Health care administration ....

Government (re health care) ....

Consumer protection and law ....

Other...........

Please briefly indicate your speciality (eg GP, retail pharmacist) and/or the capacity (eg patient) in which you write

....

....

Please use this space for further comment or to outline any particular issue of concern

Please use both sides of this **GREY CARD** to report reactions to this book, and/or air any concern (see pages 248 and 249). **Send it to Social Audit Ltd, FREEPOST, PO Box 111, London NW1 0YW**

Please tick the appropriate box to indicate how much you agree or disagree with each of the following propositions	Strongly agree	Agree	Neither agree nor disagree	Disagree	Strongly disagree
1 There is not as much wrong with pharmaceutical companies as this book suggests	☐	☐	☐	☐	☐
2 The safety of medicines depends on greater openness, scrutiny and public accountability	☐	☐	☐	☐	☐
3 The medicines control system deserves public trust	☐	☐	☐	☐	☐
4 The pharmaceutical industry can be relied upon to put its own house in order	☐	☐	☐	☐	☐
5 The quality of drug prescribing is not nearly good enough	☐	☐	☐	☐	☐
6 Where standards of prescribing are too low, this is not the fault of the pharmaceutical companies	☐	☐	☐	☐	☐
7 Review and reform of medicines law seems essential	☐	☐	☐	☐	☐
8 Much could be done to reduce levels of iatrogenic disease	☐	☐	☐	☐	☐

To help us analyse Grey Card reports, please give some information about yourself. It will be treated IN THE STRICTEST CONFIDENCE

Name.................................

Address..............................

....

....

Tel no (may we?)....................

If you have professional experience in any of these areas, please indicate how many years'

Clinical practice ....

Medical research ....

Pharmaceutical industry ....

Health care administration ....

Government (re health care) ....

Consumer protection and law ....

Other.................................

Please briefly indicate your speciality (eg GP, retail pharmacist) and/or the capacity (eg patient) in which you write

....

....

Please use this space for further comment or to outline any particular issue of concern

BIBLIOGRAPHY

ABPI (Association of the British Pharmaceutical Industry); Code of practice for the pharmaceutical industry; 1st Edition, 1958; 2nd, 1962; 3rd, 1967, revised 1969; 5th, 1978, revised 1982, 1983; 6th, 1984, revised 1986, 1988; 7th, 1988.

- Data Sheet Compendium (annually); [London: Datapharm Publications Ltd, 1972 - 1990/91]

- statement on Social Audit report; press release, 29 October 1980.

- comments on the new edition of the BNF; press release, January 1981.

- Information to patients on medicines [London: ABPI, 1987].

Abrahams MJ; Armstrong J, Whitlock FA: Drug dependence in Brisbane; Med J Aust, 29 August 1970, 397-404.

Adams BG,   Horder EJ, Horder JP et al: Patients receiving barbiturates in an urban general practice. J Coll Gen Practit, 1966, 12, 24-31.

Adams S: Roche versus Adams [London: Jonathon Cape, 1984]

Aivazian GH: Clinical evaluation of diazepam; Dis Nerv Sys; August 1964, 491-6.

Alexander EJ: Withdrawal effects of sodium amytal; Dis Nerv System, 12, 1951, 77-82.

Allen S, Oswald I: Anxiety and sleep and fosazepam; Brit J Clin Pharmac, 1976, 3, 165-8.

Allgulander C: Dependence on sedative and hypnotic drugs; Acta Psychiat Scand, 1978, Supp 270.

American Medical Association Council on Drugs: New Drugs; [Chicago, American Medical Association, 1966]. See also: JAMA, February 28, 1966, 195, 9, 149.

- (Committee on Alcoholism and Addiction and Council on Mental Health): Dependence on barbiturates and other sedative drugs; JAMA, 23 August 1965, 193, 8, 107-111.

- AMA New Drugs [Chicago: AMA, 1966]

Anderson AA: Zopiclone and nitrazepam: a multicenter placebo controlled comparative study of efficacy and tolerance in insomniac patients in general practice; Sleep, 1987, 10 Suppl. 1, 54-62.

Anderson RM: The use of repeatedly prescribed medicines; J Roy Coll Gen Practit, October 1980, 609-163.

Anstie FE: Physiological and therapeutical action of alcohol; Lancet, 23 September 1865, 343.

- The hypodermic injection of remedies; Practitioner [1868], 1, 32-41.

- On the effects of the prolonged use of morphia by subcutaneous injection, Practitioner, 1871, 6, 148-157.

Antonelle M, Katz D: Lorazepam in the long-term treatment of anxiety associated with gastro-intestinal disorders: an open comparison with diazepam; Clinical Therapeutics, 1977, 1, 2, 140-151.

Ashton H: Benzodiazepine withdrawal: an unfinished story; Brit Med J, 14 April 1984, 288, 1135-1140.

- Adverse effects of prolonged benzodiazepine use; Adverse Drug Reaction Bulletin, June 1986, 118, 440-443.

- Dangers and medico-legal aspects of benzodiazepines, Journal of the Medical Defence Union, Summer 1987, 6 - 8. (a)

- Problems with lorazepam (unpublished paper), 6 March 1987. (b)

Asscher W: Risk/benefit analysis in medical treatment; BIRA Journal, 1985, 4, 3, 54-56.

- Strategy of risk-benefit analysis; in D'Arcy PF, Griffin JP (Eds) 1986, 108-116.

- Risk management: regulatory responsibilities (in) Burley D, Inman WHW: Therapeutic Risk - Perception, measurement, management [Chichester, UK: John Wiley & Sons, 1988], 53-59.

Athinarayanan P, Pierog SH, Nigam SK, Glass L: Chlordiazepoxide withdrawal in the neonate; Am J Obstet Gynecol, 15 January 1976, 124, 2, 212-3.

Bargmann E, Wolfe SM, Levin J: Stopping Valium [Washington DC: Public Citizen Health Research Group, 1982]

Barton DF: More on lorazepam withdrawal; Drug Intell and Clin Pharmacy, 15, February 1981, 133-4.

Batchelor IR, (Cit. Glatt, 1962): Practitioner, 184, 718.

Beardshaw V: Conscientious objectors at work - Mental hospital nurses; a case study [London: Social Audit, 1981]

Bennett JR (Chairman, Campaign on the Restriction and use of Barbiturates): Barbiturate abuse (circular letter to doctors), May 1976.

- Goodbye ! (circular letter) May 1977,

Benson P: Too much or too little compassion; Brit Med J; 24 September 1988, 297, 801.

Berridge V: Professionalisation and narcotics: the medical and pharmaceutical professions and British narcotic use, 1868-1926. Psychological Medicine, 1978, 8, 361-372.

Berridge V, Edwards G: Opium and the People: Opiate Use in Nineteenth Century England [New Haven: Yale University Press, 1987].

Berridge V: The origins of the English drug "scene", 1890-1930. Medical History, 1988, 32, 51-64.

Bianchi M, Musch B: Zopiclone discontinuation: review of 25 studies assessing withdrawal and rebound phenomena; Int Clin Psychopharmacol, April 1990, 5 Suppl 2, 139-145.

Birley JLT: Drug advertisements in developing countries. Lancet, 28 January 1989, 220.

Bitnun S: Possible effects of chlordiazepoxide on the fetus; Canad Med Ass J, 15 February 1969, 100, 351.

Bixler EO, Kales A, Manfredi RL et al: Next-day memory impairment with triazolam use; Lancet, 6 April 1991, 827-831.

Bleich A, Grinspoon A, Garb R: Paranoid reaction following alprazolam withdrawal; Psychosomatics, November 1987, 28, 11, 599-600.

Bleyer WA, Marshal RE: Barbiturate withdrawal syndrome in a passively addicted infant; JAMA, 10 July 1972, 221, 2, 185-6.

Blinick G, Wallach RC et al: Drug addiction in pregacny and the neonate; Am J Obstet Gynecol, 15 May 1976, 125, 2, 135-142.

Blyth AW: Poisons: their effects and detection; 2nd Edition. [London: Charles Griffin, 1884]

Bonney G: Defending cases of medical negligence (letter); The Independent, 2 September 1989, 21.

Bowes HA: The role of Librium in an out-patient psychiatric setting; Dis Nerv Syst, March 1960, 20-22.

- The role of diazepam (Valium) in emotional illness; Psychosomatics, Sept/Oct 1965, 6, 336-340

Braithwaite J: Corporate Crime in the Pharmaceutical Industry [London: Routledge & Kegan Paul, 1983].

Brecher EM: Licit and Illicit Drugs [Mount Vernon, NY: Consumers Union, 1973]

Breitner C: Drug therapy in obsessional states and other psychiatric problems; Dis Nerv Syst, March 1960, 31-5.

Brier A, Charney DS, Nelson JC: Seizures induced by abrupt discontinuation of alprazolam; Am J Psychiatry, December 1984, 141, 12, 1606-7.

British Encyclopaedia of Medical Practice, 2nd edition [London: Butterworths, 1967].

British Medical Association: Secret Remedies: what they cost and what they contain [London: BMA, 1909]

- More Secret Remedies: what they cost and what they contain [London: BMA, 1912]

British Medical Journal: (Cit. Glatt, 1962) Editorial, 1954, II, 1534.

- Stimulants and depressants, 28 April 1956, 969-70.

- Any questions ? 1958, I, 954

- Drugs of addiction - 2; 31 October 1964, 1119-1120

- Sound sleep; 30 May 1970, 492-3.

- Adverse drug reactions, 6 June 1981, 282, 1819-1820

- Benzodiazepine 'addicts' to sue; 26 January 1991, 302, 2000.

British National Formulary; a joint publication of the British Medical Association and The Pharmaceutical Society of Great Britain; published twice yearly since 1981.

Brockington CF: Public Health in the Nineteenth Century [London: Livingstone, 1965].

Browne L, Hauge KJ: A review of alprazolam withdrawal; Drug Intell and Clin Pharmacy, November 1986, 20, 837-841.

Brun JP: Zopiclone: a cyclopyrrolone hypnotic: review of properties; Pharmacol Biochem Behav, April 1988, 29, 4, 831-832.

Burley DM: Risk in broad perspective; Centre for Pharmaceutical Medicine, 1986 manuscript [CPM, 50 Guilford Road, West End, Woking, Surrey GV24 9PW].

Byck R: Cocaine Papers [New York: Stonehill, 1974]

Caldwell AE: Origins of Psychopharmacology from CPZ to LSD [Springfield, Illinois, CC Thomas, 1970].

Canadian Pharmaceutical Association: Compendium of Pharmaceuticals and Specialties, 1981.

Cantopher T, Olivieri S, Edwards JG: Rates of tranquilliser prescribing in primary care; Brit J Addiction, 1988, 83, 969-970.

Carney MWP: Five cases of bromism; Lancet ii, 523-524.

CBS Television Network: A study of attitudes, concerns and information needs for prescription drugs and related illnesses [New York: CBS Inc, June 1984]. Chemist and Druggist: Dangers of chloral; 1886, 28, 293.

Chetley A: A Healthy Business [London: Zed Press, 1990]

Clarke K (Minister of Health): Letter to Dr J Marks, Chairman of the BMA Council [London: DHSS Press statement, 8 November 1984]

Clarke MJ: Chloral Hydrate: Medicine and Poison ? Pharm. Historian, 1988, 18, 4, 2-4.

Clift AD: Factors leading to dependence on hypnotic drugs. Brit Med J, 1972, 3, 614-617.

Cochran PW: Drugs for Anxiety; JAMA, 29 July 1974, 29, 5, 521

Cohen M (Wyeth Laboratories): Lorazepam: the manufacturer's reply; Pulse, 9 November 1985

- Wyeth statement for BBC-TV Brass Tacks Programme on lorazepam; Document Ref pr6/be 8 October 1987.

Cohen S, 1976: See Hollister LE (Chairman), 1977

Cohen SI: Are benzodiazepines useful in anxiety ? Lancet, 7 November 1987, 1080.

Cohn JB, Noble EP: Effect of withdrawing treatment after long-term administration of alprazolam, lorazepam, or placebo in patients with an anxiety disorder; Psychopharmacology Bulletin, 1983, 19, 4, 751-2. Collier J: The Health Conspiracy [London: Century, 1989].

Committee on Safety of Medicines; Unpublished data (aggregated from Yellow Card reports), 1972, 1976.

- Midazolam (Hypnovel) - respiratory depression and hypertension; Current Problems No 14, February 1985, 1-2.

- Dangers of newer antidepressants; Current Problems No 15, July 1985, 2.

- Benzodiazepines, dependence and withdrawal symptoms; Current Problems No 21, January 1988, 1-2.

- Fenbufen and mucocutaneous reactions; Current Problems No 23, September 1988, 2.

- Fenbufen, rash and pulmonary eosinophilia; Current Problems No 24, January 1989, 1-2.

- Xamoterol (Corwin) - revised indications, contraindications, dose schedule and warnings; Current Problems No 28, May 1990, 1-2.

- Zopiclone (Zimovane) and neuro-psychiatric reactions; Current Problems No 30, December 1990, 2.

- Fenoterol (Berotec, Boehringer Ingelheim) - new dosage recommendations; Current Problems No 31, June 1991, 2.

Committee on the Review of Medicines: Recommendations on barbiturate preparations; Brit. Med. J., 22 September 1979, 2, 719-720.

- (1980) Systematic review of the benzodiazepines, Brit. Med. J., 29 March 1980: 910 - 912.

Connor S: Cocaine 'first used 2,000 years ago'; Independent on Sunday, 16 June 1991.

Council of Europe: Resolution AP (90) 3; On the prescription of benzodiazepines [Strasbourg: Council of Europe, 1990].

Covi L et al: Factors affecting withdrawal response to certain minor tranquillisers. In Cole J O and Wittenborn J R [Eds.] Drug abuse: social and psychopharmacological aspects [Springfield, Illinois: Charles C Thomas, 1969], 93 - 108.

- Length of treatment with anxiolytic sedatives and response to their sudden withdrawal, Acta Psychiatr Scand, 1973, 49: 51-64.

Craig M: Letter; Lancet, 29 December 1917, 978.

- (Cit. Glatt, 1962): Lancet, 1934, 1, 708.

Critchley EMR, Vakil SD, Hayward HW, Owen VMH: Dupuytren's disease in epilepsy: result of prolonged administration of anticonvulsants; J Neurology, Neurosurgery and Psychiatry, 1976, 39, 498-503.

Crossman RH: (HC Deb on Thalidomide, 8 May 1963); cit. Forthcoming legislation on the safety, quality and description of drugs and medicines (Cmnd 3395); [London: HMSO, September 1967].

Curran HV: Tranquillising memories: a review of the effects of benzodiazepines on human memory; Biological Psychology, 1986, 23, 179-213.

Cushny AR: A textbook of Pharmacology and Therapeutics; 3rd Edition. [London: Rebman, 1903].

- A textbook of Pharmacology and Therapeutics; 10th Edition. [London: Churchill, 1928].

D'Arcy PF: Epidemiological aspects of iatrogenic disease; in D'Arcy PF, Griffin JP (Eds), 1986, 29-58.

D'Arcy PF, Griffin JP (Eds): Iatrogenic Diseases, 3rd Edition, [Oxford, OUP, 1986]

Davies DM (Ed.): Textbook of Adverse Drug Reactions [Oxford: OUP, 1981]

De Buck R: Clinical experience with lorazepam in the treatment of neurotic patients; Curr Med Res Opin; 1973, 1, 5, 291-5.

Deitch R: Dr Griffin's departure from the the department; Lancet, 21 July 1984, 176.

De la Fuente JR, Rosenbaum AH: Lorazepam related withdrawal seizures; Mayo Clin Proc, 1980, 55, 190-192.

Dennis PJ: Monitoring of psychotropic drug prescribing in general practice; Brit Med J, 3 November 1979, 2, 1115-6.

Department of Transport: Increased value for death in a road accident; Press notice No 506, 18 October 1988.

- Road Accidents in Great Britain: the casualty report; [London: HMSO, December 1988]. Also: provisional data for 1990, provided by DoT Press Office, July 1991.

De Quincey T: Confessions of an English Opium-Eater (1821) [London: Walter Scott, 1886].

Desmond MM, Schwanecke RP, Wilson GS et al: Maternal barbiturate utilisation and neonatal withdrawal symptomatology. J. Pediatr, 1972, 80, 190-197.

Diethelm O: On bromide intoxication. J Nerve and Mental Diseases, 1930, 71, 151-165.

Drill VA (Ed): Pharmacology in Medicine, 2nd Edition [New York: McGraw-Hill, 1958].

Drug and Therapeutics Bulletin (DTB): - Labelling drugs - a big step forward, 7 January 1972, 10, 1, 1

- Lorazepam - another benzodiazepine, 30 March 1973, 11, 7, 27-8.

- Is the patient a fast or slow acetylator? 15 March 1974, 12, 6, 21-22.

- Action from the CRM: Barbiturates, 1 February 1980, 18, 3, 9-11.

- The CRM on benzodiazepines; 5 December 1980, 18, 25, 97-8.

- Three more benzodiazepines; 12 August 1983, 21, 16-17.

- Some problems with benzodiazepines, 25 March 1985, 23, 6, 21-3.

- Lorazepam - a benzodiazepine to choose or avoid ? 12 August 1985, 23, 16, 61-2.

- Xamoterol - more trouble than it's worth ? 9 July 1990, 28, 14, 53-54

- Fenoterol and asthma deaths, (20 August 1990), 28, 17 (reprint)

Dukes MNG: The moments of truth; [in] Dukes MNG (Ed): Side Effects of Drugs Annual 1 [Amsterdam: Exerpta Medica, 1977], v - ix.

Dukes MNG, Lunde I: Controls, common sense and communities. Pharmaceutische Weekblad, 1979, 114, 1283-94.

Dukes MNG: The van der Kroef syndrome; [in] Dukes MNG (Ed): Side Effects of Drugs Annual 4 [Amsterdam: Exerpta Medica, 1980], v - ix.

- (Ed.): Meyler's Side Effects of Drugs [Amsterdam, Elsevier, 1988]

Dukes MNG and Swartz B: Responsibility for drug-induced injury [Amsterdam, Elsevier, 1988] Dunlop DM, (Cit. Glatt, 1962); Practitioner, 1957, 178, 26.

Dunlop DM: Drug Control and the British Health Service: Ann Intern Med, August 1969, 71, 2, 237-244.

- The use and abuse of psychotropic drugs; Proc Roy Soc Med, December 1970, 63, 1279-82.

Dunnell K, Cartwright A: Medicine takers, prescribers and hoarders [London: Routledge & Kegan Paul, 1972].

Einarson TR: Lorazepam withdrawal seizures; Lancet, 19 January 1980, 151

- Comment on lorazepam withdrawal; Drug Intell and Clin Pharmacy, 15, February 1981, 133-4.

English DC: Librium, a new non-sedative neuroleptic drug: a clinical evaluation; Curr Ther Res, March 1960, 2, 3, 88-91

Erlichman J: Drug firm made threats; The Guardian, 3 November 1986.

- 'Risky' heart drug kept on sale; The Guardian, 13 June 1990, 1. See also: Deaths from ICI heart drug raise questions on testing (Ibid. p. 3); and Corwin: a suitable case for debate; (editorial) ibid, 22.

- Risk alert after drug go-ahead; The Guardian, 14 June 1990, 2.

Evans JG, Jarvis EH: Nitrazepam and the elderly; Brit Med J, 25 November 1972, 487.

Evans NJB, Cunliffe PW: Study of control of medicines [London: HMSO, 1987].

Evans JI, Lewis SA, Gibb IAM, Cheetham M: Sleep and barbiturates: some experiments and observations; Brit Med J, 2 November 1968, 291-3.

Evans JI, Ogunremi O: Sleep and hypnotics: further experiments, Brit Med J, 8 August 1970, 310-313.

Fabre LF, Mclendon DM, Gainey A: Double-blind comparison of ketazolam administered once a day with diazepam and placebo in anxious out-patients; Curr Ther Res, December 1978, 24, 8, 875-883.

Farb HH: Experience with Librium in clinical psychiatry; Dis Nerv Syst, March 1960, 27-30

Farwell JR, Lee YJ, Hirtz DG, Sulzbacher SI, Ellenberg JH, Nelson KB: Phenobarbital for febrile seizures - effects on intelligence and on seizure recurrence; N Eng J Med, 8 February 1990, 364-369

FDA: Use in Pregnancy Ratings - X category; cit. Physicians Desk Reference 1990, 336.

File SE, Pellow S: Behavioural pharmacology of minor tranquillisers; Pharmac Ther, 1987, 35, 265-290.

Finer MJ: Habituation to chlordiazepoxide in an alcoholic population; JAMA, 24 August 1970, 213, 8, 1342.

Fisher H: Sleeping pills; Brit Med J, 19 September 1970, 711

Fishman RH; Yanai J: Long-lasting effects of early barbiturates on central nervous system and behaviour; Neurosci Biobehav Rev, Spring 1983, 7, 1, 19-28.

Floyd JB, Murphy CM: Hallucinations following withdrawal of Valium; J Kentucky Med Assoc, November 1976, 74, 11, 549-550

Fort J: The problem of barbiturates in the USA; Bull Narcotics, 1964, 16, 17.

Fraser HF, Wickler A, Essig CF, Isbell H: Degree of physical dependence induced by secobarbital or pentobarbital; JAMA, 11 January 1958, 166, 126-9.

Freed A: Prescribing of tranquillisers and barbiturates by general practitioners; Brit Med J, 1976, 2, 1232-3.

Freedman AM: Opiate Dependence; in Kaplan A, Freedman A (Eds); Comprehensive Textbook of Psychiatry [Baltimore, Williams & Wilkins, 1980]; 1591-1614.

Fruensgaard K: Withdrawal psychosis: a study of 30 consecutive cases; Acta Psychiat Scand, 1976, 53, 105-118.

Fyer AJ, Liebowitz MR, Gorman JM et al: Discontinuation of alprazolam treatment in panic patients; Am J Psychiatry, March 1987, 144, 3, 303.

Fyfe RM (Hoffman LaRoche, Canada): Comment in reply to letter from Slater J: Suspected dependence on chlordiazepoxide hydrochloride (Librium); Canad Med Ass J, 27 August 1966, 95, 416

Garattini S, Mussini E, Marcucci F, Guaitani A: Metabolic studies on benzodiazepines in various animal species; (in)

Garattini S et al (eds) The Benzodiazepines [New York: Raven Press, 1973], 75-97.

Gathorne-Hardy J: Doctors [London: Weidenfeld & Nicholson, 1984]

General Medical Council: The teaching of behavioural sciences, community medicine and general practice; report of a working party, March 1987.

General Medical Services Committee: Guidance on benzodiazepines, October 1988.

General Practitioner: Counter access to psychotropic drugs; 24 October 1975, 13

Gibb R: Letter; Lancet, 20 August 1864, 299.

Gillespie RD (Cit. Glatt, 1962) : Lancet, 1934, 1, 337 and 482.

Glatt MM: The abuse of barbiturates in the United Kingdom; Bull Narcot, 1962, 14, 20, 19-38.

Goedde HW: Ethnic differences in reactions to drugs and xenobiotics: outlook of a geneticist; Prog Clin Biol Res, 1986, 214, 9-20.

Goldsmith V: Sleep without fear, General Practitioner, 26 September 1975, 8.

Goodman L, Gilman A (Eds) The Pharmacological Basis of Therapeutics [New York: Macmillan, 1941].

Gordon B: I'm dancing as fast as I can [New York: Bantam, 1979]

Gordon EB: Addiction to diazepam (Valium); Brit Med J, 14 January 1967, 112.

Grahame-Smith DG: Self-medication with mood-changing drugs; J Med Ethics, 1975, 1, 132-7.

Greenblatt DJ and Shader RI: Benzodiazepines in clinical practice; [New York: Raven Press, 1974].

Greenblatt DJ, 1976: See Hollister LE (Chairman), 1977

Greenblatt DJ and Shader RI: Dependence, tolerance and addiction to benzodiazepines: clinical and pharmacokinetic considerations, Drug. Metab. Rev, 1978, 8, 1, 13-28.

Greenfield PR (Chairman): Report to the Secretary of State for Social Services of an informal working group on effective prescribing [London: DHSS, 1983]

Griffin JP: Is better feedback a major stimulus to spontaneous adverse reaction reporting ? Lancet, 10 November 1984, 1098.

Griffin JP, Diggle GE: A survey of products licensed in the United Kingdom from 1971-1981; Brit J Clin Pharmac, 1981, 12, 453-463.

Griffin JP, D'Arcy PF: Adverse reactions to drugs - the information lag; (in) Side Effects of Drugs Annual 5 [Amsterdam: Elsevier, 1981].

- Iatrogenic Diseases, 3rd Edition [Oxford: OUP, 1986].

Grinspoon L, Bakalar JB: Coca and cocaine as medicines: an historical review; J Ethnopharmacology, 1981, 3, 149-159.

Gross AJ: Observations on long-term administration of lorazepam in anxiety states: an open comparison with diazepam; Curr Therapeutic Res, November 1977, 22, 5, 579-604.

Gross F: Constraints of drug regulation on the development of new drugs. Arch Toxicol, 1979, 43, 9-17.

Guile LA, Rapid habituation to chlordiazepoxide ("Librium"); Med J Australia; 13 July 1963, 56-7.

Gulevich G: Convulsive and coma therapies and psychosurgery (in) Barchas JD et al (Eds): Psychopharmacology - from theory to practice [New York: OUP, 1977], 514-526.

Haizlip TM, Ewing JA: Meprobamate habituation - A controlled clinical study. N Eng J Med, 258, 24, 12 June 1958, 1181-6.

Hallstrom C, Lader M: Benzodiazepine withdrawal phenomena; Int. Pharmacopsychiat, 1981, 16, 235-244.

- The incidence of benzodiazepine dependence in long-term users; J Psychiatric Treatment and Evaluation; 1982, 4, 293-6.

Hallstrom C: Benzodiazepine dependence: who is responsible? J Forensic Psychiatry, 1991, 2, 1, 5-7.

Hamilton M: A rational approach to clinical trials of psychotropic drugs; in James B (Ed), Drugs and the mind [Dunedin NZ: University of Otago Medical School, 1967], 21-8.

Hampton JR: The end of clinical freedom; Brit Med J; 29 October 1983, 287, 1237-1238.

Hanna SM: A case of oxazepam (Serenid D) dependence. Brit J Psychiatry, 1972, 120, 443-5.

Harris TH: Methaminodiazepoxide, JAMA, 12 March 1960, 128, 1162-3.

Harry TVA (John Wyeth & Brother Ltd): Oxazepam (Serenid D) dependence. Brit J Psychiatry, 1972, 121, 235-6.

- Abuse of benzodiazepines; Lancet 11 September 1978, 1045.

Haskell D: Withdrawal of diazepam; JAMA, 14 July 1975, 233, 2, 135.

Hawkins CF: Presentation of results, in Good CS (Ed): The principles and practice of clinical trials [London: Churchill Livingstone, 1976], 138-146.

Henderson LJ, circa 1935. Attributed in: Blumgart HL: Caring for the patient; N Eng J Med, 27 February 1964, 270, 9, 449-456.

Hendler N, Cimini C, Terence MA, Long D: A comparison of cognitive impairment due to benzodiazepines and to narcotics; Am J Psychiatry, July 1980, 137, 7, 828-830.

Herxheimer A, Collier J: Promotion by the British pharmaceutical industry, 1983-8: a critical analysis of self-regulation; Brit Med J, 3 February 1990, 300, 307-311.

Hines LR (Hoffmann La Roche Inc): Methaminodiazepoxide (Librium): A psychotherapeutic drug; Curr Ther Res, 1960, 2, 6, 227-236.

Hinton D: Warning on Drug; Mind Out, No. 43, November 1980, p. 10.

Hodgkin C: 1992 - is harmonisation healthy? Critical Public Health, 1991, 1, 11-17.

Hollister LE, Motzenbecker FP, Degan RO: Withdrawal reactions from chlordiazepoxide ("Librium"); Psychopharmacologia, 1961, 2, 63-8.

Hollister LE, Bennett JL, Kimbell I et al: Diazepam in newly admitted schizophrenics; Dis Nerv Sys, December 1963, 746-50.

Hollister LE: The prudent use of antianxiety drugs; Rational Drug Therapy, March 1972, 6, 3, 1-6.

- (Chairman, proceedings of a roundtable discussion on diazepam held in Chicago, 20 May 1976): Valium: A discussion of current issues; Psychosomatics, 1977, 18, 1, 44-58. (a)

- Withdrawal from benzodiazepine therapy; JAMA, 4 April 1977, 237, 1432. (b)

Howe JG: Lorazepam withdrawal seizures; Brit Med J, 10 May 1980, 1163-4.

Hunter RA, Greenberg HP: Barbiturate addiction simulating spontaneous hyperinsulism, Lancet, 10 July 1954, 58-62.

Hunter RA: "Minor" Addictions; Lancet 18 June 1955, 1265.

- The abuse of the barbiturates, Lancet, 28 July 1956, 176

- The abuse of barbiturates and other sedative drugs with special reference to psychiatric patients, Brit J. Addiction, 1957, 53, 2, 93-100.

Hurst DL, Hurst MJ: Bromide Psychosis: A Literary Case. Clinical Neuropharmacology, 1984, 7, 3, 259-264.

Hussey HH: Insomnia: JAMA, 4 February 1974, 227, 554-5.

Idestrom CM: Sedative-hypnotic drug abuse among adults; in Zarafonetis C J D (Ed): Drug Abuse: Proceedings of an international conference, November 1970 [Philadelphia: Lea and Febinger, 1972], 217-222.

Illich I: Limits to medicine - Medical nemesis: the expropriation of health; [Harmondsworth: Penguin, 1976].

Imoto RM: Benzodiazepine withdrawal reaction; Drug Intell and Clin Pharmacy, March 1980, 14, 187

Inglis B: The Forbidden Game [London: Hodder & Stoughton, 1975]

Ingram IM, Timbury GC: Side effects of Librium; Lancet, 1 October 1960, 766

Inman WHW: Detection and investigation of drug safety problems (in) Gent M, Shigamatsu I (Eds): Epidemiological issues in reporting drug-induced illness [Hamilton, Ontario: McMaster University, 1976].

- Risks in medical intervention - balancing therapeutic risks and benefits; Wolfson College Lecure, Oxford, 31 January 1984.

- Let's get our act together; [in] Dukes MNG (Ed): Side Effects of Drugs Annual 9 [Amsterdam: Exerpta Medica, 1985], xiv - xxiii.

Institute of Medicine: Sleeping pills, insomnia and medical practice [Washington DC: National Academy of Sciences, 1979].

Isbell H, Altschul S et al: Chronic barbiturate intoxication - An experimental study. Archives of Neurology & Psychiatry, 64, 1, July 1950, 1 - 28.

Isbell H, Chrusciel TL: Dependence liability of 'non-narcotic' drugs [Geneva: WHO: 1970]

Jacobson B, Nyberg K et al: Opiate addiction in adult offspring through possible imprinting after obstetric treatment; Brit Med J, 10 November 1990, 301, 1067-1070.

Jacqz E; Hall SD; Branch RA: Genetically determined polymorphisms in drug oxidation; Hepatology, Sept-Oct 1986, 6, 5, 1020-1032

Johnson J, Clift AD, Dependence on hypnotic drugs in general practice; Brit Med J, 7 December 1968, 4, 613-7.

Jones E: Sigmund Freud: Life and work, Vol. 1. [London: Hogarth, 1953].

Jones G, Mann R: Better reporting of adverse drug reactions; Brit Med J, 4 April 1987, 901-902.

Jones L, Simpson D, Brown AC et al: Prescribing psychotropic drugs in general practice: three year study; Brit Med J, 20 October 1984, 289, 1045-8.

Journal of the American Medical Association (JAMA): New tranquilizer; 10 September 1960, 198.

- The use of the terms habituation and addiction; 2 February 1963, 183, 5, 363.

- Skeleton in the cupboard, 14 September 1963, 185, 11, 902

- Dependence on barbiturates and other sedative drugs, 23 August 1965, 193, 8, 673-7.

- Abuse drugs listed; 31 January 1966, 195, 5, 21-2.

- A new minor tranquilliser - Oxazepam (Serax); 28 February 1966, 195, 9, 149.
- "Suit ... the word to the action"; 12 June 1967, 200, 11, 176.
- Sleep now, pay later, 26 May 1969, 208, 8, 1485
- Insomnia, 4 Feruary 1974, 227, 5, 554-5

Juergens SM, Morse RM: Alprazolam dependence in seven patients; Am J Psychiatry, May 1988, 145, 5, 625-7.

Kagan F et al (eds): Hypnotics; [New York: Spectrum Publications, 1975].

Kahan BB, Haskett RF: Lorazepam withdrawal and seizures; Am J Psychiatry, August 1984, 141, 8.

Kales A (Ed): Sleep: physiology and pathology; [Philadelphia: JP Lippincott Co, 1969].

Kales A, Bixler EO, Tjiauw-Ling Tan, Scharf MB, Kales JD: Chronic hypnotic drug use - ineffectiveness, drug-withdrawal insomnia and dependence; JAMA, 4 February 1974, 227, 5, 513-7.

Kales A, Soldatos CR, Bixler EO, Kales JD: Rebound insomnia and anxiety: a review; Pharmacology, 1983, 26, 121-137

Kales A, Bixler EO, Soldatos CR, Jacoby JA, Kales JD: Lorazepam: effects on sleep and withdrawal phenomena; Pharmacology, 1986, 32, 121-130.

Kales A, Kales JD et al: Hypnotic efficacy of triazolam: sleep laboratory evaluation of intermediate-term effectiveness; J Clin Pharm; 1986, 16, 396-406.

Kales A, Manfredi RL et al: Rebound insomnia following only brief and intermittent use of rapidly eliminated benzodiazepines. Clin Pharm Ther, 1991, 49, 468-476.

Katz R: Drug therapy: sedatives and tranquillisers. N Eng J Med, 6 April 1972, 286,14, 757-760.

Kellett JM: The benzodiazepine bonanza (letter); Lancet, 19 October, 1974, 964.

Kemper N, Poser W, Poser S: Benzodiazepin-Abhangigkeit; Dtsch med Wschr, 1980, 105, 1707-1712

Khan A, Joyce A, Jones AV: Benzodiazepine withdrawal syndromes; NZ Med J, 13 August 1980, 94-96

Kinross-Wright J, Cohen IM, Knight JA: The management of neurotic and psychotic states with Ro 5-0690 (Librium); Dis Nerv Syst, March 1960, 23-6.

Kirby J: Help patients find release from benzodiazepines; General Practitioner, 27 August 1982, 22.

Klein DF, Davies JM: Diagnosis and Drug Treatment of Psychiatric Disorders [Philadelphia: Williams and Wilkins, 1969]

Koeppen D (Hoechst AG): Review of clinical studies on clobazam; Br J Clin Pharmac, 1979, 7, 139S-150S.

Korsgaard S: Misbrug af lorazepam (Temesta). Ugeskr. Laeg., 1976, 138, 164-5.

Lacey R, Woodward S: That's Life! Survey on Tranquillisers [London: BBC in association with MIND, 1985].

Lader M: Benzodiazepines - the opium of the masses ? Neuroscience, 1978, 3, 159-165

- Benzodiazepine dependence (in) Murray R, Ghodse H, Harris R et al (Eds): The Misuse of Psychotropic Drugs [London: Gaskell (Royal College of Psychiatrists), 1981].

- (cited in BBC-TV programme, That's Life!) SCRIP No 804, 20 June 1983, 19.

Lader M, Frcka G: Subjective effects during administration and on discontinuation of zopiclone and temazepam in normal subjects; Pharmacopsychia-
try, March 1987, 20, 2, 67-71.

Laidlaw J, Richens A: A Textbook of Epilepsy [Edinburgh: Churchill Livingstone, 1982]

Lancet: The habitual use of alcohol, 27 September 1862, 2, 333-5.

- Editorial; 26 March 1864, 357

- Editorial, 11 February 1865, 153-4

- Medical annotations, 29 August 1868, 287

- Editorial, 1 January 1870, 15.

- The peril and plague of narcotics; 1 May 1886, 845-6.

- Editorial; 1889, ii, 1047

- Medical men and the morphia habit; 27 October 1900, 1219.

- Editorial, 1947, ii, 583 (Cit. Glatt, 1962).

- Editorial, 1954, ii, 75 (Cit. Glatt, 1962).

- How safe does a drug have to be ? 1981, i, 1297-1298.

- UN Commission on Narcotic Drugs - benzodiazepines and pentazocine
scheduled under convention on psychotropic substances; 17 March 1984, 637.

- Lessons from nomifensine; 5 November 1988, 1059-1060.

- Zopiclone: another carriage on the tranquilliser train; 3 March 1990, 507-508

- European drug regulation - anti-protectionism or consumer protection ? 1991,
337, 1571-1572

Lasagna L, (Cit. Medical Letter, 1959): J Chronic Diseases, 1957, 3, 122.

Laties VG, Weiss B (Cit. Medical Letter, 1959): J Chronic Diseases, 1958, 7, 500.

Laughren TP, Battey Y, Greenblatt DJ, Harrop DS: A controlled trial of
diazepam withdrawal in chronically anxious patients; Acta Psychiat Scand, 1982,
65, 171-9.

Laurence DR, Bennett PN: Clinical Pharmacology (6th edition) [London:
Churchill Livingstone, 1987].

LeBlanc AE: Perspectives in drug abuse with particular reference to sedative hypnotics; (in) Kagan F et al (eds), Op. Cit.

Lemere F: Habit-forming properties of meprobamate; Arch Neurol, 1956, 76,
205-6.

- Toxic reactions to chlordiazepoxide; JAMA, 15 October 1960, 174, 7, 893.

Levinstein E: Morbid craving for morphia [London: Smith, Elder, 1878]

Levy AB: Delirium and seizures due to abrupt alprazolam withdrawal: case
report; J Clin Psychiatry, 1984, 141, 1606-7.

Lewis A: Sleeping pills; Brit Med J, 22 August 1970, 463.

Lock S: Misconduct in medical research: Does it exist in Britain ? Brit Med J; 10
December 1988, 297, 1531-1535.

Locket S, (Cit. Glatt, 1962): Brit J Addiction, 1957, 53, 105.

Lumley CE, Walker SR, Hall GC et al: The under-reporting of adverse drug reactions seen in general practice; Pharmaceut Med, 1986, 1, 205-212.

Lumley JA: The British pharmaceutical industry, 1868-1968; Practitioner, July 1968, 201, 217-223.

Macleod N: Triazolam: Monitored release in the United Kingdom; Brit J Clin Pharmac, 1981, 11, 51S-53S.

Maillard G, Renard G: Un nouveau traitment de l'epilepsie; Presse Medicale, 1925, 20, 1-4.

Maletzky BM and Klotter J: Addiction to diazepam; The International Journal of the Addictions, 1976, 11, 1, 95 - 115.

Management Sciences for Health: Managing drug supply [Boston, Mass: MSH, 1981]

Mann RD: letter to Dr Vernon Coleman [Life without Tranquillisers newsletter No 3, 1986]

Mansell-Jones D, 1972; in Parish PA et al (Eds), 1973.

Marinker M L, 1972; in Parish PA et al (Eds), 1973.

Marks J: Methaminodiazepoxide ("Librium") A new psychotropic drug; Chemother Rev, 1960, 141-3, 173.

- The benzodiazepines: use, overuse, misuse, abuse; [Lancaster UK, MTP Press, 1978].

- The benzodiazepines - use and abuse; Arzneim.-Forsch, 1980, 30, 1, 5a, 898-901.

- The benzodiazepines - for good or evil; Neuropsychobiology, 1983, 10, 115-126

Martin EA (Ed): Concise Medical Dictionary, 2nd edition [Oxford: OUP, 1985]

Mattson RH; Cramer JA; McCutchen CB and the Veterans Administration Epilepsy Cooperation Study Group: Barbiturate-related connective tissue disorders; Arch Intern Med, April 1989, 149, 911-914.

Maudsley H: Insanity and its treatent (Presidential address to the Medico-Psychological Association), Journal of Mental Science, October 1871.

- The pathology of mind, [London: Macmillan, 1895].

Mazzi E: Possible neonatal diazepam withdrawal; Am J Obstet Gynecol, 1 November 1977, 129, 5, 586-7.

McMahon FG: How safe should drugs be? JAMA, 28 January 1983, 249, 481-482

McNair DM: Antianxiety drugs and human performance; Arch Gen Psychiatry, November 1983, 29, 611-7.

Medd B (Roche Laboratories): Comment - Valium Addiction ? ; Drug Therapy, August 1975, 147.

- Manufacturer's views on Valium; FDA Consumer, October 1980, 5.

- Considerations when prescribing minor tranquillisers; New Physician, October 1980

Medawar C: Insult or Injury ? An enquiry into the promotion of British food and drug products in the third world [London: Social Audit, 1979].

- Drug Disinformation [London: Social Audit, 1980]

- The Wrong Kind of Medicine? [London, Consumers' Association and Stodder & Houghton, 1984]. (a)

- One Drug at a time - a report on the limitations of fixed-ratio combination drugs; [IOCU: The Hague, 1984]. (b)

- Data sheets: a consumer perspective, Lancet 2 April 1988, 777 - 778.

- On our side of the fence; [in] Dukes MNG, Beeley L (Eds): Side Effects of Drugs Annual 13 [Amsterdam: Exerpta Medica, 1989], xviiii - xxx.

- What We Know We Don't Know; in Mitchell C: (Ed.): Vision and Values in Pharmaceutical Innovation; ALZA Conference Series, Vol. 3 [Palo Alto, Cal: ALZA Corporation, 1990], 123-140.

Medawar J: A very decided preference - Life with Peter Medawar [Oxford: Oxford University Press, 1990].

Medical Economics Co: 1988 PDR Usage study [Oradell NJ: Medical Economics Co, 1988]

Medical Letter on Drugs and Therapeutics: Meprobamate, 23 January 1959, 1, 1, 3-4

- Librium; 13 May 1960, 2,10, 37-8.

- Librium and Valium, 3 October 1969, 11, 20, 81-4.

Medicines Control Agency: Medicines Act Information Letter No 68; July 1991.

Melrose D: Bitter Pills - Medicines and the Third World Poor [Oxford: Oxfam, 1982].

MIMS India (Monthly Index of Medical Specialities [New Delhi: A E Morgan Publications (India) Private Ltd, January 1987].

Misra PC: Nitrazepam (Mogadon) dependence; Brit J Psychiat, 1975, 126, 81-2.

Monopolies Commission: Chlordiazepoxide and Diazepam [London: HMSO, 1973]

Montgomery AW (Hoffman La Roche, Canada): About Valium; Canadian Doctor, April 1980, 8 - 12.

Morgan K, Oswald I: Anxiety caused by a short-life hypnotic; Brit Med J, 27 March 1982, 942.

Movat FG: The ethics of opium and alcohol. Lancet, 12 November, 1892, 1091.

Multi-centre study: A double-blind comparison of ketazolam given once each day with diazepam given in divided doses and placebo in the treatment of anxiety; Br J Clin Practice, 1980, 34, 107-113.

Murphy SM, Tyrer P: A double-blind comparison of the effects of gradual withdrawal of lorazepam, diazepam and bromazepam in benzodiazepine dependence; Brit J Psychiatry, 1991, 158, 511-516.

Murray D, O'Leary D: Recommendations on data sheets for benzodiazepines ignored; Brit Med J, 3 March 1984, 288, 717

Musto DF: Iatrogenic Addiction: the problem, its definition and history, Bull NY Acad Med, 1985, 61, 8, 694-705.

Nebert DW: Possible clinical importance of genetic differences in drug metabolism; Brit Med J, 22 August 1981, 283, 537-542.

New England Journal of Medicine: Current concepts in therapy - sedative hypnotic drugs V. The non-barbiturates (Unsigned), 14 February 1957, 314-6.

- Drug abuse control amendments of 1965; 25 November 1965, 273, 22, 1222-3.

Noyes R, Clancy J, Coryell WH et al: A withdrawal syndrome after abrupt discontinuation of alprazolam; Am J Psychiatry, January 1985, 114-6.

Noyes R, Perry PJ, Crowe RR: Seizures following the withdrawal of alprazolam; J Nervous and Mental Disease, 1986, 174, 1, 50-2,

Observer: Original report on institutional treatment of the mentally ill on Leros was published on 10 September, 1989; further reports were published on 17-09-89;

15-10-89; 12-11-89; 11-03-90; 04-03-90; 29-07-90 and 26-08-90.

O'Donnell VM, Balkin TJ et al: Effects of triazolam on performance and sleep in a model of transient insomnia; Human Performance, 1988, 1, 3, 145-160.

O'Dowd JJ, Spragg PP, Routledge PA: Fatal triazolam poisoning; Brit Med J, 22 October 1988, 297, 1048

Office of Health Economics: Medicines which affect the mind [London: OHE, 1975]

- Sources of information for prescribing doctors in Britain [London: OHE, 1977]

- 'Innovative chemical extensions' - the economic basis of pharmaceutical progress; [London: OHE, 1990]

Olajide D, Lader M: Depression following withdrawal from long-term benzodiazepine use: a report of four cases; Psychological Medicine, 1984, 14, 937-940.

Olivieri S, Cantopher T, Edwards JG: Two hundred years of dependence on antianxiety drugs; Human Psychopharmacology, 1986, 1, 117-123.

Oswald I (Discussant at a symposium at St Bartholomew's Hospital, London; 7/8 September 1964) in Marks J and Pare CMB (Eds): Drug Therapy in Psychiatry [London: Pergammon, 1965], 47-9. (a)

Oswald I, Priest RG: Five weeks to escape the sleeping-pill habit; Brit Med J, 6 November 1965, 1093-5. (b)

Oswald I: Drugs and Sleep; Pharmacological Reviews, 1968, 20, 4, 273-303

- Dependence upon hypnotic and sedative drugs; Brit J Hosp Med, August 1970, 272-7.

- Triazolam syndrome 10 years on; Lancet, 19 August 1989

- Rules for drug trials; Brit Med J, 28 October 1989, 299, 1103.

Palmer HD, Paine AL: Prolonged narcosis as therapy in psychoses. Am J Psychiat, 1932, 12, 143-164

Palmer HD, Braceland FJ: Six years experience with narcosis therapy in psychiatry. Am J Psychiat, 1937, 94, 37-53.

Parish PA: The prescribing of psychotropic drugs in general practice; J Roy Coll Gen Practit, November 1971, Vol 21 (92), Supp 4.

Parish PA, Williams WM, Elmes PC (Eds): The medical use of psychotropic drugs, A report of a symposium, sponsored by the Department of Health and Social Security and held at University College, Swansea, 1-2 July 1972; J Roy Coll Practit, 1973, 2 (Suppl), 23.

Parssinen TM, Kerner K: Development of the disease model of drug addiction in Britain, 1870-1926. Medical History, 1980, 24, 275-296.

Pekkanen J: The American Connection [Chicago, Follett Publishing, 1973]

Peters D: The British medical response to opiate addiction in the nineteenth century. J History of Medicine, 1981, 455-488.

Peters von UH, Boeters U: Valium-Sucht - Eine Analyse anhand von 8 fallen; Pharmakopsychiatrie Neuro-Psychopharmakologie, November 1970, 3, 6, 339-348.

Peters von UH, Seidel M: Medikamentenmissbrauch und Sucht bei Diazepam; Artzneim Forsch (Drug Res), 1970, 7, 876-7.

Peterson F: Insanity. The Encyclopaedia Britannica, 11th Edition, Vol XIV [Cambridge: University Press, 1910], 597-618.

Petursson H, Lader MH: Withdrawal from long-term benzodiazepine treatment; Brit Med J, 5 September 1981, 283, 643-5

- Benzodiazepine dependence; Brit J Addiction, 1981, 76, 133-145.

Physicians Desk Reference [Oradell, NJ: Medical Economics Co Inc, annual].

Pilowski L, O'Sullivan G: Mental illness in doctors, Br Med J, 298, 4 February 1989, 269-270.

Practitioner: The barbiturate menace, 1953, 171, 230

- The barbiturate problem; July 1964, 193, 1153, 1-2.

Prescribers Journal: New drugs - 1. Diazepam ("Valium"); 1964, 3, 126-7.

Price FW (Ed): Psychological Medicine; in A Textbook of the Practice of Medicine, Sixth Edition; [Oxford: University Press, 1942] p. 1862.

Priest RG (Chairman, Psychopharmacology working party): Benzodiazepines and dependence: A college statement; Bull Roy Coll Psychiatrists, March 1988, 12, 107-9.

Rashid K, Patrissi G, Cook B: Multiple serious symptom formation with alprazolam; Unpublished paper from USAF Medical Center, Keesler Air Force Base, Mississippi USA), 1987.

Rassaby ER: Personal communication, 1991

Rawlins MD: Adverse reactions to drugs; Brit Med J, 1981, 282, 974-6.

- Spontaneous reporting of adverse drug reactions 1: the data; Brit J Clin Pharmac, 1988, 26, 1-5.

- Spontaneous reporting of adverse drug reactions 2: Uses; Brit J Clin Pharmac, 1988, 26, 7-11.

Rawlins MD, Jefferys DB: Study of United Kingdom product licence applications containing new active substances, 1987-1989; Brit Med J, 26 January 1991, 302, 223-225.

Ray WA, Griffin MR, Shaffner W et al: Psychotropic drug use and the risk of hip fracture, N Eng J Med, 12 February 1987, 316, 7, 363-9.

Reber AS: Dictionary of Psychology [Harmondsworth: Penguin, 1985].

Regent TA, Wahl KC: Diazepam abuse: incidence, rapid screening, and confirming methods; Clinical Chemistry, 1976, 22, 6, 889-891.

Reggiani G; Hurlimann A, Theiss E (Hoffman La Roche): Some aspects of the experimental and clinical toxicology of chlordiazepoxide; in Proc. Eur. Soc. for the study of drug toxicity, Vol IX, [Amsterdam: Exerpta Medica, 1968], 79-97.

Rementeria JL, Bhatt K: Withdrawal symptoms in neonates from intrauterine exposure to diazepam; J Pediatrics, January 1977, 90, 1, 123-6.

Retterstol N, Ropstad O: Misbruk av lette ataractica. Nord Psyckiat T, 1969, 23:477

Richards DJ (Wyeth Laboratories): Clinical profile of lorazepam, a new benzodiazepine tranquillizer; J Clin Psychiat, October 1978, 58-66.

Rickels K: Drug use in outpatient treatment; Amer J Psychiatr, 124, 8, February 1968 Supp., 20-31.

Ridley H: Drugs of choice, A report on the drug formularies used in NHS hospitals [London: Social Audit, 1986]

Ringer S: The therapeutic action of drugs. Lancet, 20 March 1869, 392-4.

Rivington W: The Medical Profession [Dublin, Fawin & Co., 1879]

Robertson W (DHSS Medicines Division): Remarks made at Royal Society of Medicine conference on Patient Information, 1 November 1988.

Robinson K (Minister of Health): Prescriptions for barbiturates (Parliamentary answer); Lancet, 5 November 1966, 1032.

Robson J, 1972; in Parish PA et al (Eds), 1973.

Roche Products Ltd: A life of anxiety ... and the place of Valium Roche; brochure ref. M51OUK, December 1968

- Whatever the diagnosis - Librium; advertisement in Br Med J, 1 March 1969.

- The Sixties; advertisement, circa 1970

- The neurotic skin; advertisement in Brit Med J, 14 November 1970.

- The anxious heart; advertisement in Brit Med J, 17 October 1970.

- brochure ref M556008/5 OS, June 1973

Rodrigo EK, King MB, Williams P: Health of long-term benzodiazepine users; Brit Med J, 27 February 1988, 296, 603-6.

Ross M: Lorazepam-associated drug dependence; J Roy Coll Gen Practit, February 1986, 86.

Royal Commission on Opium, 1893-1894. Final Report, 1895

Rucinski J, Cybulska E: Mentally ill doctors; Brit J Hosp Medicine, 1985, 33, 90-94.

Ryan HF, Merrill FB, Scott GE et al: Increase in suicidal thoughts and tendencies - association with diazepam therapy; JAMA, 25 March 1968, 203, 13, 135-7.

Sainsbury, Lord (Chairman): Report of the commitee of enquiry into the relationship of the pharmaceutical industry with the National Health Service, 1965-7. [London: HMSO, 1967]

Salive M, Wolfe SM (Public Citizen Health Research Group): Letter to FDA Commissioner, Dr FE Young, 30 November 1987.

Sargant W: On chemical tranquillisers; Brit Med J, 28 April 1956, 939-943.

- Discussion on sedation and stimulation in man. Proc Roy Soc Medicine [1958], 51, 353, 13-18.

- 1972; in Parish PA et al (Eds), 1973.

- Prescribing Mandrax, Brit Med J, 23 June 1973, 716.

Scharf MB, Jacoby JA: Lorazepam - efficacy, side effects and rebound phenomena; Clin Pharmacol Ther, February 1982, 175-9.

Schwartz H: Improving the industry's image. SCRIP No 1620/21, 29/31 May 1991, 22-3.

Schweigert BF: Neonatal barbiturate withdrawal; JAMA, 11 September 1972, 221, 1282

SCRIP: ADR fatalities: the cost of prevention, 1 December 1982, 3.

- Wyeth on benzodiazepine withdrawal, 23 May 1983, 16.

- New ABPI Director's p-i concern, 27 August 1984, 1.

- UK benzodiazepine prescribing, 7 January 1985, 4.

- ADRs from CSM and ABPI, 25 March 1985, 4.

- Under-reporting of ADRs in UK, 17 April 1985, 1.

- Risks in risk assessment, 28 August 1985, 17.

- Acceptable degrees of therapeutic risk, 24 June 1987, 22.

- UK ABPI call for accuracy, 16 September 1987, 3
- Wyeth files for half-strength lorazepam, 24 August 1988, 13.
- Prozac dosage too high ? 12 October 1990, 25
- Hoechst agrees to US fine over Merital, 19 December 1990, 8.
- Norway rejects fluoxetine on appeal, 22 May 1991, 26
- FDA workforce at 17,000 in 1997 ? 5 July 1991, 14

Seevers MH: Psychopharmacological elements of drug dependence; JAMA, 4 November 1968, 206, 6, 1263-6.

Seguin EC: The abuse and use of bromides. J. Nerve and Mental Diseases, 1877, 445-462.

Seidel WF, Cohen SA et al: Dose-related effects of triazolam and flurazepam on a circadian rhythm insomnia. Clin Pharm Ther, 1986; 40, 314-320.

Selig JW: A possible oxazepam abstinence syndrome, JAMA, 21 November 1966, 198, 8, 279-280.

Sharkey S: Morphinomania; Nineteenth Century, 1887, 22, 335-42.

Shepherd M: The benzodiazepines; Prescribers Journal, 1972, 12, 144-147.

Siassi I, Thomas M, Vanov SK: Evaluation of the safety and therapeutic effects of lorazepam on long-term use; Curr Ther Res, July, section 2, 1972, 18, 1, 163-171.

Singer C: A short history of medicine [Oxford: Clarendon Press, 1928].

Slater J: Suspected dependence on chlordiazepoxide hydrochloride (Librium); Canad Med Ass J, 27 August 1966, 95, 416

Smiley A: Effects of minor tranquillisers and antidepressants on psychomotor performance; J Clin Psychiatry, December 1987, 48, 12 Supp, 22-8.

Smith AJ: Nitrazepam ("Mogadon"); Prescribers' Journal, 1966, 6, 31-2.

- Self-poisoning with drugs: a worsening situation. Brit Med J, 1972, 4, 157-159.

Smith HL: Ethical considerations in research involving human subjects; Soc Sci Med, October 1980, 5, 453-8.

Smith MC: Small Comfort - A history of the minor tranquillisers; [New York: Praeger, 1985

Snell ES: Systematic review of the benzodiazepines; Brit Med J, 12 April 1980, 1053-4.

- Recommendations on data sheets for benzodiazepines ignored (Comment on letter); Brit Med J, 3 March 1984, 288, 717

Solomon K: Benzodiazepines and neurotic anxiety; NY State J Medicine, December 1976, 76, 2, 2156-2164.

Steering Group on Undergraduate Medical and Dental Education, 2nd report [London: Doh and DES, June 1990]

Sternbach LH (Hoffman La Roche Inc): Chemistry of 1,4 benzodiazepines and some aspects of the structure-activity relationship (in) Garattini S et al (eds) The Benzodiazepines [New York: Raven Press, 1973], 1-26.

- The benzodiazepine story (in) Benzodiazepines today and tomorrow; Preist RG et al (eds); [Lancaster: MTP Press, 1980], 5-17.

- The discovery of CNS active 1,4-benzodiazepines; in Costa E (Ed): The benzodiazepines: from molecular biology to clinical practice [New York: Raven Press, 1983].

Stevens J: Hypnotics - A GP's view, Prescribers Journal, October 1973, 13, 5, 104.

Stevens M: Signal generation in multinational pharmaceutical companies - a clinical approach; Proceedings of a symposium on signal generation and analysis, organised by WHO Collaborating Centre for International Drug Monitoring, and Department of Drugs, National Board of Health and Welfare; Uppsala, Sweden, 22-23 September 1988.

Stevens R: Medical practice in modern England [New Haven, Conn: Yale University Press, 1966]

Stewart RB, Salem RB, Springer PK: A case report of benzodiazepine withdrawal; Am J Psychiat, September 1980, 137, 9, 1113-4.

Stimson GV: The message of psychotropic drug ads; J Communication, Summer 1975, 153-160.

Stough AR: Possible habituating properties of meprobamate, JAMA, 22 February 1958, 882-8.

Sunday Times Insight Team: Suffer the children: The story of thalidomide [London: Deutsch, 1979].

Sunter JP, Bal TS, Cowan WK: Three cases of fatal triazolam poisoning; Brit Med J, 17 September 1988, 297, 719.

Sussex JN: The use of Librium in office treatment of mixed neurotic states; Dis Nerv Syst, March 1960, 53-6.

Svenson SE, Hamilton RG (Hoffman La Roche Inc): A critique of overemphasis on side effects with the psychotropic drugs: an analysis of 18,000 chlordiazepoxide-treated cases; Curr Ther Res, October 1966, 8, 10, 455-464.

Svensson CK: Lorazepam withdrawal; Drug Intell and Clin Pharm, September 1980, 14, 628.

Swan C: Doctor Knows Best; General Practitioner, 22 November 1985, p. 33.

Swann JP: Academic scientists and the pharmaceutical industry [Baltimore: Johns Hopkins University Press, 1988]

Swanson DW, Weddige RL, Morse RM: Abuse of prescription drugs; Mayo Clin Proc, May 1973, 48, 359-367.

Teal JS: Comments on benzodiazepine reaction; Drug Intell and Clin Pharm, October 1980, 14, 723.

Teeling-Smith G, 1972; in Parish PA et al (Eds), 1973.

Temple RJ: The DESI Programme, in Proc. 3rd International Conference of Drug Regulatory Authorities, Stockholm, 10-15 June 1984, 13-18.

Thomas L: The Medusa and the Snail: more notes of a biology watcher [New York: Bantam, 1979].

- Late night thoughts on listening to Mahler's ninth symphony [New York: Viking, 1983].

- in Briggs A, Shelley J (Eds): Science Medicine and the Community: the last hundred years; (Amsterdam, Exerpta Medica, 1986)] 19.

Tien AY, Gujavarty KS: Seizure following withdrawal from triazolam; Am J Psychiatry, December 1985, 142, 12, 1516-7.

Tobin JM, Bird IF, Boyle DE: Preliminary evaluation of Librium (Ro 5-0690) in the treatment of anxiety reactions; Dis Nerv Syst, March 1960, 11-19.

Tobin JM, Lewis NDC: A new psychotherapeutic agent, chlordiazepoxide; JAMA, 5 November 1960, 1242-9.

Toll N: Librium as an adjunct to psychotherapy in private psychiatric practice; Dis Nerv Syst, March 1960, 264-6.

Torrey EF: The Mind Game: Witchdoctors and Psychiatrists, [New York, Emerson Hall, 1972].

Towler ML: The clinical use of diazepam in anxiety states and depressions; J Neuropsychiatry, August 1962, 3, Supp 1, 68-72.

Tucker D: The World Health Market - the future of the pharmaceutical industry [London: Euromonitor Publications, 1984].

Turner T: Henry Maudsley - psychiatrist, philosopher and entrepreneur; Psychological Medicine, 1988, 18, 551-574.

Tyrer P: The benzodiazepine bonanza; Lancet, 21 September 1974, 709-710.

- Drug treatment of psychiatric patients in general practice; Brit Med J, 7 October 1978, 1008-1010.

Tyrer P, Steinberg B, Watson B: Possible epileptogenic effect of mianserin. Lancet, 13 October 1979, 798-9.

Tyrer P: Lorazepam withdrawal seizures (reply to letter); Lancet, 19 January 1980, 151

- Dependence on benzodiazepines; Brit J Psychiat, 1980, 137, 576-7.

Tyrer P; Rutherford D; Huggett T: Benzodiazepine withdrawal symptoms and propanolol, Lancet, 7 March 1981, 520-522

Tyrer P, Owen R: Gradual withdrawal of diazepam after long-term therapy, Lancet, 25 June 1983, 1402-6.

Tyrer P, Murphy P et al: The Nottingham Study of Neurotic disorder: comparison of drug and psychological treatments; Lancet, 30 July 1988, 235-240.

Tyrer P: Risks of dependence of benzodiazepine drugs: the importance of patient selection; Brit Med J, 14 January 1989, 298, 102-5.

Upjohn Ltd: Xanax (alprazolam) - New Government restrictions on benzodiazepine prescribing; Circular letter, March 1985

- Halcion tablets reregistered in the Netherlands; news release dated 8 August 1990.

US Senate Subcommittee on Health and Scientific Research of the Committee on Labor and Human Resources (1979) Use and misuse of benzodiazepines, Washington, US Government Printing Office, 1980.

Van der Kroef C: Halcion, a harmless hypnotic ? Nederlands Tijdschrift voor Geneeshunde, 1979, 123, 1160-1161.

- Reactions to triazolam; Lancet, 1979, ii, 526.0

Vilkin MI, Lomas JB: Clinical experience with diazepam in general psychiatric practice; J Neuropsychiatry, August 1962, 3, Supp 1, 139-144.

Vital-Herne J, Brenner R, Lesser M: Another case of alprazolam withdrawal syndrome, Am J Psychiatry, December 1985, 142, 12, 1515.

Volgyesi FA: School for patients' hypnosis-therapy and psychoprophylaxis. Br J Med Hypnotism, 1954, 5, 8

Von Wartburg WP: Drugs and the perception of risks; Swiss Pharma, 1984, 6, 11a, 21-3.

Wagner CP, Bunbury DE: Incidence of bromide intoxication among psychotic patients. JAMA, 1930, 95, 23, 1725-8.

Waldron I: Increased prescribing of Valium, Librium, and other drugs - an example of the influence of economic and social factors on the practice of medicine; Int J Health Services, 1977, 7, 1, 37-62.

Warner JH: Physiological theory and therapeutic explanation in the 1860s: the British debate on medical use of alcohol. Bulletin of the History of Medicine, 1980, 54, 235-257.

Watts CAH, 1972; in Parish PA et al (Eds), 1973.

Waugh E: The ordeal of Gilbert Pinfold [Boston: Little, Brown, 1957].

Webb P: "I just want to talk to someone"; Nursing Mirror, 15 December 1982, 18-22.

Weiss S: The clinical use and dangers of hypnotics. JAMA, 1936, 107, 26, 2104-9.

Wells FO: Nitrazepam and the elderly, Brit Med J, 27 January 1973, 235.

- Prescribing barbiturates: drug substitution in general practice; J. Roy Coll Gen Practit, 1973, 23, 164.

- The moral choice in prescribing barbiturates; J Med Ethics, 1976, 2, 68-70.

Wells N: Innovative chemical extensions - the economic basis of pharmaceutical progress [London: Office of Health Economics, 1988].

Werry JS: Drugs, learning and cognitive function in children; J Child Psychol Psychiat, 1988, 29, 2, 129-141.

Wheatley D: New hypnotic agents: clinical studies in general practice; Pharmacol Biochem Behav, April 1988, 29, 4, 811-813.

Whitlock FA: The syndrome of barbiturate dependence; Med J Aust, 29 August 1970, 391-396.

Wickler A: Diagnosis and treatment of drug dependence of the barbiturate type; Amer. J Psychiat; December 1968, 125, 6, 758-765.

Wilks J M: The use of psychotropic drugs in general practice; J Roy Coll Gen Practit, 1975, 25, 731-744.

Willcox W: Proc. Roy Soc Med, 1927, 20, 1479

- Proc. Roy Soc Med, 1934, 27, 498

- Lancet, 1934, i, 370.

Williams MW: Clinical impressions on the use and value of chlordiazepoxide in psychiatric practice; Southern Med J, August 1961, 921-6.

Wills WK: Brit Med J; 1906, 1, 498

Winfield M: Minding your own business - self regulation and whistleblowing in British companies [London: Social Audit, 1991].

Wingate P: Medical Encyclopedia, Second edition; [Harmondsworth: Penguin, 1985]

Winokur A, Rickels K, Greenblatt DJ et al: Withdrawal reaction from long-term, low-dosage administration of diazepam; Arch Gen Psychiatry, January 1980, 37, 101-105.

Winokur A, Rickels K: Withdrawal and pseudowithdrawal from diazepam therapy; J Clin Psychiatry, November 1981, 42, 11, 442-4.

Wolfe JR: Lancet, 5 May 1866, 503.

Wolfe SM: Press statement on Hoffman-LaRoche Bookburning Lawsuit; Public Citizen Health Research Group, 4 May 1982.

Wolfe SM, Fugate L, Hulstrand EP, Kamimoto ME: Worst Pills - Best Pills [Washington DC: Public Citizen Health Research Group, 1988]

Wolfe SM (Ed): Versed - another dangerous drug slips through the FDA's sieve; Health Letter, March 1988, 4, 3, 1-4.

- (Ed): The Halcion story; Health Letter, January 1990, 6, 1, 1-3 & 8.

- Letter to David Kessler MD LLB, (Commissioner, US Food and Drug Administration); [Washington DC: Public Citizen, 31 July, 1991]

Womans Own: Tranquillisers, 1 September 1984, 20-22.

Woods JH, Katz JL, Winger G: Use and abuse of benzodiazepines: JAMA, 16 December 1988, 260, 23, 3476-3480.

World Health Organisation [Expert Committee on drugs liable to produce addiction - report of the second session] (TRS No. 21). [Geneva, WHO, 1950].

- [Expert Committee on drugs liable to produce addiction - third report (TRS No. 57). [Geneva, WHO, 1952].

- [Expert Committee on addiction-producing drugs - seventh report (TRS No. 116). [Geneva, WHO, 1957].

- [Expert Committee on addiction-producing drugs - thirteenth report (TRS No. 273). [Geneva, WHO, 1964].

- [Report of a WHO scientific group] Evaluation of dependence-producing drugs. (TRS No. 287). [Geneva, WHO, 1964].

- [WHO Expert Committee on Drug Dependence; Seventeenth report]. (TRS No. 437). [Geneva, WHO, 1970].

- [WHO Expert Committee on Drug Dependence; Eighteenth report]. (TRS No. 460). [Geneva, WHO, 1970].

- [Report of a WHO Expert Committee]: New approaches to health education in primary health care (TRS No. 690). [Geneva, WHO, 1983].

- 33 tranquillizers placed under international control; Press release WHO/4 dated 22 February 1984.

Zbinden G, Randall LO: Pharmacology of benzodiazepines: Laboratory and clinical considerations; in Garattini S and Shore PA (Eds); Advances in pharmacology, vol 5, 1967; London and New York, Academic Press

Zipursky RB, Baker RW, Zimmer RB: Alprazolam withdrawal delirium unresponsive to diazepam: case report. J Clin Psychiatry, 1985, 46, 344-345.

ABOUT SOCIAL AUDIT

Social Audit's job is to ask timely questions about the organisations whose decisions and actions shape our lives. What, in social terms, do these organisations give to and take from the community, and how do they explain and justify what they do ? Social Audit publishes reports which explain why these questions seem worth asking, and what the answers to them might be. Social Audit's concern applies to all organisations and to any government, whatever its politics. The issues may differ, but the conclusions tend to be the same: there is not enough accountability in the major centres of power. There is too much secrecy in government and in the other organisations that direct and manage our lives.

These organisations go to great lengths to persuade us that they are good and do good - but they also suppress evidence of the harm they do. Unless and until there is proper accountablity, these organisations will operate by their standards - which may be completely unacceptable by yours.

Social Audit is a small, independent non-profit-making body which operates in its own name as well as through campaigning organisations such as Health Action International and the Campaign for Freedom of Information. Social Audit also acts as the publishing arm of Public Interest Research Centre Ltd, a registered charity which carries out research into the use and abuse of corporate power. Public Interest Research Centre was set up in 1972, with grants from the Joseph Rowntree Charitable and Social Service Trusts. Individual projects have since been supported by the 1970 Trust, Consumers Association, Social Science Research Council, Allen Lane Foundation, Dag Hammarskjold Foundation, Nuffield Foundation, Ford Foundation, MIND, Trocaire, War on Want and other organisations and individuals. Social Audit's work has been funded mainly by sale of publications and more recently by consultancy work in legally-aided drug injury actions. We have undertaken generic research for solicitors acting for plaintiffs in a number of cases, including those involving Opren (benoxaprofen), Factor VIII (Haemophilia/HIV), Myodil (X-Ray contrast medium), Merital (nomifensine) and benzodiazepines. Public Interest Research Centre and Social Audit are run by Christopher Zealley (Chair), Andrew Phillips, Anthony Sampson and Oliver Thorold (PIRC only); and by Charles Medawar and Elaine Rassaby (executive).

Charles Medawar's background is in consumer protection. He now specialises in questions relating to drug policy and rational drug use, and writes, lectures and broadcasts regularly on such issues. He was rapporteur of the World Health Organisation's working group of experts on national drug policy (1987); is a trustee of Health Action International (Europe); and a member of the advisory council of the Drug & Therapeutics Bulletin. Elaine Rassaby was trained as a clinical psychologist and joined Social Audit after 10 years' work with MIND (National Association for Mental Health). She is an acknowledged expert on drug injury research. She was appointed a Mental Health Act Commissioner in 1991.

Publications

Most of our recent published work on pharmaceuticals has been published externally (see bibliography in this book, under Medawar C). A number of the books and pamplets published in-house are available from us (at the prices shown, post-free) but others are out of print. Many reports are available at large discounts if ordered in multiples of 10.

MINDING YOUR OWN BUSINESS - Self regulation and whistleblowing in British companies, by Marlene Winfield (1990). The Director-General of the Confederation of British Industry, John Banham, has recommended this book as "essential reading for all corporate managers". It reports the results of a survey of 53 companies; recommends ways companies might develop more deliberately ethical cultures; considers why and how to make employees into self-regulators; examines how key decisions by courts or tribunals hinder self-regulation; looks at possible new roles for trades unions and professional associations; examines the phenomenon of "whistleblowing" and interviews

British whistleblowers; and provides British and American reading lists. Book (96 pages): £6.50; Pamphlet (25 page summary): £2.50. For both: 50% off if ordered in multiples of 10.

DRUGS OF CHOICE - A report on drug formularies used in NHS hospitals, by Helen Ridley (1986). This report surveys the numbers and types of drugs (in particular therapeutic categories) used in 30 major UK hospitals. It shows that these expert and specialist drug prescribers choose not to use about two-thirds of the drugs available to GPs. It discusses why and how limiting the numbers of drugs improves prescribing standards and saves money - and argues that drug formularies are essential to better medicine in developed and developing countries alike. Price: £5 (£15 for ten)

DRUGS AND WORLD HEALTH - An international consumer perspective, by Charles Medawar (1984) ... remarkably concise, well-documented and challenging: it will give food for thought to all who care about health" (*Self Health,* March 1986). This report was launched as "a major consumer policy on medicines" at the 1984 world congress of the International Organisation of Consumers Unions, and is available from them at 9 Emmastraat, 2595 eg The Hague, Netherlands.

THE WRONG KIND OF MEDICINE? by Charles Medawar (1984) This is a critical guide to over 800 medicines that are ineffective, or inappropriately or extravagently prescribed. Five introductory chapters discuss why different kinds of drugs don't work - and why such products are promoted, permitted, prescribed and consumed. Published by Consumers' Association and Hodder & Stoughton, and now out of print.

DRUG DIPLOMACY: Decoding the conduct of a multinational pharmaceutical company and the failure of a Western remedy for the third world, by Charles Medawar and Barbara Freese (1982). "Social Audit's investigation into the anti-diarrhoeal drug, Lomotil, is a model of the genre - well researched and worrying" (*New Society,* 1982). "This little book is an excellent case study of the conduct of multinational drug companies. It shows both the possibilities and the limitations of a struggle against them" (*Tropical Doctor,* 1984). Price: £4 post free (£12 for 10)

CONSCIENTIOUS OBJECTORS AT WORK: Mental hospital nurses - a case study, by Virginia Beardshaw, with a chapter by Oliver Thorold (1981). What role should employees play in stopping harmful practices at work ? This report discussed the dilemmas confronting nurses who question standards of care in mental hospitals. "Compulsory reading ... not just by those in nursing, but by those in all institutions where public whistleblowing has become the only way to draw attention to abuse" (*New Statesman*). "This is a superb book" (*MIND Out*). Sorry: out of print.

A WORD OF WARNING: The quality of chemical suppliers' health and safety information, by Maurice Frankel (1981). This report - based on a survey of information from 200 UK suppliers - shows that while many companies do what is required of them, others fall far short of minimum legal requirements, providing information that is misleading or dangerously inadequate. It "... gives examples of how dangers are masked by deceptive phrasing, left out, or blatantly lied about" (*The Guardian*); and "...makes horrifying reading" (*British Journal of Hospital Medicine*). Price: £5 (£20 for 10).

CHEMICAL RISK: A worker's guide to chemical hazards and data sheets, by Maurice Frankel (1981) This is a small companion volume to *A Word of Warning,* and is a guide to how to interpret and use information provided by suppliers of chemicals. It includes a specially designed model data sheet for use in obtaining information. This guide was designed specifically for use by trade union representatives; and recommends information policies for trade unions. Price: £2.40 (published by Pluto Press)

International regulation of the supply and use of pharmaceuticals - paper by Charles Medawar (published in the Dag Hammarskjold Foundation's journal, *Development Dialogue,* Advance offprint, 1985).

Report on investment in the UK tobacco industry, by David Gilbert (British Medical Association, 1985).

Parliamentary questions and answers, by Charles Medawar (Social Audit, 1980). 30p pamphlet. Price: £1

Consumers of Power - a report on lack of accountability in the London Electricity Board, by Charles Medawar (1979). Price: £3

A review of the Bingham Report - a re-appraisal of the evidence of illegal supply of oil to Rhodesia under UDI, by Andrew Phillips (1978). Out of print.

The Social Audit Pollution Handbook - A layperson's guide to toxic hazards in the workplace and beyond, by Maurice Frankel (Macmillan, 1978). Out of print.

The Social Audit Consumer Handbook - A guide to the social responsibilities of busines to the consumer, by Charles Medawar (Macmillan, 1978). Out of print.

Between 1973-1976, our reports were published in the periodical journal, *SOCIAL AUDIT*. A few copies are still available, but some are out of print. Details on request.

Social Audit Ltd, PO Box 111, London NW1 8XG. (071 586 7771).

INDEX